RAILS NORTH

ON THE WHITE PASS AND YUKON ROUTE

Constructed during the height of winter storms of 1898-99, the tunnel at Tunnel Mountain was one of the several difficult tasks for builders of the White Pass and Yukon. A bridge at the mouth of the tunnel had to be constructed for workers and equipment to reach the site. A work train with rarely photographed locomotive No. 3, a Grant 2-8-0 built in 1882, is seen entering the tunnel. (University of Washington Historical Library—Northwest Collection)

RAILS NORTH

The Railroads of Alaska and the Yukon

by Howard Clifford

SUPERIOR PUBLISHING COMPANY-SEATTLE

Box 1710, Seattle WA 98111

Copyright 1981 by Howard Clifford
Seattle, Washington

Library of Congress Cataloging in Publication Data
Clifford, Howard.

Rails north.
Bibliography: p.187
Includes index.
1. Railroads—Alaska—History. 2. Railroads—Yukon
Territory—History. I. Title.
HE2771.A4C54   385′.09798   80-23828
ISBN 0-87564-536-4

FIRST EDITION

Photographic reproduction by Artcraft Colorgraphics - Seattle, WA.
Layout and book design by Phyllis Berg
Jacket concept and design by Joe Salisbury
Typography by Nova Typesetting Co.

Printed and bound in the United States of America

TABLE OF CONTENTS

The Alaska Juneau Gold Mine in all its glory. The mine was one of the most productive in Southeast Alaska and was a mainstay of the Juneau economy for many years. Most of the mine buildings (upper right) have been torn down since the facility was closed shortly after World War II. Miles and miles of track ran through the many tunnels, with battery powered locomotives pulling ore trains. The mine docks on the waterfront are still used for commercial purposes. (H. Clifford)

FOREWARD

Millions of words telling the story of Alaska and the Yukon have been written over the years, relating the discovery of gold and other valued minerals, the development of the State and the Territory, the battle with the elements, a never-ending thing in the North.

Little, however, has been done to tell the story of the railroads of this vast and wild territory—or of the men who built them at the risk of lives and fortunes; of the harrowing and exciting story of the development and financing of these pioneering lines; the battle with the elements, not for just a month or so during the winter, but for a full 12 months of the year; the great rivalry between the various railroad companies; the battle for the "one and only route"; intrigue, politics, even warfare and murder.

This is the story of railroads in Alaska and the Yukon. The story which has intrigued us for two decades as we have researched throughout the north for tid-bits of information and gradually pieced it all together to write this book.

The writing and researching of a book such as this could only be accomplished with the generous aid and assistance of scores of knowledgeable and informative people, who have given their time and effort to help on this project. Literally there are hundreds who have "lent a hand" one way or another. To list them all would be impossible, but our sincere thanks go to each and every one.

There are a few who really went well beyond the call, they spent hours and went way out of their way to help and supply valuable materials and information. They are such as Bob Monroe and his staff at the University of Washington Library Northwest Collection, Seattle; Paul McCarthy and his staff at the University of Alaska Rasmussen Library, Fairbanks; Diane Johnston, archivist, Yukon Archives, Whitehorse; Phyllis Nottingham, State of Alaska Historical Library, Juneau; M. Diane Brenner, Museum Archivist, Anchorage Historical and Fine Arts Museum; Mrs. Dorothy Clifton, Valdez, with much valued material from the Clifton private collection of Alaskana; H.L. Berry of Homer, Ak., and Sequim, Wash., who dug into his own collection to bring up valued information and photographs; Louise Bremmer, assistant to the general manager of the Alaska Railroad, Anchorage, who made possible the use of railroad archives and collections of photographs; Cornelius W. Hauck, Cincinatti, railroad historian and editor and one of the founding fathers of the Colorado Railroad Museum; Omar LaValle, author and historian, Montreal; the staff of the Canadian Pacific Railroad archives; Lone Janson, Anchorage, railroad historian and author; Frank Downey, White Pass & Yukon Route, Seattle; Bruce LeRoy, director, and Frank Green, librarian, Washington State Historical Society, Tacoma; and Bruce Campbell, former Commissioner of Highways, State of Alaska, Juneau.

There are others—far too many to mention. Our sincere thanks to all. They made this book possible.

Chapter 1

White Pass & Yukon Route

The White Pass & Yukon Route — "the road that couldn't be built" — started as a dream of an old sea captain who suffered from gold fever to the extent that he had engaged in close to a dozen gold rushes over a 50-year period extending from California to the Bering Sea.

He was Captain William (Billy) Moore, pioneer of pioneers. A colorful old gentleman who had made and lost three fortunes and had hopes of making a fourth, which actually came about in the declining years of his extraordinary and colorful life.

During the summer of 1887 Captain Moore was hired by the Canadian government survey party headed by William Ogilvie to provide the necessary know-how of packing over wilderness trails and to build and navigate a barge with supplies down the Yukon River. A rather formidable assignment for a man 65 years of age.

At that time, entry into the Upper Yukon Valley was via the Chilkoot Pass, a precipitous and rugged route that taxed the strength of the best of men. Captain Moore, who had visited and traveled in the area over a period of years, had heard that there was another route from sea-level to the Upper Yukon — a route some 600 feet less in altitude than the Chilkoot, a route that could be reached from the placid waters of Skagway Bay. Captain Moore was determined to test the feasibility of the new route, so while the main Ogilvie party took the old trail, he started up the Skagway River, accompanied by an old Indian friend, Skookum Jim (Mason), who was destined to be one of the discoverers of the Klondike gold fields which was to make possible the fulfillment of Captain Moore's dream.

It took Moore and his companion many days to make the perilous trip over the 45-mile pass, traveling where there was no trail of any kind, over precipitous switchbacks, hillsides and canyons. When they reached Lake Bennett, one of the headwaters of

the Yukon, the main Ogilvie party had been waiting for them for several days.

Despite the hardships of the trip, Captain Moore was enthusiastic about the new route. Accepting Moore's report that the route was passable and showed promise of easing the trek to the Upper Yukon, Ogilvie named the pass after Thomas White, Canadian Minister of the Interior.

As Ogilvie recalled years later, the old man's imagination was inspired. "Every night during the two months he remained with us, he would picture tons of yellow dust yet to be found in the Yukon Valley," Ogilvie stated. "He decided then and there that Skagway Bay would be the entry point to the golden fields — and that White Pass would reverberate with the rumble of railway trains, carrying supplies in and the precious gold out."

How true that dream was to become in the next decade.

So enthusiastic was Captain Moore of his new found route, that on Oct. 20, 1887 he settled at the present site of Skagway, pitching his tent on a small knoll along a creek and staking a claim to 160 acres. Before winter, he and his son Ben, constructed a small dock or wharf out into the tideflats along the tall cliff, to enable them to land supplies and equipment for the furthering of their enterprise.

In so doing, Moore said to his son, "I fully expect before many years to see a pack trail through the pass, followed by a wagon road, and I would not be at all surprised to see a railroad through to the lakes."

Less than 10 years later the Klondike discovery triggered the greatest stampede in history, a rush which was to see more than 50,000 persons battle their way over White Pass, and to a lesser extent nearby Chilkoot Pass — the original route to the interior.

The first prospectors to go over White Pass were seven young men from California who arrived on the steamer Rustler. They started their trek with seven tons of freight on Feb. 2, 1895. They were the first to make use of two miles of Moore's trail over the ridge to avoid the falls at the junction of the upper and lower canyons.

For many years previous Captain Moore had tried without success to win financial support from the Victoria business community for his Skagway venture. Perhaps too many recalled his sorry financial history. He looked like a poor risk.

Early in 1896, however, before the Klondike discovery, Captain Moore approached E. E. Billinghurst of the British Columbia Development Co., who was an agent for the British capitalist and promotor, C. H. Wilkinson. So persuasive was Captain Moore of the future prospects of Skagway Bay as a gateway for a wagon trail and railway to the Yukon Territory, that Wilkinson arranged to advance the old sea captain $1,800 for supplies, two horses, a couple of cows, 6,000 board feet of rough lumber and other materials, in return for a lien on Moore's preemption at Skagway. From this humble beginning came the British capital that was to finance the building of the White Pass & Yukon Route.

Moore's supplies arrived in Skagway in June 1896, and since Billinghurst guaranteed the payment of wages for five men that season, Captain Moore's son, Ben, was able to improve the wharf, which is the basis of the present wharf used by passenger boats and the White Pass & Yukon Route trains. They also started work on a trail over the Pass. Later 15 men were employed to construct a pack trail along the bank of the Skagway River and bridges over the canyons.

The following gold rush resulted in Skagway becoming a town almost overnight and Captain Moore transferred 60 acres of his original preemption to the British Yukon Company which immediately laid out a townsite and through C. H. Wilkinson made an offer to the Canadian Minister of the Interior to build a wagon road through White Pass, a distance of 50 miles, at a cost of $2,000 per mile.

Before any real improvements were made on the route between Skagway and the lakes, many applications had been made to put in some form of transportation.

As early as 1887 the U.S. Secretary of the Interior received requests from promoters desirous of securing franchises for construction of trails across the Alaska panhandle from tidewater to the headwaters of the Yukon.

Edward Bean had written to the Secretary asking for a charter to construct "a practical pack trail from a point near the head of Lynn Canal to connect with the trail from Lake Bennett," for which a charter had been

Long before others even discovered gold in the Klondike Captain William (Billy) Moore had visions of a railroad over White Pass to the rich mineral fields of the Yukon. Captain Moore built the first dock at Skagway, the basis of the White Pass facilities there today, explored the route which eventually became the one taken by the White Pass & Yukon, and lived to see trains making their way over the pass, just as he had dreamed many years before. (Clifford Collection)

granted by the British Columbia government. Secretary L. Q. C. Lamar denied the request on the basis that such a franchise could only be secured through congressional action.

The next year David Flannery and Samuel O. Wheeler, having learned of Captain Moore's trip over the White Pass, attempted to steal his thunder. They were turned down by Interior Secretary William F. Vilas on a charter, "for a pack trail to be constructed from Skagway Bay . . . to the boundary line of British Columbia at Summit Lake, together with a right-of-way of one-half mile on each side."

By the time that Captain Moore had built his wharf and cabin he applied to Alaska Governor A. P. Swineford for a similar concession. The Governor replied that he was powerless to grant such a concession and referred him to the Secretary of Interior. It was three years later, in 1891, that Captain Moore finally got around to making his formal application. In April of that year he proposed to open a pack trail

Skagway as it looked in 1897-98 when work on the wagon road to the summit of White Pass was started by George Brackett. During the gold rush Skagway became a booming town of 15,000 persons. (Clifford Collection)

from Skagway Bay through White Pass to Summit Lake. This trail, to be blasted or cribbed from the mountain side, would be five feet wide and graded. All streams not fordable would be bridged. As considerable expense would be involved in construction, Captain Moore applied for a franchise to levy a toll. He requested a right-of-way of one mile either side of the trail.

Moore received the same reply as had the others.

Within six months the Interior Secretary received a request from Miner W. Bruce and Charles W. Young of Juneau for a "charter to construct a toll road up the Chilkat." Secretary John W. Noble, like the others, denied the request.

Despite earlier discouragements to obtain permits, Captain Moore had been able to obtain some financial backing from the Alaskan and Northwestern Territories Trading Company, and because of the urgency and excitement, proceeded to rough out a trail without taking the pains to secure the right-of-way and the privilege of charging tolls until a trail had been opened.

Twelve days after the first stampeders landed at Skagway, Noble Rowan of the Alaskan and Nor-

thwestern Co., wrote Secretary of Interior Cornelius N. Bliss, informing him that the company had completed "a trail from Skagway Bay . . . over the White Pass entirely at its own cost." Such was the basis of a request by Rowan "to levy a small toll of one cent per pound on the goods going over the trail." This was denied, with the warning to Rowan that "no person or persons could lawfully take possession of the White Pass Trail and charge tolls until authorized by Congress."

As it became apparent that the trail would be unable to handle the hordes that were landing at Skagway, Rowan applied to the Secretary of Interior for the priviledge of building a wagon road from Skagway Bay through White Pass to Lake Bennett. His company was prepared to begin work immediately and complete the road, if allowed to charge a reasonable toll.

Before the Secretary could reply he received a telegram from John Campbell, dated Aug. 6, 1897 stating that thousands would have to take other routes to the Klondike unless improvements were made on the trail, and such would result in great suffering and even death from privation and exposure, as winter was approaching. He also applied for permission for himself and his associate J. L. Green, for the right to build a road in the interest of the Yukon Miners Association. Both requests were denied on the basis that the Secretary lacked authority to make such concessions.

At the same time, Secretary Bliss was being pressured by Dyea interests opposed to the opening of a competing route across White Pass. One such person was Sam Herron, manager of the Healy & Wilson's Trading Post at Dyea, who stated that if Canadian interests were permitted to open the trail they soon would begin operating a line of steamers from Victoria, which would "deprive the Territory of Alaska of the Yukon trade." Land rights at Skagway, he pointed out, were held by Bernard Moore, Captain Moore's son, and a naturalized citizen. (Apparently Herron was not aware of the fact that the A&NTT Co. was incorporated in West Virginia.)

There were railroads proposed too. The first was projected by residents of Sitka and Juneau, who proposed a line through Chilkoot Pass as early as 1885, some five years after the first prospectors went through to the headwaters of the Yukon. Major M. P. Berry, Frank Myers, Abraham Cohen, W. R. Mills and George Nowell petitioned Congress for a charter for "The Chilkoot Pass and Summit Railroad Co." The company wished to be empowered to issue construction bonds to the sum of $1 million and to receive a title to one mile of land on each side of the road when completed. The undertaking failed, partly through lack of sufficient funds, but also because of the fact that there was no law under which such a project could be constructed.

Following the discovery of gold in the Yukon and the stampede that followed in 1897, Congress passed a bill permitting the use of products of the country in building railroads and provided for establishments of right-of-way, terminals and stations.

One of the first routes proposed under the new law was the Stikine Route which was to extend from Taku Arm to the Atlintoo River and the headwaters of the Yukon, thus connecting the upper Stikine with the Yukon.

In 1897 an order-in-council of the Canadian Government authorized MacKenzie & Mann of Toronto to build a railroad from Telegraph Creek, head of navigation on the Stikine River in British Columbia, to the head of Teslin Lake, a distance of 150 miles. The lake, about 85 miles in length, stretches through British Columbia into the Yukon. Four hundred men were conveyed to Telegraph Creek to start this project, but the life of this route was a short and

The infamous Chilkoot Pass, "the other way to the summit" was shorter, but more hazardous than the White Pass route later developed by the White Pass & Yukon. Stampeders landed at nearby Dyea to take the Chilkoot route as opposed to Skagway for the White Pass. (Clifford Collection.)

merry one, ending abruptly when the Canadian Parliament refused to ratify the agreement. A certain amount of work was done by the contractors in the way of clearing right-of-way and building corduroy roads on the Teslin Trail, at a cost of $280.000. Many of the employees of MacKenzie & Mann found their way to Skagway and eventually worked on construction of the White Pass & Yukon.

Another rail route was projected from Chilkat Inlet on the line of the Dalton Trail to the Yukon River, then by way of the Yukon to Dawson City.

In Aug. 1897 George W. Garside, engineer for the British-American Transportation Co., surveyed the 62 miles for a railroad running from Skagway Bay over White Pass to Lake Tagish and then through Three Mile River to Lake Atlin, headquarters of the Hootalinqua, where passengers would be transferred to steamers to be operated by the company and carried to Dawson and Forty Mile.

The same month the Sitka syndicate headed by P. L. Packard and William A. Pratt, surveyed a route from Taku Inlet on the Alaska coast to Tesline (Teslin) Lake and thence into the Yukon Territory.

The Chilkoot Railroad and Transportation Co., of Washington, proposed to build from Dyea to Camp Linderman on Crater Lake, a distance of 15.9 miles, filing for this route in Sept. 1897. In December the Chilkoot Pass Transportation Co. of West Virginia filed to build from Dyea over Chilkoot Pass to Lake Linderman.

Workmen cleared the right-of-way for the Brackett Wagon Road to the White Pass summit, using sledge hammers and crow bars, the tools of the day. Work on the wagon road started in 1897. Note the relaxed workman holding the steel chisel as the other workman is about to strike it with the heavy sledge. (National Archives)

Then came the deluge. In May 1898 filings were made by no less than five companies to construct railroads which they hoped would reach the riches of the Klondike one way or another.

The Yukon Railway Co. of New Jersey filed to build from Skagway to Lake Bennett, a distance of 39.3 miles; the Yukon Mining, Trading and Transportation Co. of West Virginia, proposed building along Taku Inlet and the Taku River to the international boundary, a distance of 20 miles; the Alaska and Northwestern Railway Co., incorporated under the laws of West Virginia, filed to build from Portage Cove on Lynn Canal to the international boundary, a distance of 36 miles; the American and Canadian Transportation Co., of Washington, proposed building from Skagway to White Pass and onward; and the Chilkat and Yukon Railway Co., of New Jersey, planned a route from Haines Mission to the head of the Klehane River.

These were in addition to the successful Pacific and Arctic Railway and Navigation Co., of West Virginia, which became the U.S. section of the White Pass and Yukon.

Other—and later filings—included the Chilkat Inlet Railway and Navigation Co., of Washington, which planned to build from Pyramid Harbor to Chilkat River and to a point on the boundary at the crossing of the Chilkat River. The company filed its routing in Nov. 1902. This was followed by the Haines Mission and Boundary Railroad Co., of Washington, which filed in Jan. 1907 to build from Haines Mission on Lynn Canal to Pleasant Camp, a distance of 41.35 miles. Another was the Lynn Canal and Short Line Railroad, which bought out the old Shellcross-Richards Telephone Line connecting Dyea and Skagway to obtain the right-of-way from Dyea Post Office to the Kelly Dry Goods Store in Skagway.

George Brackett, kneeling center, developer of the Brackett Wagon Road to the summit of White Pass, goes over plans with some of his construction crews. The conference is held on one of the log bridges which spanned the many streams in the area. The cabin in the background was constructed to house work crews along the route. (National Archives)

One of the big rivals for the White Pass for traffic to the Klondike gold fields was the aerial tramways which helped stampeders haul goods over the Chilkoot Pass route. Towers of some of these tramways may still be seen in the Chilkoot Pass area. (University of Washington Library—Northwest Collection)

Meanwhile the struggle for supremacy between Skagway and Dyea as to the favored route to the Yukon continued. In early Aug. 1897 Dyea had the edge. By mid-August it had widened its margin, as conditions over the White Pass Trail worsened. As it became impossible to get a horse to the summit of White Pass, Indian packers were being paid from $12 to $40 per hundredweight to pack goods over the Chilkoot.

As things got worse, it was estimated that there were more than 3,000 stampeders trying to get over the White Pass Trail out of Skagway, while the Chilkoot was relatively clear, with perhaps 50 or so rushers in town waiting transportation of their goods over the route.

By September packers were unable to move over White Pass, which became known as "Dead Horse Trail," and it was estimated that of about 5,000 attempting to go over this route, 10 percent made it, with many backtracking and going over the Chilkoot.

The Chilkoot with its various aerial tramways, such as the Chilkoot Railroad and Transport Co. headed by Hugh C. Wallace of Tacoma, Washington; the Dyea-Klondike Transportation Co. bucket tramway; Burns' Hoist; the Alaska Railway and Transportation Co.'s bucket tramway; all of which eventually joined under an agreement which gave the Chilkoot a big edge.

As winter came, however, and the bogs and rivers froze, the White Pass Trail gained a big edge as pack horses were able to make the entire distance with full loads. Pack trains were able to make it to the lakes in four days with 250 pounds per horse. Things swung

further in favor of White Pass when a disastrous slide at Sheep Camp on April 3, 1898 took a toll of lives on the Chilkoot route.

In the meantime, Captain Charles E. Peabody of the Washington & Alaska Steamship Co. urged George A. Brackett, former Mayor of Minneapolis and an engineer who had helped drive the rails of the Northern Pacific Railroad across the Dakotas, to seek development of better transportation over one or the other of the passes.

Heading north aboard ship in mid-September 1897, Brackett met J. A. Acklen, a Tennessee lawyer and former Congressman. They discussed transportation over the passes and visited both Dyea and Skagway. Brackett decided that Chilkoot had the most potential.

Acklen, however, learned that a Norman Smith had made a survey over the White Pass and sought to join forces with him in a proposed wagon road from Skagway. An organization meeting, with 14 potential charter members present, was held in Charles Kelly's store in Skagway. The group agreed to participate in organizing a company with capital stock of $300,000 of which $150,000 was to go to the charter members for their efforts in time and money.

Acklen and Smith returned to Washington D.C. to incorporate and on the way south again met with Brackett and convinced him to join them in their efforts. On Oct. 13, 1897 they incorporated the Skagway & Yukon Transportation & Improvement Company. C. A. Bullen of the Bullen Bridge Co., was added to the group of promotors because he owned a 250-foot steel bridge which was believed to of Skagway and opened it to traffic on Nov. 23, 1897. By mid-December eight miles had been completed. Bullen's bridge arrived and was found useless. By Dec. 20, 1897 Brackett was broke. He returned to Seattle seeking funds from Captain Peabody and others without success and continued on to Minneapolis. Starting with a small nest egg from the Great Northern, Brackett was able to raise additional funds from the Canadian Pacific and others.

He returned to Skagway in mid-January and increased his labor force only to run into trouble in the form of "outlaws" who had taken over part of the trail right-of-way, claiming they had located minerals under the roadway. Brackett called upon his old friend Jefferson Randolph (Soapy) Smith and his followers which resulted in the "outlaws" making a hasty retreat and work on the roadway continued.

Despite the fact that the road had not been completed to the summit and there was no bridge over the

Financial success of the Brackett Wagon Road to the White Pass summit depended upon tolls collected at various locations. Here is a toll bridge over one of the branches of the Skagway River, enroute to the summit. Teamsters rebelled against paying tolls and oftimes destroyed the toll gates, resulting in the calling out of Army troops to restore order at one location. (National Archives)

be suitable to span the East Fork of the Skagway River.

Work on the road started under Brackett's direction on Nov. 8, 1897 with $3,500 of Brackett's own funds the only money available despite promises of other funds from the over-ambitious promotors. Brackett was named superintendent and general manager of the company at $500 per month salary. As construction started, it became apparent that Smith's "survey" was nothing more than hand compass bearings and an outdated Canadian map that had been picked up enroute over the trail.

Acklen was unable to raise funds in the East and did not obtain support from Congress as promised, and was soon ousted from the group along with Smith and Treasurer David Samson. Brackett was put in charge of the entire operation.

Even without additional funds Brackett and his crews were able to complete four miles of roadway out

The Brackett
Wagon Road.

SKAGWAY, ALASKA

THE ONLY PRACTICAL WAGON
ROAD IN ALASKA. o o o o o o

Blockades of Traffic Impossible.

A THROUGH SLED ROUTE TO LAKE BENNETT

THE WAGON ROAD AFFORDS AN EASY MEANS
OF TRANSPORTATION FOR THE POOR MAN WHO
DESIRES TO TAKE HIS OWN OUTFIT TO THE
INTERIOR OF ALASKA.

OFFICE:

Third Ave and Main St.

Advertising a through route for both summer and winter, the Brackett Wagon Road, which preceeded the White Pass & Yukon Railroad, was a favorite and practical way to reach the lakes at the White Pass summit. (Clifford Collection.)

Tons of discarded equipment are seen along the Brackett Road, some three and one half miles below the White Pass summit. Many Klondikers gave up during the climb and tossed their equipment aside as the going got rough. Today the White Pass and Yukon Route carries tourist—and tons of freight—over much the same route, between Skagway and Whitehorse, Y.T. (Clifford Collection)

The Brackett Wagon Road was used summer and winter. When there was too much snow for wagons to operate, horses pulled sleds loaded with some 1,400 pounds of supplies over the route. At no time was there natural food for the horses enroute and during the winter there was no water. The route became known as the "Dead Horse Trail." (Hegg photo from Clifford Collection)

Packers with horses and dogs make their way through the wooded area on the lower reaches of the Skagway (White Pass) Trail. The narrow trail caused problems as those hauling loads to the summit tried to pass the oncoming traffic making its way back down the pass. (Clifford Collection)

East Fork, Brackett started charging tolls of two cents a pound for freight; a dollar each for pedestrians; a dollar for a horse, mule, or oxen; twenty-five cents for sheep; and $10 for a wagon using the completed part of the road. Hard-boiled freighters and packers refused to pay and destroyed the toll gates erected by Brackett.

Brackett wired a friend in the War Department, who explained to higher-ups that a "roudy element had seized the wagon road and had placed the country in a state of terror." This brought the troops from Dyea and order was restored.

By mid-April the bridge over the East Fork was completed and the toll road was bringing in a modest $1,000 to $1,500 a day. This was not as much as Brackett had hoped for. Despite additional financial assistance from the backers in the States and passage of the amended Lacey Bill, extending the Homestead Act to Alaska and providing for the construction of

wagon roads, trails and railroads in the Territory, Brackett was still strapped for money and faced a continuing and losing battle with packers and freighters.

Meanwhile three Victoria businessmen, who had listened to Captain Moore and his idea of building a railroad over White Pass, became interested in such a venture and obtained a charter to build a railroad over the Canadian portion of the route to the gold fields.

They obtained financing from the British firm of Close Brothers to get the project started, but were unable to build the railroad, or start work within the time allotted by their charter, and the English capitalists took over the franchise and decided to build the railroad themselves — without ever having the opportunity to look over the area — providing the proper construction experts were available for the job.

They sent Sir Thomas Tanerede to Skagway accompanied by Samuel H. Graves of Chicago, and Erastus C. Hawkins, a Seattle engineer, to determine if such a railroad was possible. Upon looking over the terrain, Sir Thomas decided that such a railroad was impossible to build and so advised his backers. He thought the mountains too massive, the sheer walls of the cliffs too difficult, and the grades too steep.

Following his report, Sir Thomas chanced to meet Michael J. Heney, a Canadian railroad contractor who had gained fame in the construction of the Canadian Pacific Railroad, and who had just completed his own survey of the White Pass route. Heney was not deterred in his plan to build a railroad over the pass, providing financing was available, and after an evening of discussion in the bar at Skagway's St. James Hotel, he convinced Sir Thomas that such a project was feasible. As dawn broke they drank a toast to the success of the operation.

The Pacific and Arctic Railway and Navigation Co., with Samuel H. Graves as president, was incorporated in the State of West Virginia to obtain the rights for the U.S. section of the route. Previously the British Columbia Yukon Railway Co., had been chartered by the Legislature of British Columbia, for construction of the portion through that Province; and the British Yukon Railway Co. chartered by an Act of Parliament of the Dominion of Canada, for the portion through the Yukon Territory.

The White Pass and Yukon Railway Co., Ltd., an English corporation, registered on July 30, 1898, to carry out the charter rights and concession of the three companies for the construction of a railway from "Skagway Harbor to Fort Selkirk on the Yukon, about 325 miles."

Graves negotiated an agreement with Brackett whereby his firm would receive $50,000 for compensation for any damages or losses suffered because of the construction of the railroad and an option to purchase his "toll road and all its franchises, appurtances and rights, etc., at any time before July 1, 1899, upon payment of an additional $50,000."

Brackett, at the time, had $185,000 in his project, but realized that it would be impossible for his company to build a railroad over the mountains, considering all the governmental red tape of the two nations involved.

Following the purchase of the right-of-way, the railroad engineers surveyed five routes over the summit, but decided that the best route was the one originally discovered and explored by Captain William Moore.

In a cost-saving move, the railroad company decided to construct a "narrow gauge" line with rails three feet apart, instead of the recently arrived at standard gauge of four feet, eight and one-half inches.

It was in the bar of this hotel, the St. James Hotel in Skagway, that Sir Thomas Tancrede and Michael Heney met and brought about the building of the White Pass & Yukon Railroad. The hotel was moved to its present location on Fourth near Broadway from its original Fourth and State location following the gold rush. (Western Airlines)

Building the White Pass & Yukon Railroad was a real challenge for turn of the century workers. There was no so-called modern equipment, only picks and shovels and blasting powder. Workers prepare for the blasting, and then after the blast move down to the wagon road below to remove the debris so that the wagons could continue to travel over White Pass. Below the wagon road is the old Moore trail. (University of Washington Historical Library—Northwest Collection)

This is Broadway, the main street in Skagway, with White Pass & Yukon Railroad tracks down the center of the street. The railroad tracks remained in the center of the street until World War II, when a by-pass was constructed, due to the heavy 24-hours a day traffic. Most of the buildings shown are still standing. (Clifford Collection)

The White Pass & Yukon was in reality three railroads. One incorporated in the United States, another in British Columbia and the third in the Yukon. The headquarters for the U.S. corporation, the Pacific and Arctic Railway & Navigation Co., was this building in Skagway photographed in June 1898. S. H. Graves was president of the P&AR&N as well as the overall project, the White Pass & Yukon. (Yukon Archives.)

This resulted in a 10-foot roadbed, instead of the normal 15-foot.

The building of the White Pass railway was attended by more than ordinary problems. It was a thousand miles from supply bases and there were no telegraph or telephone lines connecting this area with the States. Steamer traffic was irregular.

The Pacific Contracting Co., under Michael J. Heney, started construction on the railroad on May 27, 1898. The first passenger train operated a distance of four miles out of Skagway on July 21, 1898.

Construction was difficult. Workers would blow down the side of a mountain, filling the wagon road below at the bottom of the gulch, climb down, clear the trail, and then climb back up the steep cliff to the grade again. It was slow work — and expensive. Thousands of travelers went over the route at the bottom of the canyon. The railroad builders decided that it must be kept open as they wanted travel to continue over the White Pass as rivals were building an aerial tramway over Chilkoot Pass to compete with the railroad.

Nearly all of the work between Skagway and the Summit was in solid rock. Immense quantities of dynamite and blasting powder were used. In one case a rock cliff 120 feet high, 70 feet wide, and 20 feet thick was blasted away. Sometimes the mountain sides were so steep that men had to be suspended by ropes to prevent their falling off while cutting the grade. A short distance from the summit a deep V-shaped canyon was spanned by a steel cantilever bridge 215 feet in height, the most northerly bridge of its type and height in the world.

To many Jefferson Randolph "Soapy" Smith was a notorious character in Skagway, but builders of the railroad credit him with saving the project. During a strike of construction workers, radical leaders threatened to destroy much of the work that had been completed. "Soapy" and some of his followers arrived on the scene and restored order after other means failed. Smith was later killed in a shootout on the Skagway waterfront. (Denver Public Library— Western History Department.)

Prior to completion of the White Pass & Yukon Route one of the ways of traveling between Whitehorse or Dawson City and Skagway was by dog team. Here is a team from Dawson City which arrived in Skagway on Christmas Day 1898. In the background is the St. James Hotel where Sir Thomas Tanerede and Michael Heney met and formulated plans for the construction of the White Pass & Yukon Route. The hotel still stands in Skagway, although it has been moved from Fourth and State Street to a location just off Broadway. (Clifford Collection)

Workers with picks and shovels, along with a little blasting powder make a cut through the mountains on the White Pass & Yukon Railroad right-of-way. This photo was taken during the height of construction in August 1898. (Yukon Archives.)

Workers literally hung on by "the skin of their teeth" as they worked on the side of cliffs building the White Pass & Yukon Railroad. This photo was taken at Fisk's Cut on Tunnel Mountain in 1898. (Yukon Archives)

19

Key personnel involved in the building of the White Pass & Yukon Railroad pose in front of the foreman's tent at Construction Camp No. 3. Left to right are: the camp foreman, Mr. Foy; Dr. F.B. Whiting, railroad surgeon who was also active in the construction of the Copper River and Northwestern; Mike Heney, builder of the White Pass and the Copper River and Northwestern railroads; E.C. Hawkins, engineer who was also with Heney on the Copper River; Samuel H. Graves, president of the White Pass and representative of the money interests in the project; and John Hislop, chief surveyor—one of the three H's (Heney, Hawkins and Hislop) instrumental in the building of the WP&YR. (British Columbia Provincial Archives)

Construction work on the White Pass & Yukon continued through the winter months despite severe storms in the mountains. Here a bridge crew works through a blizzard building the timber bridge at Tunnel Mountain. (University of Washington Historical Library—Northwest Collection.)

One of the many difficulties faced by the builders was at Tunnel Mountain, where a tunnel was to be built. This was in late November — at the height of the storms with the weather hovering at 30 degrees below zero with gusting winds. Frequently it was impossible to shelter the men from the weather and days went by when it was impossible to go out and work. A day would be spent in clearing snow from the area, and during the night it would drift back and another day would be spent clearing the same area again.

Building the bridge at the mouth of the proposed tunnel was likewise difficult. Men became numb from the cold, and snow drifted so that it was almost impossible to see. Often they could not see across the forty-foot gap and the loudest shout could not be heard. A post would be swung up and be almost ready to drop into place, and a gust of wind would sway it out of line and out of reach of the men. But by perseverance they finally succeeded and the bridge was built.

Track was laid over the summit on Feb. 16, 1899 and the first passenger train with a load of excursionists went from Skagway to the summit of White Pass on Feb. 29, 1899. The first major hurdle had

This rather steep section of track was part of the construction facilities necessary for the building of the White Pass & Yukon. In September 1898 this section was used as a feeder track to haul supplies for the construction crews. It was located at Heney, B.C. (Yukon Archives.)

Tunnel building during the construction of the White Pass & Yukon Railroad was difficult work in 1898. Crews cut through the rock of Tunnel Mountain with picks and shovels and blasting powder. There was no power equipment in those days. This photo was taken during the cold winter months when work was almost at a standstill. (University of Washington Historical Library—Northwest Collection)

The first passenger train over the White Pass and Yukon Route to the summit of White Pass was on Feb. 20, 1899. The train crosses the East Fork of the Skagway River on one of the many trestles it was necessary to construct to carry the rails through the mountains and over the many streams and rivers. (University of Washington Historical Library—Northwest Collection)

When the White Pass & Yukon was completed to the summit of White Pass it became necessary to find a way of transportation between that point and the steamer terminus at Lake Bennett. All of the teamsters of the Skagway area were brought together under the direction of "Stikine Bill" Robinson and formed the "Red Ball Express" to meet all trains and all steamers. Horses and wagons are lined up at the rail terminus awaiting the next train. (Yukon Archives)

been overcome in less than a year since the start of work on the railroad.

One of the problems that had to be overcome by Mike Heney was "crossing" the international boundary into Canada, despite the fact that the money to finance the railroad was British.

At the time the summit of White Pass was believed to be the boundary between the United States and Canada. When Heney's spike-drivers and track-layers reached the summit they were told in courteous, but positive terms, that their "wildcat railroad" could go no further. The Royal Northwest Mounted Police visited the camp daily and were treated royally by Heney's crew, but they received instruction from Ottawa that "they shall not pass."

The "Irish Prince" as Heney was known, sent his trusted friend and co-worker, "Stikine Bill" Robinson as informal ambassador to the summit with instructions to procede in the spirit of diplomacy and untie the red tape.

The story goes that Bill's only baggage on his trip consisted of a bottle of Scotch in each pocket of his mackinaw, and a box of cigars under each arm. He found a guard pacing the supposed line. Two days later the guard woke up from a long and heavy sleep, and the first sight he saw was Heney's construction gang working like beavers, laying track well over the

international line and already a mile or so down the shore of Summit Lake.

Shortly thereafter the construction company was faced by a strike and it was not until June that trackage was laid far beyond the summit. It was during the months between the completion of the railroad to the summit and the continuation of the project to Lake Bennett, where passengers and cargo were carried to and from Dawson City and other points on the Yukon, that the White Pass sponsored the operation of the Red Line Transportation Co., known as the "Red Ball Express."

The project involved gathering together all of the teamsters who had operated over the White Pass Trail, forming them into a scheduled operation which met all trains, as well as the river sternwheelers. Such was put under the able direction of "Stikine Bill" Robinson, and operated successfully during the period between the completion of the railroad to the summit and the continuation on to Lake Bennett. More than 300 horses, with a corresponding number of wagons, teamsters and the like were involved.

Work on the railroad resumed on June 20, 1899 and from then on the track-layers put down three miles of track a day—two shifts working 12 hours a day each.

Early on the morning of July 6, 1899 a steamer that

Hundreds of workers were used to clear the track near the summit of White Pass when a winter storm hit. This photo shows the track completely buried during a storm on March 20, 1899. (University of Washington Historical Library— Northwest Collection)

Having successfully battled its way through the snow and ice over the White Pass, the WP&YR's first snowplow and its crew take a welcomed break in the continuing winter battle against the elements. The snowplow is now on display, along with an early day steam locomotive, at Lake Bennett, enroute between Skagway and Whitehorse. (University of Washington Historical Library—Northwest Collection.)

had come up the Yukon landed 200 passengers at Bennett. Across the front of a tent they saw a sign, "White Pass & Yukon R.R. Ticket Office." Many rushed in to buy tickets, but there was no railroad — not a rail or tie to be seen.

"We'll take care of you," the ticket agent blandly replied. "The train leaves at 2 p.m. sharp."

"Where abouts does it start frum?" asked a man in a broad white hat.

"It will leave from this depot at 2 p.m.," was the reply.

With that, the agent ceased to be a source of information. He gave his individual attention to the stamping of tickets, the counting of money, and the weighing of "dust."

Snow, sometimes 10 to 20 feet deep in the passes, presented a winter problem for the White Pass & Yukon trains. Locomotive No 7, a Baldwin 2-8-0 built in 1899 and which later saw service on the Klondike Mines Railway as No. 3, makes its way through drifts highter than the engine stack. The photo was taken near Glacier in December 1899. (Yukon Archives.)

The farthest north and highest steel bridge of the times (1898) was this structure over Dead Horse Gulch on the White Pass & Yukon Route over White Pass. This bridge was in daily service on the railroad until a few years ago when a cut-off was constructed, making use of the structure unnecessary. It served its purpose well for more than 75 years. (Yukon Archives.)

DRIVING THE LAST S[PIKE] [OF T]HE WHITE PASS AND YUKON R.R. AT LAKE [BENNETT]

Impressive ceremonies were held on July 6, 1899 at Lake Bennett when the "golden spike" was driven, marking completion of the White Pass & Yukon to that point. Government and business leaders of the day took part. Lake steamers stood by to take rushers on to Whitehorse and Dawson City. (University of Washington Historical Library—Northwest Collection)

When all had bought tickets, the pilgrims sat and listened to the ceaseless ring of the steel spike-mauls on the steel rails. Many went to see the men at work. The end of the track had been two miles away when they landed. It was nearer now. Some of the prospective passengers wanted to help the workmen, so eager were they to continue their journey, for many had "dust" that was spilling to be spent; and more longed to reach Seattle.

Finally amid the wildest of enthusiasm, the last spike was driven, and the first through passenger train pulled out on schedule.

On July 20, 1897 the first pack train had crossed the range from the head of Lynn Canal. A year later, on July 20, 1898, the first locomotive ran on the White Pass and Yukon line. On Feb. 20, 1899 the first passenger train went to the summit of White Pass, and the first through passenger train to Lake Bennett on July 8, 1899, only a little over a year from the commencement of building of the road.

When it was seen that the road would be completed, those who had predicted its failure began to prophesy that it would never earn operating expenses. As a matter of fact, the 20 miles from Skagway to the top of the hill earned enough to pay the cost of the expensive extension to Bennett—paid operating expenses and left a balance. The first $130,000 earned after the line was completed to Bennett showed a net profit of $100,000 over operating expenses. It cost in the neighborhood of $25,000 to run the road during the month of August, the first full month after completion of that portion of the line. The gross earnings that month were about $200,000. Not a bad month for a 40-mile road.

When the rails reached the head of Lake Bennett some method had to be devised to carry an immense quantity of rails, ties, stores, construction plants and rolling stock down Lake Bennett to Carcross (Caribou Crossing). For this purpose, a barge with a capacity of about 150 tons of freight was designed. All cargo was carried on its deck for convenience in loading and unloading. In shape it was a flat oblong box, with sloping ends which projected over the shore landings and facilitated freight handling. Again Bill Robinson was put in charge of this most important project.

When it was finished, Bill walked around it and inspected both ends carefully. Finally he said, "I think we'll make this end the stern." Whereupon the word "stern" was chalked in large letters on that end.

The next move was to install upright boilers with engine attached to three propellors. On a short trial trip the craft traveled so fast that it was named the

FIRST LOCOMOTIVE IN ALASKA - SKAGWAY, JULY 20, 1898

The White Pass & Yukon's first locomotive is serviced on Broadway, the main street in Skagway on July 20, 1898, prior to being put into service. Numbered No. 2 and later No. 52, the little Brooks, built in 1881, is now on display in Skagway. (University of Washington Historical Library—Northwest Collection)

"Torpedo Catcher." Finally Bill's flagship was ready and loaded for its maiden voyage down Lake Bennett. In the pilot house was "Stikine Bill." He blew his starboard whistle, jingled the engine-room bells, and backed out from the Bennett wharf. With all three propellors working, Bill wanted to show the crowd assembled on the bank how he could turn the "TC" in its own length. He did, but it kept turning and turning until the watchers on the bank struck up a popular tune of the day, "Waltz Me Around Again, Willie."

Bill finally got his steamship straightened out and chugged down the lake to Carcross.

Work was speeded up, with construction at both the Carcross and Whitehorse locations heading towards each other. On Aug. 8, 1899, however, 1500 employees during that day and the ensuing days to follow grabbed their picks and shovels (valued at $16 each) and started off pellmell on a gold stampede at Atlin B.C. Thus only a few hundred men were left on the job and it was necessary to fill their places. It was also necessary to break in the men who did fill the vacancies and to wait for a new supply of picks and shovels.

Construction on the railroad between Caribou Crossing and Whitehorse was completed on June 8, 1900, and the Bennett to Caribou Crossing section on July 29, 1900, joining the chain of steel from Skagway to Whitehorse.

Dignitaries of the period, both American and Canadian, took part in the Golden Spike ceremonies. An experienced trackman started the spike upright and gleaming beside the rail. The officials on hand, by this time feeling the effects of the typical Yukon hospitality marking such an auspicious occasion, struck with vigor at the spike with heavy sledge hammers, but to no avail. The spike remained battered but undriven. Calling it a most successful affair, the dignitaries, led by the company's president, retired to parttake of better things.

First Train to Lake Bennett. On July 6, 1899 the first White Pass & Yukon Railroad train made its way to Lake Bennett. Enroute back to Skagway the train carried more than $500,000 in gold from the Klondike. (University of Washington Library)

Winter Excursion Train. Local residents of Skagway took advantage of the completion of the White Pass & Yukon route to the summit of White Pass to ride an excursion train to the top on Feb. 20, 1899. Note the winter clothing of the day, and the many "tourists" with their cameras. (University of Washington Historical Library)

An early-day **White Pass & Yukon** locomotive on the turntable at the railroad shops in Skagway in 1899. Skagway has remained the major work terminal for the White Pass. (Yukon Archives)

One of the many scenic sights along the White Pass & Yukon Route is Hanging Rocks at Clifton. Steam locomotives passed this way half a century ago, just as the diesels do today. The locomotive pictured is No. 7, a Vulclain compound, one of the few of this type seen in the north. The engine is now on display at Minto Park in Dawson City. (Dedman photo from Clifford Collection.)

The track superintendent remained behind, removed the battered spike and replaced it with one less noble and drove it home, thus completing the rail link.

The building of the railroad was one of the most difficult ever engineered. There was no heavy equipment available and most of the work through the solid rock along the route was by hand drills and blasting powder.

Mike Heney and his able assistants, "Stikine Bill," E. C. Hawkins, Dr. F. B. Whiting, and others later were to be involved in the building of another northern railroad under similar difficult conditions—the Copper River and Northwestern, from Eyak (later named Cordova by Heney) to the rich copper fields of the interior.

All told there were 35,000 men at work on the White Pass from June 1, 1898 to Oct. 1, 1900, and of this number there were only 35 deaths from all causes, including sickness and accident. A very intelligent class of workmen was employed. Many of the men were anxious to reach the gold fields, but were waiting the opening of water transportation. Others who worked through the summer had exhausted their funds and wished to replenish them so they could continue prospecting. No Asiatic labor was employed on the project.

Upon one occasion the company surgeon, having an operation to perform, sent out on the grade for assistance. A skilled physician was found among the graders. He came in, assisted in the operation, and then took up his pick again.

From sea level at Skagway the WP&YR climbs to the summit of White Pass (2,885 feet) in 21 miles. The average grade to the summit is 2.6 percent, with the steepest about 4 percent. The line, from terminal to terminal, is 110.7 miles, of which 20.4 miles is in Alaska, 42.2 miles in British Columbia, and 58.1 miles in the Yukon. Cost of construction at the time the railroad was built was about $10,000,000.

In 1901 the White Pass expanded its transportation services—mainly because river service was irregular and unreliable. It bought the John Irving Navigation Co. which served the Atlin-Bennett region and the Canadian Development Co., which operated a winter stage line from Whitehorse to Dawson City. Included in the purchase were several sternwheelers and to operate them the WP&YR formed a river division, the British Yukon Navigation Co., or B.Y.N. as it was soon called. The firm built three new vessels, the 779-ton Dawson, the 777-ton Selkirk, and the 1120-ton Whitehorse, and bought several others, including the colorful Yukoner.

Concurrent with the starting of river services, the White Pass also took over the contracts for the winter hauling of both American and Canadian mail—and the many sled dog teams involved in the project.

The American contract covered the route between Juneau and St. Michael, via Whitehorse, with a branch to Nome and several other points off the Yukon River. The Canadian contract called for the carrying of Canadian mail between Skagway and Dawson City with a branch to Atlin, B.C.

The WP&YR did not want the winter routes—and the some 500 dogs involved, but it was necessary to take them over to continue with the summer routes, which payed a good portion of the operation costs of the sternwheelers on the river.

After one summer of maintaining 500 dogs, transferred with keepers, facilities and the like to a large island in Lake LaBarge, which became known as Dog Island, the company gradually changed the mail routes to horse drawn sleds, which carried passengers at the same time. Thus it was able to maintain the lucrative summer haul of the mail, and even make a little on the winter haul—thanks to the passenger service. The horse-drawn vehicles remained in service until 1921.

Jitneys line up at the right to whisk WP&YR passengers to Skagway hotels and nearby outgoing steamers when the train arrives from Whitehorse. This train is on Broadway, Skagway's main street, with Pioneer Hall in the near background. The tracks have been removed from Broadway but Pioneer Hall remains in the same location. (Yukon Archives.)

During the summer of 1899 the White Pass & Yukon terminated its run at Lake Bennett. Here trains turn around—without benefit of a roundhouse turntable—before heading back down the track to Skagway. Today Lake Bennett is a popular luncheon stop for travelers enroute between Skagway and Whitehorse. (University of Washington Historical Library—Northwest Collection.)

While the river remained open the White Pass built roadhouses at intervals along the trail and stored supplies for men and horses. When snow and ice hit, the roadhouses—small hotels of logs, heated by roaring fires provided comfortable beds and good meals. Meals were $1.50 with beds a $1 per night. Baggage up to 25 pounds per passenger was carried free, with fares $125 one-way plus roadhouse expenses between Whitehorse and Dawson City.

Service was cancelled if the temperature fell below minus 40 degrees.

By 1905 the era of pick and shovel miners was ending in the Yukon and being replaced by machinery. One firm that moved in was the Guggenheims of New York. They acquired control of the Eldorado, Bonanza and other creeks and in 1906 started construction of a $3 million, 70-mile-long ditch to bring in water for hydraulic mining. Additional millions went into construction of a fleet of seven dredges to rip up

the gravel—providing much needed traffic for the WP&YR riverboats.

Sternwheelers continued to be the main means of transportation, but scores were now ashore and abandoned. Others died more tragically. On Sept. 25, 1906, the Columbia was bound for Dawson on her last trip of the season. A crew member decided to shoot ducks from the vessel's deck, but unfortunately stumbled and fired into three tons of blasting powder on the bow.

Because of dwindling traffic, the Columbia was not replaced for five years. In 1911 the B.Y.N. launched the Casca, a 1,079-ton sternwheeler, which became the flagship of the fleet. Next was the Nasutlin and in 1913 the Yukon. By now B.Y.N. was engaged in a rate war with Northern Transportation, the major U.S. firm still on the river. Fares between Whitehorse and Dawson dropped from $26 to $5, a rate that officials of both companies knew would bankrupt them. Consequently,

During the winter months travel between Whitehorse—the terminus of the White Pass & Yukon—and Dawson City, the territorial capital, was by sledges. Passengers, well bundled in furs, stopped enroute at various roadhouses between the two cities for meals, overnight accommodations, and an occasional warm-up. No matter what the weather it was a chilly way to travel. This sledge was operated by the White Pass. (Yukon Archives)

Whitehorse was the northern terminus of the White Pass & Yukon and the "jumping off" place for the Klondike. River steamers carried the rushers down the Yukon to Dawson City during the summer months, and then were stored ashore during the winter as ice closed the river to all navigation. This was Whitehorse in 1901. (Yukon Archives)

they "reached an agreement." In April 1914 the White Pass bought out Northern Transportation.

In 1923 came new competition for the B.Y.N.—and there was no answer. The Alaska Railroad was completed from Seward on Alaska's southern coast 460 miles to Fairbanks. Additional sternwheelers joined the scores already decaying along the river and at St. Michael. The B.Y.N. operated 11 vessels on the Canadian section of the river, but these gradually dwindled. The Dawson was wrecked in Rink Rapids in 1926, the Selkirk in the fall of 1930 and in 1936 Thirty-Mile river claimed both the Klondike and the Casca.

Then in 1937 came a flurry of activity along the river. From the shipyards at Whitehorse came a new

1,363-ton Klondike and a 1,300-ton Casca. In addition the Keno was built and the Nasultin thoroughly overhauled. This was the last major sternwheeler building in North America.

World War II gave the vessels another life, but completion of the Alaska Highway and roads radiating from it once again cut into the transportation formerly supplied by these colorful vessels. In 1951 a road linked the mining community of Mayo to Whitehorse, and ore from the mine went by WP&Y trucks. In 1953 the road was completed to Dawson City, and the remaining sternwheelers were hauled onto the ways at Whitehorse, their working days over.

The Klondike was given a short reprieve following World War II when the White Pass in conjunction with

These three modes of transportation are a package of the way people traveled in the days of the Klondike gold rush and for many years thereafter. At Carcross along the White Pass & Yukon Route are: an old White Pass & Yukon stage, used to carry passengers between the railroad and the riverboats, and to interior towns in the Yukon; the sternwheeler Tutshi, which plyed the nearby waters of Nares and Tagish Lakes; and the historic little locomotive "Dutchess," which toiled for the White Pass & Yukon and for the Atlin Southern Railroad before being retired and put on display. (Yukon Travel and Information)

Canadian Pacific Airlines, spent $100,000 refurbishing her to stimulate summer tourist trade. She was fitted with a dance floor, lounge, full bar, and even a $1,000 record player. The experiment failed and in 1955 she too, was hauled ashore at Whitehorse. Today—after a disastrous fire which destroyed the Whitehorse and the Casca—only the Keno at Dawson City, the Klondike at Whitehorse, and the Tutshi at Carcross remain of the more than 200 which at on time were the key to transportation in the Yukon.

As far as the railroad itself was concerned, there were good years and bad, but by the 1920s the gold production started to fall off and the drop continued through the 1930s. The Yukon's population declined almost to the vanishing point. Some mining operations for silver, lead and zinc were developed in the Mayo district. The ore was carried to tidewater by the White Pass river and rail divisions and the Yukon communities maintained a reasonable level of business during the summer months, but business dropped to an extremely low level during the winter.

Over the years the railroad ran further and further into the red and at times barely was able to pay its bond interest. In added efforts to keep solvent in addition to the sternwheelers, horses and sleds, the firm went into the wholesale petroleum business with a pipeline long before the invention of tank cars on tracks.

Despite all this—during the winter months all senior officers of the company were forced to work without salary.

June 1934 marked the inauguration of an aviation division by the White Pass & Yukon when President Herbert Wheeler hired Vernon Bookwalter, a veteran northern pilot who was flying for Clyde Wann's Skagway Airlines, to operate the new division.

The White Pass's first aircraft was a Loening Keystone Commuter, a strange looking flying boat which soon became nicknamed "The Duck." Bookwalter first brought the aircraft to Whitehorse, where company officials lost little time in taking advantage of its time saving ability to line up wood along the

The White Pass & Yukon Route entered the air age with this Loening Keystone Commuter amphibian airacraft in 1930. Nicknamed "The Duck" this plane was the first of several operated by the railroad in competition with other "airlines" in the Yukon. The plane was operated between Whitehorse and Dawson City. (Yukon Archives.)

One of the last survivors of the hundreds of Yukon River sternwheelers which provided river transportation during the early 20th Century is the "Keno" now on display at Dawson City, Y.T. The other vessels, the Whitehorse at Whitehorse, and the Tutshi at Carcross, are all that remain of this once proud fleet owned by the White Pass and Yukon Route. (Clifford Collection.)

The White Pass & Yukon sternwheeler "Whitehorse" makes its way along the Yukon between Whitehorse and Dawson City, pushing an empty barge back to Whitehorse. The sternwheelers and barges were generally loaded to the gunwales on downstream trips to the Klondike. (Yukon Archives)

An early day White Pass & Yukon Route train crosses one of the many trestles and bridges encountered enroute to the Lake Bennett area. (University of Washington Historical Library—Northwest Collection)

Yukon River for the hungry boilers of the sternwheelers, which plied the waters between Whitehorse and Dawson. Normally such a journey took weeks. Wood-buyer Wheeler was able to make the trip in a matter of hours, saving days of valuable time. The WP&YR was in the aviation business.

Soon a 10-passenger Ford Tri-Motor, the largest such craft in the Yukon, was added and flew between Skagway, Whitehorse, Mayo and Dawson City. In July 1935, Ed Wasson, a partner in Northern Airways, was named chief pilot of the aviation division and a Fairchild 82 added to the fleet as headquarters was moved from Skagway to Whitehorse.

Other aircraft were added, the facilities at Whitehorse improved and airstrips built at Carmacks, Minto and Selkirk. As competition over the various routes increased—at times there were four or more aviation companies operating out of Whitehorse—the White Pass added a still larger plane, a Curtis Condor, which carried 18 passengers, to its fleet. The Condor was powered with two 750-horsepower Wright Whirlwind engines, turning three-bladed control-pitch propellors and cruised at 170-miles an hour.

In Oct. 1937 the White Pass received a government contract to carry the air mail between Dawson City, Mayo and Whitehorse, where it was turned over to the United Air Transport, headed by Grant McConachie, later to become president of Canadian Pacific Air while still in his 30s. Another competitor in the area, which flew from Juneau to Fairbanks, via Whitehorse, was Pacific Alaska Airways, a subsidiary of Pan American World Airways.

By 1939 more equipment was added, and like with the boats, competition beat the price on the Dawson-Whitehorse route down to $5, including luggage. None could survive at this rate, and the various operators soon got together and established a tariff of $50 one-way.

More planes came and went—as did the pilots—but bad luck and bad weather plagued the aviation division and late in 1939 President Herbert Wheeler sold out the aviation division lock-stock-and barrel to McConachie and his Yukon Southern as United Air Transport had become known.

A dramatic and sudden change came over the White Pass with the impact of World War II. The system went to war and despite being a Canadian corporation, donned the uniform of the U.S. Army. Its rail line and river system were strained to the limits to carry the hundreds of thousands of tons of military equipment and construction machinery which poured over the docks at Skagway and was carried inland to help build the Alaska Highway (Alcan) and the Canol pipeline system.

The Army took over on Oct. 1, 1942 and the soldiers landed in the north country at the beginning of one of the coldest winters on record. Temperatures dipped at Whitehorse to minus 75 degrees and stayed under 40 below for weeks at a time.

The story of the first winter is a story of hardships, privation and enduring cold which cut sharper than a razor. The men in the 770th Railway Operating Battalion came from such as the Southern Pacific, Texas Pacific and Santa Fe Railroads, and had never seen snow before, let along the most frigid weather on the continent. But an unending effort filled with hairbreath excapes and daring rescues pulled them through, and they have not been forgotten in a country where such exploits are common.

One time a train was smothered under huge snowdrifts at Fraser Loop, about 30 miles from Skagway, and a snow slide occurred a few miles behind, thus cutting off all communications in either direction. The engine ran out of water and crews were forced to draw the fires to keep from burning out the tanks. Coal for the stoves in the passenger cars ran out, and the few aboard chopped up the furniture to keep from freezing in the 30 below temperatures. Food soon became exhausted.

After seven days in this precarious position, the trapped train was reached by a tractor which had traveled 40 miles from Carcross over the Lake Bennett ice pulling three heavy sleds of supplies. The rescue was in time to prevent any casualties. Meanwhile, rotary plows working from both directions finally broke through and restored traffic over the line.

Lt. Col. William P. Wilson, who had been superintendent of the Burlington's frosty route across the Rockies in Colorado, was the commanding officer of the battalion.

As spring approached the military received help in the form of five narrow gauge locomotives from the United Nations, which the soldiers called "Gypsy Rose Lees" as they were "stripped for action." The Army purchased additional locomotives from the Colorado narrow gauge lines, and freight cars, built for services in South America, were hurriedly diverted to the north for use by the WP&YR.

This brought about a complete change. Trains were highballed over the pass every few hours. At one time

The White Pass & Yukon played an important role in construction of the Alcan Highway during the early days of World War II. Military construction equipment was landed at Skagway and transported to the Yukon via the WP&YR. A train load is seen in front of the depot, heading up Broadway. The dome of the Golden North Hotel is seen in the upper left hand corner. (Clifford Collection.)

This 18-passenger Curtis Condor was added to the White Pass fleet as competitors increased and fares dropped to as low as $5 per person between Whitehorse and Dawson City. A short time later the WP&YR got out of the airline business, selling out to Grant McConachie, who later became president of Canadian Pacific Air. (Yukon Archives.)

Two container unit trains pass at Lake Bennett enroute between Skagway and Whitehorse on the White Pass & Yukon Route. One of the trains also has a series of passenger coaches and one or two units for carrying automobiles. Cargo traffic is a most important part of the White Pass operation. Lake Bennett is the point from which sourdoughs of '98 built their boats and rafts for the trip down the Yukon River to the Klondike gold fields. (White Pass & Yukon Route)

the battalion put 34 trains through the Log Cabin station in a single day. Aug. 1943 was the record month with 45,000 tons hauled — an average of 1,500 tons a day.

The line was returned to civilian management on May 1, 1946, and it appeared as if the end was near. The equipment was worn out, business was at a low ebb, and all that remained was old and inefficient — even the employees who were long past their prime and remained on the payroll as there was no retirement plan.

The company became unpopular in both Skagway and Whitehorse. Damage claims on shipments ran high. Delayed shipments were blamed on the railroad whether it was responsible or not. The White Pass became the scrapegoat for just about everything that went wrong.

In 1947 the last steam locomotives purchased by the WP&YR, Nos. 72 and 73, were put into service. These Baldwins were also the last steamers to operate over the line, being retired from service on June 30, 1964.

In 1951 a new Canadian company, the White Pass and Yukon Corporation, was formed. The next years were ones of growth and modernization. The White Pass still remains quaint with old-fashioned coaches for the tourist trade, but its locomotives are modern, streamline diesel units. Even more important the line became a real pioneer in containerization. It made the big move in the early 1950s. Although not yet booming, prospecting and exploration were on the upswing and had produced a slight increase of transportation costs and their relationship to the future of the rail line and the territory.

The White Pass entered into containerization with the Clifford J. Rogers, the world's first ship designed specifically to handle the containers and containerized freight. The 4,000-ton Rogers was named after the president and general manager of the railroad for many years, and who had worked his way up through the ranks from an assistant in the freight office at Dawson City in 1904 to chief executive officer of the company.

The Rogers made more that 500 trips between Vancouver and Skagway in 10 years of service before it gave way to the new WP container ships of advanced

One of the White Pass & Yukon Route container ships, the Frank F. Brown, was recently converted to a barge for towing by ocean-going tugs. The vessel is pictured as it plys the waters of Lynn Canal between Skagway and Vancouver B.C. under its own power. The vessels carry rich minerals from the Yukon to markets in Western Canada. (White Pass & Yukon Route)

Today the White Pass & Yukon uses other means of transportation as well as the railroad and oil pipeline over the mountain passes. Ore is trucked from mines in the interior of the Yukon to the railroad in especially designed cargo units. The complete unit can be placed aboard the White Pass freight carriers and moved to the docks at Skagway for shipment to other parts of the world. (White Pass & Yukon Route.)

Container trucks are another means of transporting materials on the White Pass & Yukon routes. Containers can also be carried on trains, barges, and ships. (White Pass & Yukon Route.)

White Pass & Yukon Route highway division headquarters at Whitehorse. The WP&YR uses trains, trucks, barges and a pipeline to transport materials in the far north. (White Pass & Yukon Route)

design, the Frank H. Brown and the Klondike. Both are 6,000-ton vessels, with the Brown (named for the president of the White Pass Corporation) launched in April 1965 and the Klondike a few months later. Both since have been converted to barges and are towed between Vancouver and Skagway by ocean-going tugs.

On Oct. 15, 1969 a fire which started in a caboose being repaired destroyed six buildings in the White Pass & Yukon roundhouse and shop complex, including the roundhouse, blacksmith shop, boiler room, oil room, and the workmen's wash and lunch room building. Also lost in the blaze were two of the new diesel locomotives, Nos. 102 and 105; a switcher, No.

White Pass & Yukon Route roundhouse and shop facilities at Skagway as they appeared prior to the fire of Oct. 15, 1969, which destroyed six buildings, two new diesel locomotives and other equipment. (Dedman Photo Shop.)

3; an old steam engine, No. 72; one caboose, one parlor car, and a flat car. Loss was estimated in the millions of dollars.

Earlier, in Dec. 1943, a fire in the roundhouse at Whitehorse had damaged two locomotives, Nos. 10 and 14, which were later returned to Seattle and scrapped in Dec. 1945.

Federal Industries Ltd., a Winnipeg-based firm, acquired the White Pass and Yukon Corp., Ltd., in June 1973, including the shares of the major stockholder, Angelo American Corporation of Canada Ltd., and is owner of the Neptune Terminals Ltd., Vancouver area mineral terminal.

A reorganization program was put into effect which is still being carried out. In recent months, a slacking off in the mining industry in the Yukon and the recent opening of the Skagway-Carcross highway has cut into traffic and revenues. The company headquarters has been moved to Whitehorse.

Little remained of the roundhouse after the fire of Oct. 15, 1969 destroyed the WP&YR facility at Skagway. Here are remains of two new diesel locomotives, and a switcher which were totally destroyed. Little No. 52 steam locomotive at the far left was out of reach of the flames. Six buildings were destroyed in the blaze and the damage was estimated in the millions (Anchorage Historical and Fine Arts Museum)

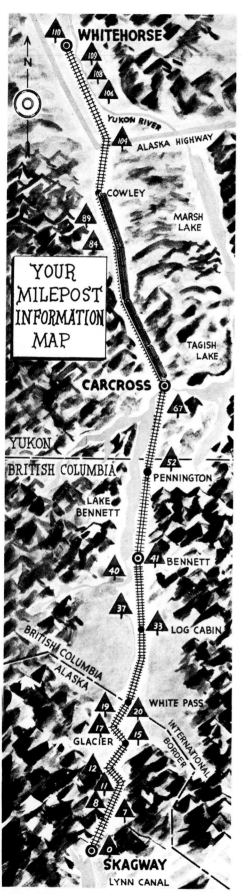

YOUR MILEPOST INFORMATION MAP

POINTS OF INTEREST

(Numbers represent miles from Skagway)

67 CARCROSS Famous old Yukon town on the Trail of '98.

41 LAKE BENNETT Old sourdough stopping place where boats were built to float down the Yukon to the Klondike. Famous "home style" meals served.

40 LAKE LINDERMAN Head of navigation during the gold rush.

37 BEAVER LAKE Home of many beaver.

33 LOG CABIN Start of the Fan Tan Gold Trail to Atlin. Once a gold rush town.

20 WHITE PASS SUMMIT Elevation 2,900 feet. International Boundary.

19 DEAD HORSE GULCH Named for 3,000 pack animals that died here during the gold rush of '98.

17 INSPIRATION POINT "Camera Stop" Magnificent scenery — historical spot.

15 TUNNEL MOUNTAIN White Pass Railway tunnel 1,000 feet above the floor of the gulch. Magnificent view.

12 BRIDAL VEIL FALLS As many as twenty-two cataracts have been seen tumbling down the gorge.

11 BLACK CROSS ROCK 100-ton granite block buried two men during blasting in 1898. The Black Cross marks their resting place.

8 CLIFTON See huge overhanging rock.

7 ROCKY POINT Magnificent view. Railway crosses Trail of '98.

0 SKAGWAY The Gateway to the Yukon. Once a city of 15,000 during the gold rush. Headquarters for the White Pass & Yukon Railway.

Map of the White Pass & Yukon Route from Mile 0 in Skagway to Mile 110 in Whitehorse. Most of the map, and explanations are of the sections between Skagway and Carcross, probably some of the most interesting and most historic trackage in North America. (Clifford Collection.)

This Brooks 2-6-0 locomotive, the first to arrive in Alaska for the White Pass and Yukon, is on display in downtown Skagway. Numbered No. 2 and later changed to No. 52 when remodeled in 1900, this historic narrow gauge locomotive also saw service with the Atlin Southern before being retired in 1940. (H. Clifford)

Two modes of White Pass & Yukon Route transportation are seen here. The Brooks 2-6-0 locomotive No. 51, built in 1881 and acquired in 1898 by the WP&YR from the Columbia & Puget Sound, was originally No. 1 on the railroad but numbered No. 51 following rebuilding in 1900. The engine was retired in 1941 and put on display at Whitehorse along with one of the White Pass horse-drawn sledges, which were used between Whitehorse and Dawson City during the winter months. (H. Clifford)

White Pass & Yukon locomotive roster.

"Georgiana" 0-6-0T Baldwin #3713, April 1875. Seattle & Walla Walla 1878. Sold to WP&YR 1898 but never shown on engine roster. Believed to have been lost with other equipment in shipwreck enroute to Skagway.

"Dutchess" 0-6-0T Baldwin #4424, Sept. 1878. Built for Dunsmuir, Diggle & Co. as 2'6" gauge "Dutchess." Wellington Colliery Ry. No. 2; WP&Y "Dutchess" 1899; Atlin Southern Ry. "Dutchess" 1899-1919. Retired and on display at Carcross. When widened to 3' gauge in 1899, the first driver was not coupled to the rods, making the engine an 0-(2)4-0T.

No. 1-51 2-6-0 Brooks 1881 Seattle & Walla No. 3; Columbia & Puget Sound No. 3; believed to be Ex-Utah & Northern. To WP&Y 1898. Rebuilt and renumbered No. 51 in 1900. To Atlin Southern 1919 and back to WP&Y in 1931. Retired in 1941 and on display at Whitehorse, Y.T.

No. 2-52 2-6-0 Brooks 1881. Seattle & Walla, No. 4; Columbia & Puget Sound No. 4; believed to be Ex-Utah & Northern. To WP&YR 1898 as first WP&Y locomotive. Arrived in Skagway July 20, 1898. Rebuilt and renumbered No. 52 in 1900. To Atlin & Southern 1931, back to WP&Y in 1937. Retired in 1940 and on display at Skagway.

No. 3-53   2-8-0 Grant 8/1882. Cincinnati & St. Louis No. 63; Dayton & Ironton No. 63, 1884; Columbia & Puget Sound No. 9, 1887. WP&Y 1898. Remodeled and renumbered No. 53 in 1900. Scrapped 1918.

No. 4-54   4-4-0 Baldwin #4294, 3/1878. Olympia & Tenino (later Olympia & Chehalis Valley) No. 1, "Quimette"; Columbia & Puget Sound No. 10, 1890; WP&Y 1898. Rebuilt and renumbered No. 54 in 1900. To Tanana Mines Ry. (Tanana Valley) No. 50, 1905; Alaska Engineering Commission (Alaska Railroad) 1917. Scrapped 1930.

No. 4 (2nd) 2-6-2 Baldwin #37564, 3/1912. Klondike Mines Ry. No. 4. WP&Y No. 4 (2nd) 1942. To Oak Creek Central Ry. 1952; Petticoat Junction RR, Sevierville, Tenn., 1965.

No. 5-55   2-8-0 Baldwin #7597, 5/1885. Columbia & Puget Sound No. 8. WP&Y 1898. Rebuilt and renumbered No. 55 1900. To Klondike Mines No. 2 1904. On display at Dawson City Y.T.

No. 6-56   2-8-0 Baldwin #16455, 1/1899. First new locomotive on WP&YR. Renumbered in 1900. Rebuilt from Vauclain compound to simple in 1907. Scrapped 1938.

No. 7-57   2-8-0 Baldwin #16456, 1/1899. Renumbered No. 57 1900. To Klondike Mines Ry No. 3 1906. On display in Dawson City Y.T. - last remaining Vauclain compound in Canada.

Locomotive No. 5, a Baldwin built in 1885, saw a lot of action on the White Pass before being sold to the Klondike Mines Railroad in 1904. The locomotive, KM's No. 2, is now on display at Minto Park in Dawson City (Clifford Collection)

White Pass & Yukon locomotives Nos. 4 and 5, along with some passenger coaches seen on the Seattle docks before being shipped to Skagway in 1897. No. 4, a Baldwin built in 1878, was obtained from the Columbia & Puget Sound, and later went to the Tanana Valley and Alaska Engineering Commission. No. 5 was also obtained from the Columbia and Puget Sound and eventually went to the Klondike Mines Railway. (Yukon Archives)

This Baldwin 2-6-2, built in 1912 for Klondike Mines Railway as their No. 4, later became a White Pass & Yukon No. 4 (2nd). It is seen here as it came out of the WP&YR shops in Skagway in 1942. It was later shipped east to Wisconsin for use on scenic railroads in the Mid-West and East. (H.L. Berry Collection)

A train load of little Porter saddle-tankers is enroute to Whitehorse on the White Pass & Yukon. The little locomotives were used by the Northern Light, Power, Coal and Transportation Co., near Dawson City. One of them eventually made its way to Fairbanks and the Tanana Valley (Mines) Railroad. The locomotive is No. 59, a Baldwin 4-6-0 built in 1900 for the White Pass. (Yukon Archives)

No. 8-58   3-truck. Climax #167, 12/1897. Columbia & Northwestern No. 2; Pacific Contract Co. (WP&Y) No. 8 1899; Renumbered No. 58 1900. Sold to Maytown Lumber Co. 1903. Scrapped.

No. 10   4-6-0 Baldwin #42766, 1/1915. East Tennessee & Western North Carolina No. 10; United States Army Transportation Corps., assigned to WP&Y No. 10 1942-45. Damaged in Whitehorse roundhouse fire Dec. 1943, returned to Seattle and scrapped 12/1945.

No. 14   4-6-0 Baldwin #52406, 9/1919. East Tennessee & Western North Carolina No. 14; USATC No. 14 1942-45. Damaged in Whitehorse roundhouse fire Dec. 1943, returned to Seattle and scrapped 12/1945.

No. 20   2-8-0 Baldwin #11355, 12/1890. Denver, Leadville & Gunnison No. 272; Colorado & Southern No. 69 1899; USATC No. 20 1943. Retired 1944 and scrapped in Seattle 12/1945.

No. 21   2-8-0 Baldwin #11356 1890. Denver, Leadville & Gunnison No. 273; Colorado & Southern No. 70 1899; USATC No. 21 1943. Scrapped in Seattle 12/1945.

No. 22   2-8-0 Baldwin #24109 4/1904. Silverton Northern No. 3; USATC No. 22 1943. Retired 1944 and scrapped in Seattle 12/1945.

No. 23   2-8-0 Baldwin #27977 4/1906. Silverton Northern No. 4; USATC No. 23, 1943. Retired and scrapped in Seattle 12/1945.

No. 24   2-8-0 Baldwin #24130 12/1904. Silverton Gladstone & Northerly No. 34; Silverton Northern No. 34, 1915; USATC No. 24, 1943-47. Retired 1944 and scrapped in Skagway 1951.

No. 59   4-6-0 Baldwin #17749 5/1900. Scrapped 1941.

No. 60   4-6-0 Baldwin #17750 5/1900. Retired 12/1942; used as riprap fill in Skagway River MP 2.5 in 1949.

Now with the Nebraska Northern, this locomotive was known as "Klondike Casey" when it was used by the White Pass & Yukon. It was retired from the WP&YR in 1954 after almost a half century of service. (Dedman Photo from Clifford Collection.)

One of the locomotives acquired by the WP&Y during World War II was this Baldwin 2-8-0, dubbed "Klondike Kate." These locomotives were originally built for use in Iran by the Army Corps of Engineers, but were converted to use on the White Pass. "Klondike Kate" was retired in 1960 and acquired by the Rebel Railroad as a tourist attraction in 1961. (Dedman Photo from Clifford Collection.)

No. 61	2-8-0 Baldwin #17814 6/1900. Retired 1944; used as riprap fill Skagway River MP2.5 in 1949.
No. 62	4-6-0 Baldwin #17895 6/1900. Retired 1945; used as riprap fill Skagway River MP 2.3 in 1949.
No. 63	2-6-0 Brooks #522 1881. Kansas Central Ry. No. 102 & No. 7. WP&Y, June 1900. Klondike Mines Ry. No. 1 in 1902. On display at Dawson City, Y.T.
No. 64	2-6-0 Hinkley 1878. Purchased 1900 from Canadian Pacific Railroad. Ex-Columbia & Western (Trail Tramway) No. 2. Scrapped 1918.
No. 65	2-6-0 Brooks #578 1881. Kansas Central No. 8; Union Pacific No. 102, 1885; Columbia & Western No. 3; Utah & Northern; Columbia & Western (Trail Tramway) No. 3; Canadian Pacific; White Pass & Yukon No. 65, 1900; Tanana Mines (Valley) No. 51, 1906; AEC (Alaska Railroad) No. 51, 1917. Scrapped by Alaska RR 1930.
No. 66	4-6-0 Baldwin #18964 5/1901. Retired 1953. Cab to No. 69.
No. 67	4-6-0 Baldwin #18965 5/1901. Retired 1941, used as riprap in Skagway River 1951.
No. 68	2-8-0 Baldwin #30998 6/1907. Destroyed by rock slide at MP 15.6 Aug. 17, 1917.
No. 69	2-8-0 Baldwin #32962 6/1908. Retired 1954. Sold to Black Hills Central RR No. 69 "Klondike Casey" 1954; Nebraska Northern No. 69.
Nos. 70 & 71	2-8-2 Baldwin #62234-57 5/1938 and 1/1939. Retired 1963 and stored. Sold to "Whistle in the Woods" Corp. for restoration.
Nos. 72 & 73	2-8-2 Baldwin #73351-52. 5/1947. Retired June 30, 1964 and stored. No. 72 destroyed in roundhouse fire, Skagway, Oct. 15, 1969.
Nos. 80 & 81	2-8-2 Alco #61980-81 5/1920. Sumpter Valley No. 20 & No. 19 and No. 102 & No. 101. To WP&Y 1940. Retired 1958 and 1957 and stored. Returned to Sumpter Valley RR for restoration.
No. 152	4-6-0 Baldwin #53269. 6/20 Alaskan Engineering Commission for Tanana Valley No. 152. Retired in 1932 and stored. To U.S. Army No. 152 for use on WP&YR. To Lathrop Transportation Corps Depot, Calif., 1945; Davidson Scrap Metals Co., Stockton, Calif.; Hal Wilmunder (Antelope & Western Ry. No. 3), Roseville, Calif.; Camino, Cable & Northern, Camino, Calif. CC&N ceased operation in 1974 and disposed of to unknown operation in Penn.

It wasn't many years ago that this scene was a familiar one on the waterfront at Skagway. Still using the dock area originally developed by Capt. Billy Moore, White Pass and Yukon Route trains picked up cruise ship passengers on the dock for their scenic trip over the historic White Pass to Lake Bennett and Whitehorse. The steam locomotive, No. 70, a Baldwin 2-8-0 built in 1938 and retired in 1963, has been sold to "Whistle in the Woods" for restoration and use on an East Coast tourist railroad. (Dedman's Photo Shop)

White Pass snowplow No. 2 and locomotive No. 81 loaded aboard a train in Seattle enroute to Sumpter Valley Railroad in Oregon. No. 81, formerly Sumpter Valley Nos. 19 and 101, was shipped north to Skagway for use on the White Pass in 1940 and following retirement in 1957 was stored and only recently returned to the Sumpter Valley—now a tourist type operation—where it will be restored and put back into service. (H. Clifford.)

White Pass snowplow No. 1 and steam locomotive No. 73 are part of the display of early day railroad equipment at Lake Bennett, on the White Pass & Yukon Route. The locomotive is a Baldwin 2-8-2 built in 1947. Lake Bennett was the building and launching point for a fleet of boats and scows which the Klondike stampeders made their way down the various lakes to the Yukon River and Dawson City. (H. Clifford.)

Nos. 190-200	2-8-2 Baldwin #69425-35 incl. 2/1943. Built for U.S. Army Corps of Engineers as meter-gauge for use in Iran, diverted and converted to 3' gauge. All USA same numbers.
	190 1943-46, retired 1946. Sold Tweetsie RR No. 190 "Yukon Queen" in 1960.
	191 1943-47, retired 1946, scrapped 1951.
	192 1943-46, retired 1960, sold Rebel RR No. 192 "Klondike Kate" 1961.
	193 1943-47, retired 1946, scrapped 1951.
	194 1943-47, retired 1946, scrapped 1951.
	195 1943-47, retired 1946, on display in Skagway.
	196 1943-45, retired 1961, stored unserviceable.
	197 1943-47, retired 1944, scrapped 1951.
	198 1943-44, scrapped Seattle 1945.
	199 1943-44, scrapped Seattle 1945.
	200 1943-44, scrapped Seattle 1945.
Nos. 250-256	2-8-2 Alco #64981 −82, −83, −85, −86, −88, −90. 9/1923. Ex-Denver & Rio Grande Western Nos. 470, 471, 472, 474, 475, 477, 479. USA 1942/44 Nos. 250-256. No. 250 scrapped Seattle 1944; 251 Seattle 1945; 252 Ogden 1945, boiler to Pueblo; 253-256, Seattle 1945.

Similar to the scene above is the Skagway waterfront today. The dock is the same, the cruise ship little different, the train coaches the same, but with a modernized diesel locomotive providing the motive power. The General Electric diesel No. 90 was built in 1954 for the narrow gauge White Pass operation. (Dedman's Photo Shop)

Early records of the White Pass & Yukon fail to show this little 0-4-0 switcher pictured on the docks of Skagway. Identification of the workers or date of the photo are not known, but the little saddle-tanker apparently was a real workhorse during construction of the railroad over White Pass. (University of Washington Historical Library—Northwest Collection)

Diesels

Nos. 90-91   General Electric #32060-61. 800 hp. June 1954.
Nos. 92-94   General Electric #32709-11. 890 hp. Dec. 1956.
Nos. 95-97   General Electric #34592-94. 890 hp. March 1963.
Nos. 98-100 General Electric #35790-92. 990 hp. May 1966.
Nos. 101-107Alco #602301, 03, 04, 06, 07. 1200 hp. 1969.
Nos. 108-110Alco #605401-03. 1200 hp. 1972.

Switchers

No. 1   General Electric #28109. 150 hp. 1969.
No. 81   General Electric #32933. 800 hp. 1957.

Built in 1898-99 this steel bridge over Dead Horse Gulch was just one of the many marvels of the White Pass & Yukon Route. The bridge was recently by-passed by a shorter cut-off but was in use for more than 75 years. A small roundhouse, used to protect the locomotives during winter storms, is seen at the far left. (Dedman's Photo Shop)

The skeleton of the old log church at Lake Bennett is a constant reminder of the romance and history that remains from the gold rush days of 1898. Bennett was the jumping off point for thousands as they took their boats, scows and barges into the unknown waters of the North to make their way to the Klondike. The church today is a popular visitor attraction during the luncheon stop at Bennett on WP&YR trains traveling between Skagway and Whitehorse. (Yukon Travel and Information.)

A White Pass & Yukon Route passenger train along the shores of scenic Lake Fraser in the Yukon. The White Pass follows the original Trail of '98 from Skagway to Whitehorse, Y.T. Modern diesel locomotives pull trains formerly headed by little narrow gauge steam locomotives, but much of the romance of such a trip over historic White Pass and down the Yukon to Whitehorse remains. (White Pass & Yukon Route)

Passengers in front of the old log depot at Whitehorse wait the arrival of the daily White Pass & Yukon Route train from Skagway. The railroad connects the two historic gold rush towns with one of the most scenic rail trips in the world. The little narrow gauge trains follow closely the route taken by the gold seekers of 1898. (Yukon Travel and Information.)

Except for the locomotives, these two photographs, taken almost a half-century apart, are almost identical. They show a White Pass & Yukon passenger train in front of the depot in Skagway. One was taken in the early 30's, the other in the mid-70's. (Dedman photos from Clifford Collection)

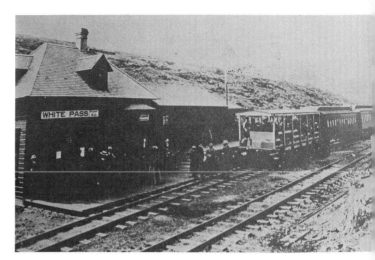

Brand-spanking new, the first diesel-electric locomotive on the White Pass & Yukon is tested outside the railroad shops at Skagway. Locomotive No. 90 was acquired by the White Pass in June 1954, following the retirement of much war-weary equipment. (Dedman Photo from Clifford Collection.)

Early-day White Pass & Yukon excursion train at White Pass summit. Sightseeing cars were constructed from flat cars with open sides and a roof. Passengers sat on benches. (Clifford Collection.)

A modern day White Pass & Yukon Route train at Carcross (formerly Caribou Crossing), hauling teardrop ore containers of lead-zinc concentrate to the terminal at Skagway. It is shipped to U.S. and Canadian smelters for processing. (White Pass & Yukon Route)

Chapter 2

Atlin Southern

Just as the Atlin gold rush was a spin-off of the larger Klondike rush, the Atlin Southern Railway was a spin-off of the larger White Pass & Yukon Railroad.

The Atlin gold strike came in Aug. 1899, with the resultant rush of some 1,500 White Pass construction workers to abandon their jobs with the railroad, but hang onto their railroad picks and shovels, to join the stampede. At first the Atlin rush showed signs of being the "real thing" and in Feb. 1899, a group of Victoria businessmen obtained a charter from the British Columbia Legislature to build a tramway or railroad, to be known as the Atlin Short Line Railway and Navigation Co., across the isthmus from Taku Arm, near the mouth of the Atlin River, to Scotia Bay on the west shore of Atlin Lake. This was a short-cut from the headwaters of the Yukon River, reached by the White Pass & Yukon from Skagway, to the gold fields of the Atlin area.

The new company also acquired powers to construct telegraph lines, to utilize the Atlin River for electric power purposes, and to build wharves and other facilities for steamship services.

To reach the communities on Atlin Lake it was necessary to transfer passengers and freight from the White Pass to the sternwheeler Tutshi at Carcross for the trip through Nares Lake, then some 70-miles down Tagish Lake to Taku where a portage of two miles was necessary before reloading at Scotia Bay aboard another lake steamer for the trip across the lake to the community of Atlin.

On June 6, 1899, J.H. Brownlee, the company president, officially opened the tramway, in the form of a wagon road used to haul freight across the portage from Scotia Bay to Taku. Brownlee's firm also constructed wharves at Scotia Bay and Taku.

The John Irving Transportation Co. temporarily acquired control of the Atlin Short Line during the navigation season of 1899, but Brownlee reassumed direction of the line in the fall of the same year.

Not to be outdone, Captain John Irving planned to construct a second tramway across the peninsula in competition with the Brownlee concern, and in March 1900 construction began on the John Irving Tramway. Protests from Brownlee's group, however, led to the temporary suspension of work on the Irving tram. In June 1900 the dispute between the two groups was settled by the intervention of the White Pass & Yukon, which bought out the assets, steamers, wharves and tramway of the Irving Navigation Co., and completed the railway across the isthmus as planned by Brownlee, and known as the Atlin Southern or the "Taku Tram."

Continued disruption of service by disputes in other areas, plus confusion and dissatisfaction with the hodge-podge of independently owned and operated river and lake boats on the Yukon downstream to Whitehorse and Dawson City, resulted in the WP&YR also acquiring all such independent companies, and thus gain control of transportation to the mining camps between Atlin, Carcross and other areas in British Columbia and the Yukon.

Following the acquisition by the WP&YR a narrow gauge rail system was completed between Taku and Scotia Bay and on July 18, 1900 the first train ran across the isthumus, over what was probably the shortest railroad in Canada. The fare, oneway was $2, one of the highest per mile rates in the world. Passengers sat on their baggage during the journey. There was no turn-table or roundhouse, so it was necessary for the train to go forward from Taku to Scotia Bay and backwards on the return trip. Grades on the run were up to seven percent, and oftimes it was necessary for the locomotive to take a run at the hill in order to pull the 12-ton passenger car over the summit. At times the passengers disembarked and helped push.

Another "unusual" feature of the Taku Tram was that the lone passenger car was fully "air conditioned"

Early day transportation across the Taku Isthmus was via horse cars on wooden rails as seen here. Later the Atlin Southern Railroad, known as the Taku Tram, carried passengers and freight across this narrow arm of land between the Atlin River and Atlin Lake. (University of Washington Library)

with no windows. Swallows built their nests in the inside corners, and when the car moved from one end of the line to the other, they flew alongside. The moment the train stopped, they reboarded. A swallow sitting on eggs in its nest would not move off when the train started. When nests had their young in them mature birds flew alongside catching insects and fed them to their youngsters when the train came to a stop.

The first locomotive acquired by the Atlin Southern, which like the rest of the rolling stock would have been fit for a museum in those days, was a little engine which had seen hard useage since it was built 22 years earlier by the Baldwin Locomotive Works in Sept. 1878, Shop #4424, for the Dunsmuir & Diggie Co. It later became #2 for the Wellington Collier Railway on Vancouver Island, and was acquired by the Atlin Southern in 1899. The little 11-ton wood-burner built as a two-foot, six-inch gauge, was widened out to three feet narrow gauge and in the conversion the leading drivers were not reconnected, thus making the

0-6-0T in effect a 0-(2)4-0T. The little locomotive was immediately dubbed the "Dutchess" a name it still carries today.

The other original equipment consisted of a passenger car seating 48 people and six flat cars, of 10-ton capacity each.

After more than 15 years use on the Taku Tram, the Dutchess was converted to an oil burner in 1917 and then in 1919 was taken out of commission, and later moved to Carcross where she was sidetracked, refurbished with new paint, and put on display for tourists. For years, however, she still served a useful purpose as the White Pass agent at Carcross burned papers and refuse in her firebox.

The Dutchess was followed in 1919 by WP&YR locomotive No. 1, a Brooks 2-6-0 built in 1881. In 1931 she blew a piece out of her main steam pipe and was replaced by a sister locomotive, the former WP&YR No. 2, a Brooks 2-6-0 built in 1881. She served on the Atlin Southern until 1937 when she was replaced by a Ford tram, a home-made piece of rolling stock which consisted of a flatcar powered with a Ford V-8 truck engine, which operated until 1951 when Atlin was connected by road to the Alaska Highway.

Number 51 was repaired and used by the White Pass until 1941 when it was retired and put on display at Whitehorse. Number 52 was retired in 1940, but it was not until 1964 that efforts were made to recover the locomotive (which had been left in the brush near Taku), restore it and put it on display. White Pass employees, under direction of Carl Mulvihill, a dispatcher and third generation White Pass man, started "Project 52" to purchase, recover and restore the historic engine. As the drive gained momentum the White Pass donated the locomotive to the project.

After a lengthy and difficult project, including the moving of the locomotive over the ice of Lake Atlin, using a low-boy truck to move the 29½-ton engine to Whitehorse, then by train to Skagway, where it was restored, only to be damaged in a fire that destroyed the roundhouse and yards in Oct. 1969.

The roundhouse repairs and other urgent projects delayed the final restoration until late 1971, when #52 was moved to its place of honor in downtown Skagway.

In 1953 the Tutshi was pulled up on the beach at Carcross and the rails at Taku-Scotia Bay removed, leaving the rolling stock in the bush. Today, the Tutshi, the Dutchess and one of the White Pass stages is on display at Carcross, a momento to early days of transportation in the area.

Other railroads for Atlin have been projected, but none of them materialized. In 1899 the Atlin Southern Railway Co. proposed to build a line from Log Cabin, via Atlin to Telegraph Creek. Between 1900 and 1902 the Pacific Northern and Omineca Railway Co. evolved ed plans to construct a railway from Kitimat Inlet, via Hazelton, Teslin and Atlin to Dawson City. The Atlin Claim, the community newspaper, repeatedly urged both the Provincial and Federal Governments to support these railroad projects. The Claim argued that an all-Canadian railway route to the Yukon was essential, and that any of the proposed routes would keep northern trade in the hands of the Canadian businessmen. The arguments of the Claim, however, were fruitless. The period between 1900 and 1915 was a booming one for railroad construction in Canada, but the major portion of the construction was on an east-west basis rather than to the northland. Not one of the railways which planned to originate from, or pass through Atlin ever materialized. The only real railway Atlin ever had was the Atlin Southern.

Atlin Southern locomotives.

"Dutchess" 0-6-0T Baldwin #4424. 1378. Built as a 2'6" gauge for Dunsmuir Diggie & Co.; Ex-Washington Colliery Ry., Vancouver Island; White Pass & Yukon "Dutchess." Converted to 3-foot gauge and 0-(2)4-0T. Atlin Southern in 1899. Back to WP&Y in 1919 and retired. On display at Carcross.

No. 1 2-6-0 Brooks. 1881. Ex-Utah & Northern; Seattle and Walla Walla No. 3; Columbia and Puget Sound No. 3; White Pass & Yukon No. 1 in 1898. Rebuilt in 1900 and renumbered No. 51. Atlin Southern 1919. Back to WP&Y 1931. Retired 1941 and on display at Whitehorse.

No. 2 2-6-0 Brooks. 1881. Ex-Utah & Northern; Seattle and Walla Walla No. 4; Columbia and Puget Sound No. 4; First locomotive for White Pass & Yukon as No. 2 on July 20, 1898. Rebuilt and numbered No. 52 in 1900. Atlin Southern in 1931. Abandoned at Taku in 1937. Recovered and restored 1964. On display at Skagway.

One of the North Country's most historic locomotives is the little "Dutchess" which saw service on both the White Pass & Yukon and Atlin Southern. Here the little narrow gauge locomotive is seen in service pulling the Atlin Southern's one and only passenger car. In the background is one of the lake steamers which brought passengers and freight to the Atlin area. The "Dutchess" is now on display at Carcross. (Canadian Pacific Archives)

Chapter 3
Whitehorse Tramways

The gold rush in the Klondike brought thousands of prospectors to the north, and whether they went through Chilkoot Pass out of Dyea or over the White Pass from Skagway, they eventually found their way through the lake country and down the Yukon River.

One of the major hazards of this route was Miles Canyon, a danger few desired to risk their lives or their possession to tackle. On top of that, the Northwest Mounted Police made a rule that stampeders would have to hire experienced pilots to take them through the canyon, and fixed a fee of $20 - so that they would not be fleeced. One of those early day pilots was Jack London, who is reported to have made $3,000 in 1897 before continuing on to the Klondike.

In the spring of 1897 Norman D. Macaulay arrived at White Horse Rapids and a year later with five other men constructed a tramway, known as the Canyon & White Horse Rapids Railway, on the east side of the Yukon (also known as the Lewes or Fifty Mile River at this point) from Canyon City, one mile above Miles Canyon where he operated a roadhouse, to a point about four miles downstream from the Canyon, where a community eventually known as White Horse (Whitehorse) was being built. (The town moved across the river to its present site when the White Pass and Yukon Railroad came down the west side of the river).

The tramway was constructed of rough hewn poles about eight inches in diameter, laid three feet apart and at intervals of from five to 12 feet cross pieces or ties were place. A truck with concave surfaced iron wheels was drawn by a horse. Thus, boats, supplies and the like were transferred past the treacherous rapids.

A group of stampeders with a horse-drawn tram car move their goods over the wooden rails of the Miles Canyon and Lewes River Tramway, Inc. This tramline was constructed by John Hepburn on the east side of the river and extended about a half-mile above the Macaulay tram with the hopes of tapping the river traffic. In the background are the Northwest Mounted Police buldings and stacks of freight awaiting transportation. The trams operated in the 1897-98 period, prior to the building of the White Pass & Yukon Railroad. (Yukon Archives)

Loaded horse-drawn tram cars are pulled along the Miles Canyon-Whitehorse tramline dock, with piles of freight awaiting movement seen in the background. The sternwheeler "Bailey" is docked nearby. The line, known as the Macaulay Tramline, was on the east side of the river and later became known as the Canyon and Whitehorse Rapids Railway. The tramline enabled stampeders to by-pass the treacherous White Horse-Rapids, one of the most dangerous spots enroute to the Klondike. (Yukon Archives)

Macaulay did a land-office business, charging three cents a pound and $25 for boats. The little wagons or cars were not over-steady on the rails and many oldtimers recall riding high on top of a load of freight on one of the cars, watching with bated breath as boats and barges zoomed through the canyon.

Shortly thereafter another tramway, this one on the west side of the river, was constructed by John Hepburn. His tram about six and one-half miles in length, and was designed to "tap" the river traffic about a half mile or so above Macaulay's. A crude windlass was rigged to hoist the gear from boats to the top of the bank. Hepburn's route was along the line of the old portage trail and was known as the Miles Canyon and Lewes River Tramway, Inc.

Hepburn eventually sold out to Macaulay for a reported $60,000 and he successfully operated both tramways until the White Pass & Yukon tracks neared Whitehorse. He sold both rights-of-way to the Canadian Development Co., a subsidiary of the Alaska Steamship Co., (C.E. Peabody and associates) who later sold out to the White Pass & Yukon.

Macaulay later operated three roadhouses on the route between Whitehorse and Dawson City, which he eventually sold to the C.D. Co., and built the White Horse Hotel.

Chapter 4

Klondike Mines Railway

Deemed necessary for the proper development of the Klondike mining district, the British Columbia government in Victoria passed an act on July 10, 1899 to incorporate the Klondike Mines Railway and Stage Co. Incorporators were Thomas W. O'Brien of Dawson City; James A. Seybold, Ottawa; William R. Rose, New Glasgow, N.S.; Llewellyn N. Bates, Ottawa; and Harold McGiverin, Ottawa.

The act provided for incorporation for $1,000,000 and granted the company the right to build a single or double line railway or tramway or both from Klondike City to Bonanza Creek, then along the divide to Dominion Creek, to Indian River, the Yukon and then back to Dawson City. Branch lines on the Klondike River to Hunker Creek, Bear Creek, Quartz Creek, Sulphur Creek, Eldorado Creek, and other creeks were provided for along with telegraph and telephone lines and electricity.

Shortly after the papers were granted, O'Brien made application on behalf of the Klondike Mines Railway to lease waterfront lots in Klondike City for the terminus of the railway, but this action was cancelled in 1904. In 1902 William White, on behalf of the railroad, started negotiations for property for railway shops at Ogilvie Bridge, but this too was dropped because the railway was unable to obtain surface rights for the property from those people who held placer claims on the property.

In 1902 O'Brien, along with W.H. Parsons and E.C. Hawkins (who had made a name for himself in railroad construction circles as a result of his work on the White Pass & Yukon) appeared before the city council of Dawson City for a franchise for the right-of-way for the railroad to enter the city via First Avenue to Queen Street where a passenger depot was to be erected; then along the waterfront to King Street and to First Ave. again and then to Albert Street, where

the terminus was to be located. The franchise application was brought about by Dawson City businessmen who could see dollars slipping through their fingers if the terminus was allowed to stay in Klondike City as originally planned.

Another plan called for the railroad to run into the White Pass & Yukon docks in Dawson City where freight and passengers could be transferred without effort or delay. Neither plan came about, however, as the government incorporation did not call for such a terminus, and the cost of bridging the Klondike River would have been prohibitive for the railroad.

Nothing further was done in the mad rush of the early day excitement in the Klondike and it was not until May 23, 1903, when the initial rush had petered out, that the Yukon Council, in a communication to the Governor General of Canada, reported that cheap transportation (rail) would allow the reworking of claims at a profit if large machinery could be brought in. The report went on to state that at present such transportation in the Klondike was inadequate.

In 1905 further negotiations were carried on between J.A. Chute representing the railroad, and the Klondike City council regarding waterfront property in that community being used as a terminus of the railroad. Such leases were finally forthcoming, first at $1.00 per year per front foot and later $10.00 a year for all the property required.

Following the letter from the Yukon Council considerable grading was done and three or four miles of track laid. This grade was afterward abandoned and work started on a new grade on July 18, 1906 with financing of construction and operation provided by a British company, the Dawson, Grand Forks & Stewart River Railway Company of London.

On Aug. 16, 1906 the railroad applied to open the first 15 miles out of Klondike City. At that time the first

The construction crew working on a bridge for the Klondike Mines Railway in the Dawson City area in 1902 takes a break for the photographer. The railroad eventually ran from Klondike City to Dome Mountain, a distance of 31 miles. (Yukon Archives)

13 miles of narrow gauge track had been constructed of 52-pound rails and then tapered off to 45-pound for the remainder of the trackage. The first 15 miles was opened to traffic on Nov. 5, 1906 after various governmental agencies certified that traffic over that section would be "reasonably safe" to the public.

Work was continued and eventually 31 miles of track was laid to the summit of Dome Mountain at a cost of $2,000,000. Work on this line was completed on Oct. 16, 1906, and from then on the railway engaged in transporting large amounts of cord wood, freight and mining equipment to the creeks. Passenger traffic was also included with the cargo handled by the company's own freighting outfits from the railroad to its various destinations. Daily stages carried the passengers and express to and from all creek points.

The Klondike Mines Railway acquired its first locomotive in 1902, A 2-6-0 Brooks freight engine

known as a Mogol, from the White Pass & Yukon. The second locomotive was also acquired from the White Pass. It was a 2-8-0 consolidated type freight engine built by Baldwin Locomotive Works. Klondike Mines' No. 3 was also a 2-8-0 consolidated built by Baldwin as a Vauclain compound. An oddity of the time with this engine was the fact that the driving wheels were inside the main frame.

These three locomotives are on display at Minto Park at Dawson City, having been moved there from Klondike City in the early 1960s.

The Klondike Mines' No. 4 locomotive was built new for the railroad by Baldwin. It was a 2-6-2 Prairie type and was used very little during its two years of service. It was later sold to the White Pass & Yukon.

From the opening of service in 1906 until May 31, 1908, the railway lost $121,596.65 on revenue of $128,058.82. The loss was due largely to the fact that costs skyrocked during the winter months, and the railroad was able to operate a regular schedule only from April to November.

The Klondike Mines Railway ceased operation as such in July 1914 and was acquired by the Yukon Consolidated Gold Corp., Ltd. Trackage was later removed, and Sept. 6, 1928, permission was given to the government to use the right-of-way from Six Below to Bonanza as a highway. That highway is still in use today.

During the entire operation of the railway, pressure was put upon the owners to extend their trackage into Dawson City, and negotiations for a lease of property there was a continuing program, but nothing came of it.

Following the discontinuation of service the KM equipment was moved to Klondike City along with some acquired by YCGC in the taking over of the Northern Light, Power, Coal and Transportation Co. In the 1960s this equipment was moved across the ice to the present location in Minto Park, Dawson City.

Hauling cordwood to the mining areas where giant furnaces generated steam to thaw the permafrost was one of the major operations for the Klondike Mines Railway. Here a train, headed by KMR No. 3, a Vauclain compound Baldwin, is pulling out of Klondike City enroute to the gold fields. Dawson City is across the river. (H.L. Berry Collection)

The first train on the Klondike Mines Railway makes its way out of the Klondike City on Nov. 5, 1906 after the first 15 miles of track received approval from government officials. The locomotive is a Brooks 2-6-0 acquired from the White Pass & Yukon. (H.L. Berry Collection)

THE KLONDIKE MINES RAILWAY COMPANY

Operating daily trains between **Dawson** and **Sulphur Springs** and connecting with our own stages running on **Sulphur, Dominion** and **Quartz Creeks.**

We operate our own freighting outfits in connection with the railway and quote passenger and freight rates to any claim on Bonanza, Eldorado, Hunker, Sulphur, Dominion, Gold Run and Quartz Creeks, or any of their tributaries. For rates or other information address

E. A. MURPHY, Manager
Dawson, Y.T.

An advertisement for the Klondike Mines Railroad Company as it appeared in the July 21, 1909 edition of the Dawson Daily News. This was the period that the Klondike Mines operation was at its peak. (Clifford Collection.)

Klondike Mines Railway locomotive No. 1, a Brooks 2-6-0 acquired from the White Pass & Yukon is on display at Minto Park in Dawson City.

Three locomotives from the Klondike Mines Railway, plus a little Porter narrow gauge, are on display at Dawson City's Minto Park. They are a vivid reminder of early day railroading in the Yukon. (H. Clifford)

Klondike Mines locomotives.

No. 1   2-6-0 Brooks #522 4/1881. Ex-Kansas Central Nos. 102 and 7; White Pass & Yukon No. 63, 1900. Klondike Mines No. 1, 1902. Now on display Minto Park, Dawson City.

No. 2   2-8-0 Baldwin #7597 5/1881. Ex-Seattle and Walla Walla No. 8; Columbia & Puget Sound No. 8; White Pass & Yukon Nos. 5 and 55, 1898. Klondike Mines No. 2, 1904. On display at Minto Park, Dawson City.

No. 3   2-8-0 Baldwin #16456, Vauclain compound #1602. 1/1899. Ex-White Pass & Yukon No. 7 and 57. Klondike Mines No. 3, 1906. Now on display at Minto Park, Dawson City.

No. 4   2-6-2 Baldwin #37564 2/1912. White Pass & Yukon No. 4 (2nd), 1912; To Oak Creek Railroad 1952; Petticoat Junction RR, 1964.

The pontoon section of a giant gold dredge under construction is seen in the center of this photo of a Klondike Mines Railway construction camp at Bonanza Creek. The photograph was taken in August 1912. The railroad ceased operation two years later when gold production fell off. (Yukon Archives)

Dawson City looking north from Queen Street at midnight June 10, 1904. The Klondike Mines Railroad started operating about two years later from across the Klondike River to the gold fields. (Clifford Collection.)

Chapter 5

Northern Light, Power, Coal and Transportation Co.

One of the more unusual little railroads to spring up as a result of the Klondike gold rush was the Northern Light, Power, Coal & Transportation Co. which operated from the Yukon River at a point some six miles below Forty Mile, 12 miles up Coal Creek to a coal mine.

Built in 1904 at a cost of $400,000 the little narrow gauge served the mine and power plant which provided electricity to the city of Dawson. Coal from the mine was also brought down to the river for use in the Yukon River steamers. The entire operation went bankrupt when the North Fork Power Plant was put into operation in the Dawson City area.

The narrow gauge operated with an undetermined number of saddle-back locomotives built by the H.K. Porter Co., Pittsburg, Pa. and brought to Whitehorse from Skagway on the White Pass & Yukon Railroad and transshipped to Forty Mile on one of the sternwheelers operating on the river at that time.

Following the closing down of operations, one of the little Porter 0-4-0T's, #1792, was barged down the river to Fairbanks in 1905 where it was the first locomotive put into service by the Tanana Mines Railroad, later the Tanana Valley Railroad.

The Porter was acquired by the Alaska Railroad in 1917 when the U.S. Government took over the Tanana Valley operation. For many years it was on display as Alaska R.R. No. 1 at the Alaska Railroad depot in Fairbanks, located at what was known as Garden Isle in the early days. In 1967 it was moved to the Alaska Centennial grounds (Alaskaland) where it is still on display, although the ARR No. 1 designation has been removed.

In later years the Yukon Consolidated Gold Corp., Ltd. acquired the NLPC & T Co. facilities and right-of-way.

A second Porter, #3025, designated No. 1 was removed from the Yukon in 1965 when it was acquired by Roger Burnell of a Vancouver, B.C. and trucked to Whitehorse where it was loaded aboard a White Pass & Yukon rail car for shipment south. Another locomotive, Porter #3022, and bearing the Northern Light designation No. 4, was moved first to Klondike City and then early in the 1920s taken across the river to Dawson City's Minto Park where it is on display along with three of the four locomotives which served the Klondike Mines Railroad.

In the winter of 1968-69 three Whitehorse men, Harry C. Cooper, Gunnar Nielson and D.F. Howian, discovered another Porter 0-4-0T on the Coal Creek property, believed to be No. 3, along with two Porter 0-6-0Ts, which were not known to have existed in this operation. All three were brought out in the middle of winter, by sledding them down the ice and snow from the mine into Dawson City, a distance of about 75 miles, and then trucked into Whitehorse. Plans call for the rebuilding and eventually putting them into service.

Northern Lights engine roster.

No. 1   0-4-0 Porter #3025. Northern Lights, Power, Coal and Transportation Co., 1904. To Yukon Consolidated Gold Corp.; Roger Burnell, Vancouver, B.C., 1965.

No. 2(?)   0-4-0 Porter #1792. First locomotive acquired by NLPC&T. Ex-North Transfer & Trading Co., Vancouver B.C. To Tanana Mines (Tanana Valley) No. 1, 1905; Alaska Engineering Commission; U.S. Government Railroad (Alaska Railroad) No. 1, 1917. Retired 1930. Now on display at Alaskaland, Fairbanks.

No. 3(?)   0-4-0 Porter. To Yukon Consolidated Gold Corp; Harry Cooper, Gunnar Nielson and D. F. Howian, Whitehorse in 1969 for restoration.

No. 4   0-4-0 Porter #3022. To Yukon Consolidated Gold Co.; Klondike City, 1920s. Now on display at Minto Park, Dawson City.
             Also two 0-6-0 Porters. To Yukon Consolidated Gold Co.; Harry Cooper, Gunnar Neilson and D. F. Howian, Whitehorse in 1969 for restoration.

A little Porter saddle-tanker is busy hauling coal from the Northern Light, Power Coal and Transportation Co. mines to the power station to supply Dawson City with power. The photo was taken in 1904 when things began to taper off a bit in the Klondike. (Yukon Archives)

Locomotives from the Klondike Mines Railway and Northern Light Power, Coal & Transportation Co., are on display at Minto Park in Dawson City, along with other mining equipment from the Klondike gold rush. (Blaine Freer)

Proudly carrying No. 1, this Porter saddle-tanker, which saw service with the Northern Light, Power, Coal and Transportation Co. near Dawson City, is headed south to Vancouver B.C. for restoration. It was acquired by Roger Burnell of Vancouver, from the Yukon Consolidated Gold Co., which took over Northern Light properties. Burnell hauled the little giant out of the bush at Bear Creek. (Whitehorse Star)

Chapter 6

Alaska Central Railroad

With the Klondike booming at a $20 million a year rate, American interests were seeking an all-American route between the gold fields and the United States proper. Such a route would save many days. The need was based on a variety of resources to support a permanent population and to provide profitable increasing traffic.

With such a program in mind, the Alaska Central Railroad Co. was organized on March 31, 1902 under the laws of the State of Washington with capital of $30 million by a group of Seattle businessmen. There were 550,000 shares of common stock at par value of $50 a share, and 50,000 shares of five percent preferred stock. General headquarters was in the Denny Building in Seattle with C.W. Dickinson, Seattle, former general manager of the Northern Pacific Railroad, president and general manager; John H. McGraw, former governor of the State of Washington, vice president; J.W. Godwin, president of the Alaska Fisheries Union, treasurer; George Turner, U.S. Senator from Washington State, general counsel; and John F. Ballaine, Spanish-American war veteran who had much to do with the initial groundwork on the project and a former secretary to Gov. McGraw, secretary and auditor. Others included Charles W. Peck of Omaha; Captain E.C. Caine, Charles L. Denny and C.M. Andrews, all of Seattle.

The original route selected was from the present site of Seward on Resurrection Bay, through the Susitna Valley and Broad Pass to the Tanana River, where Nenana has since been built. The plan was to reach the rich coals fields of the Matanuska Valley as soon as possible. The distance of the originally planned route was 412 miles. Fairbanks did not enter into the program until 1903.

The route followed a preliminary survey completed in 1899 under the supervision of C.M Andrews, civil engineer from Seattle. The survey was adopted and approved by the Board of Directors and filed with the Interior Department in Washington D.C.. The route was much the same as that later used by the present day Alaska Railroad.

The site on Resurrection Bay selected as the terminus and seaport for the railroad was the same location that had been recognized by the Russians 135 years earlier when they established a shipbuilding facility in Alaska in 1767. They built on the bay, from native timber, one of the largest frigates of the Russian navy prior to 1800.

The original American surveyors for the townsite - to be named Seward - arrived in mid-summer of 1903. In the surveying of the town, Alaskan ingenuity was used as the surveyor's chain for measuring had been lost in shipment, so links were cut from baling wire, using a tailor's cloth measuring tape as a standard. Later, when the proper equipment arrived, the measurements were found to be only a few inches off.

Prior to the establishing of the town, a Mrs. Lowel had homesteaded the site and John Ballaine acquired the homestead for $4,000 cash and $2,000 in soldier's script. John Ballaine and his brother, Frank, along with W.M. Whittlesey laid out the city.

The panic of 1901 made it impossible to sell the Alaska Central bonds or have them underwritten as planned, so in July 1903 the Tanana Construction Co. was organized with John Ballaine owning all of the stock except four qualifying shares for the other directors. Ballaine was president and manager. The Tanana Company then took a contract from the Alaska Central to build the railroad from Resurrection Bay to

The construction headquarters building of the Alaska Central Railroad as it looked in 1904 when work started on the railroad. The company headquarters was located in Seattle. The Alaska Central later became the Alaska Northern, then the U.S. Government Railroad and finally the Alaska Railroad. Today the ARR trains operate over the same routing as survey by early Alaska Central crews. (University of Washington Library—Northwest Collection)

the Tanana River, receiving $35,000 a mile in Alaska Central bonds and a majority of the Alaska Central stock.

E.A. and C.B. Shedd and four of their Chicago associates provided Ballaine with $200,000 in funds to construct the first 20 miles with a tentative agreement to finance additional sections. Ballaine was required to put up $50,000, which he raised in Seattle. He later raised another $75,000 in Chicago to go with the $200,000.

On Aug. 23, 1903 some 30 workers were landed at Seward along with horses and supplies and on Aug. 28 the town of Seward was actually founded. The advance construction crew built a dock and got out bridge timbers during the fall and winter in preparation for the start of railroad building in the spring.

Construction on the standard gauge line started on April 16, 1904, with the driving of the first spike on the previously completed dock. Additional workers arrived that same week and the first locomotive for the railroad was landed from the Pacific Navigation Co.'s Santa Ana a few days later. Frank Ballaine was placed in charge of business management and Colonel A.W. Swartz was named chief engineer. E.R. Kesler was designated by the Shedd syndicate as treasurer. A contract was awarded by the Tanana Company to the Seward Construction Co., of Chicago., for railroad construction and to J.M. Moore of Seattle for right-of-way clearing. General manager for the project was John Dowdle of the contracting firm of Nash and Dowdle.

In the early days of construction men were so eager to work they made wooden rails and dogs pulled cars carrying supplies. The first tunnel was driven by hand at a per-foot cost less than those driven by machinery later on. Beginning wages were $2.00 per day with

board figured at an additional $1.00 per day. There was a medical plan which cost $1.50 per month.

Cost of the first 20 miles, including some heavy rock work was $16,000 per mile, including rolling stock and equipment—considered tremendous at the time. It cost over $50 per ton to buy rails and ship them to Seward. Labor rates went to $4 and $5 per day and even at these figures men would work only long enough to earn "grub stakes" so they could go prospecting nearby and perhaps discover ground that would pay them $20 a day.

In the early 1900s the railroad workers filled the town. There were churches, stores, a hospital, schools, restaurants, bakeries, and saloons where the hard working laborers could refresh themselves. From the first, Seward which by now had a population of 4,500 persons, was a social town with parades, parties, picnics and ball games shared by all.

Some 20 miles of trackage was completed during the first year. During 1904 John Ballaine negotiated with several groups of capitalists for money to complete the road to the Tanana Valley. Two eastern financiers, A.C. Frost of Chicago, and H.C. Osborne of Toronto made a survey of the company and routing and negotiations started with them for $2.5 million. They offered to purchase Ballaine's stock in the Tanana Construction Co., which also carried ownership and control of Alaska Central. Ballaine sold out in 1905, after Frost and Osborne had secured backing of the Sovereign Bank of Canada to the extent of $3.5 million with a contingent promise of more up to $18 million.

The Shedds and all other original investors were paid off in full.

Frost and Osborne bound themselves individually in a contract with Ballaine to complete the Alaska Cen-

Seward was a booming seaport town during the construction of the Alaska Central and later the Alaska Northern Railroad. A bright summer day finds citizens strolling out on the city's dock. (Seattle Historical Society)

tral. Frost became president of both the Alaska Central and the Tanana Construction Co., and Frost vice president. Ballaine continued to hold a minority share of stock.

Additional construction contracts were let to P. Welch & Co., Spokane, in the amount of $1.2 million for construction of 30 miles along Turnagain Arm and to Rich Harris, Prosser, for a 2,500-foot tunnel at Placer River Canyon, some 50 miles from Seward for $300,000. Rails and supplies for 70 to 80 miles of track were on hand along with 1,800 men and 170 horses working on the project.

By June 1906 Alaska Central had four locomotives, 30 flat cars, 10 box cars and cabooses, a snow plow and a large number of side dump construction cars and 350 horses.

The panic of 1907 saw the failure of the Sovereign Bank of Canada and with it the failure of Frost and Osborne and their Alaska Central and Chicago and Milwaukee Electric railroads. During the next three years efforts were made by receivers of the bank to reorganize the Alaska Central without success. The

railroad operated in receivership until 1910 when it was finally reorganized as the Alaska Northern.

By that time the line had been extended some 51 miles from Seward and included grades over two passes at 705 and 1,063 feet elevation, considerable trackage with grades of 2.2 percent, and numerous trestles and curves. At one point, between Miles 50 and 51 the track passed near Bartlett Glacier and made a complete loop, a marvelous engineering feat for that day.

During the construction of the Alaska Railroad years later, an old plaque making note of a location survey for the Alaska Central was found carved in a spruce tree near Mile 245 of the Government Railroad.

Listed among those whose names appeared on the plaque as having been members of the survey party were such as: Slumgullion Joe, stomach robber (cook); Moose Liver Jackson, dog musher; Long Shorty, dog musher; and Long Shafter Murphy, dog musher. There were others too, such as Cy Perkins, Al Miller and the like.

Another early locomotive on the Alaska Central was this 4-4-0 Baldwin built in 1881 for the Northern Pacific Railroad. All four locomotives obtained by the Alaska Central came from the Northern Pacific, which also supplied the railroad's first president and general manager, C.W. Dickinson of Seattle. This locomotive later became No, 11 on the Alaska Railroad roster. (University of Washington—Northwest Collection)

An Alaska Central work train with the old reliable locomotive No. 1, a Portland 4-4-0 built in 1883 for the Northern Pacific, pulling flat cars loaded with ties. (University of Washington Library—Northwest Collection.)

Early day "cheesecake." Even in the early 20th Century a pretty girl added much to a promotional photograph for a budding railroad. Here a young lady is pictured with the Alaska Central Railroad locomotive No. 1, newly acquired from the Northern Pacific. (University of Washington Library—Northwest Collection.)

The first locomotive for the Alaska Central, a Portland 4-4-0 built in 1883 for the Northern Pacific, arrived in Seward in mid-April 1904 aboard the Santa Ana of the Pacific Navigation Co. The locomotive later was used by Alaska Northern and transferred to the Alaska Engineering Commission. (Anchorage Historical and Fine Arts Museum —Alaska Railroad Collection)

The first snowplow operated by the Alaska Central Railroad is seen in storage at Seward during the summer months. During the winter heavy snows in some areas made it necessary to use a snowplow in an attempt to keep the right-of-way open. (Oregon Historical Society.)

Work continued at a fast pace on the Alaska Central during the summer of 1905. Locomotive No. 1 is seen pulling a work train along the waters edge with snow capped mountains along Turnagain Arm in the background. Rails and supplies for 70 to 80 miles of track were on hand by this time, along with 1,800 men and 170 horses. (University of Washington Library—Northwest Collection)

With a full head of steam and smoke pouring from the stack, a northbound special highballs along the rickety tracks of the Alaska Central Railroad. This photo was taken in 1906, before the panic brought an end to the dreams of the backers of the Alaska Central. (Alaska Railroad Archives photo)

OFFICIAL PROSPECTUS
OF THE

ALASKA CENTRAL RAILWAY

COMPANY

Organized under the Laws of the State of Washington.

The Purpose of this Company is to build an All American Railroad from Resurrection Bay to Rampart, opening up the richest part of Interior Alaska.

CAPITAL - - $30,000,000

Par Value of Shares $50, non-assessable and without liability to holder.

Common Stock - - - - 550,000 Shares
Five per cent Preferred Stock - 50,000 Shares

The 50,000 shares of 5 per cent preferred stock have been set aside for public subscription at a low rate, in order to raise a fund for the completion of the permanent survey, for the location of terminals, the erection of wharves, and the prompt beginning of construction. So much as necessary of the common stock will be used in the floating of bonds for the completion of the entire road.

Nine crews of engineers have been at work all summer making the permanent survey.

OFFICERS.

President and Gen. Man'gr, G. W. DICKINSON. Vice President, JOHN H. McGRAW.
Sec'ty-Auditor, JOHN E. BALLAINE. Treasurer, J. W. GODWIN.
General Counsel, GEORGE TURNER.

DIRECTORS.

G. W. DICKINSON, Ex-GOVERNOR JOHN H. McGRAW, F. AUG. HEINZE,
UNITED STATES SENATOR GEORGE TURNER, CAPT. E. E. CAINE, MAJ. JOHN. E. BALLAINE,
J. W. GODWIN.

DEPOSITORY.

Puget Sound National Bank, Seattle.

GENERAL HEADQUARTERS:

215-216 DENNY BUILDING, SEATTLE, WASH.

Title page for the prospectus of the Alaska Central Railroad Co. C.W. Dickson of Seattle was the company's first president. He was formerly general manager of the Northern Pacific Railroad. Initial financing was furnished by the Shedd Brothers of Chicago, who with their associates provide $200,000 to start construction. (Clifford Collection.)

Builders of the Alaska Central Railroad are pictured at Mile 49, the start of the famed loop trestle, an engineering marvel of the time. The trestle was in use by the Alaska Central, Alaska Northern, U.S. Government and Alaska Railroad until 1951. It was one of the great scenic attractions on the route. (University of Alaska Archives—McKeown Collection.)

Chapter 7

Alaska Northern

The Alaska Northern Railway Co. was chartered on Oct. 9, 1909 under laws of the State of Washington as a reorganization of the Alaska Central Railway Co., whose properties were sold under foreclosure on Oct. 11, 1909. Successful bidder was F.C. Jemmett, of Toronto, representing the interests that liquidated the Sovereign Bank of Canada, which had owned a majority of the $4 million in bonds of the Alaska Central.

Others associated with Jemmett included O.G. Larabee, Seattle, president; J.D. Williams, Seattle, vice president; J.A. Haight, Seattle, secretary. Jemmett was named treasurer; and A.H. Weatly, Seward, auditor. General offices were in the Alaska Building, Seattle.

The Alaska Northern took over three locomotives from the Alaska Central (some reports indicate that one of the original four was sold to the Copper River and Northwestern Railroad. Other reports show all four being taken over by the government in the transfer of properties when the government purchased the Alaska Northern in 1915). Other properties included two baggage or mail cars; 33 freight cars, including seven box cars and 26 flat cars; and one service car; plus other rolling stock.

Construction work was resumed on the single track, standard gauge line using 65-pound rails and another 21 miles of track was added to the old Alaska Central right-of-way. When taken over by the reorganized Alaska Northern the wooden trestle supporting the upper track of the loop was nearly 100 feet high. Alaska Northern finished the loop and brought the track to Kern Creek, 52 miles from Seward to Tunnel siding, and 19 miles from Tunnel siding. In addition there was 16 miles of siding—with another 40 miles partially completed.

This section of track was put into operation and the trains were met by boats that came up Turnagain Arm, and freight went out over the Iditarod Trail from this point.

It was projected that the railroad would be constructed north to the Fairbanks area on the Tanana River—a total overall distance of 450 miles. Also planned was another division of 300 miles of track through the Kuskokwim country in the new field at Iditarod, leaving the main line at Susitna. Stock on hand included an additional 10 miles of graded right-of-way, 40 miles of ties and 10 miles of rails. The survey had been completed to the Tanana River.

Once again, however, the railroad ran short of money. An attempt was made by John F. Ballaine to regain control, but in his efforts to obtain funds from J.P. Morgan interests he was turned down on the basis that they were in partnership with the Guggenheim brothers in the development of the Copper River and Northwestern Railroad to the copper holdings in the Kennecott district and a planned extension to the Tanana.

With money not forthcoming, rails and equipment began to deteriorate and for a time a gasoline-powered speeder was about the only rolling stock operating on the track.

By now all of Alaska was pleading for help with the railroad, and Walter Fisher, Secretary of the Interior, made his 1911 visit to the Territory, examining the routes from Valdez, Cordova and Seward. In his report for the year he officially recommended that the government purchase the Alaska Northern and complete it to the Yukon River.

President Howard Taft sent a special message to Congress in Feb. 1912, asking authorization for $35 million to carry out Secretary Fisher's recommenda-

Seward was headquarters for the Alaska Central and Alaska Northern railroad construction and later was the operations base for the U.S. Government Railroad. This is Seward pictured sometime during the first decade of the 1900s, when railroad construction was at its height. (Anchorage Historical and Fine Arts Museum—Alaska Railroad Collection)

tion, but opponents to such a purchased attached a rider to the Alaska Territorial Act creating an Alaska Railroad Commission to investigate such a program.

In 1915 the government finally purchased the Alaska Northern's 71 miles of standard gauge track, advance gradings and surveys, shops and equipment under the government's own appraisement as provided in the Alaska Railroad Act, giving it the power of appraisal and commendation.

The Canadian owners of the railroad had asked $6 million for the Alaska Northern, but the government set a price of $1,150,000 which was approximately the amount finally paid.

The cash cost of the property including advance work, surveys, and seven tunnels at Mile 48 and 52 had been $4,125,000. The government purchase price was 25 cents on the dollar. The Canadian owners had frozen all interests in it except those held by the defunct Sovereign Bank.

The cost to the government—despite the poor con-

Alaska Northern Railroad construction headquarters at Seward. This facility also served as headquarters for the Alaska Railroad before the offices were moved to Anchorage. (Anchorage Historical and fine Arts Museum —Alaska Railroad Collection)

dition of the road and the money needed to bring it up to standard was less than it would have cost for new construction over another routing.

By the end of 1916 the line was in very good condition as far as Mile 45, having been considerably improved and many of the old trestles renewed or filled in. In Jan. and Feb. 1917 there were three trains per week operating from Seward to Mile 40, and by June with the reconstruction completed on the Alaska Northern Railroad, one train a week ran to Kern, Mile 71.

In Sept. 1917 a most destructive storm hit Seward and washed out most of the year's work, with a loss estimated at $100,000. The line was closed down for several weeks, but by November two trains a week were again operating between Seward and Kern Creek.

The Alaska Northern turned over to Alaskan Engineering Commission three locomotives, a rotary snow plow, 2 cabooses, 5 boarding cars, 1 observation car, 3 box cars, 24 flat cars, 1 large Fairbanks Morse gasoline car No. 22 with Sheffield motor, and 1 Fairbanks Morse gasoline car No. 24A with Sheffield motor.

One other locomotive and six flat cars were destroyed in a fire at Seward shortly before the properties were turned over to the Alaskan Engineering Commission.

Alaska Northern gravel train at Mile 71 during the height of construction. Alaska Northern took over from Alaska Central on April 15, 1910 and complete construction to Mile 71 where it was possible for travelers to meet boats that came up Turnagain Arm. Freight also went over the Iditarod Trail from this point. (Clifford Collection)

Alaska Northern tram car No. 2 at Mile 52 in 1913. Such cars were used for passenger travel when light traffic did not warrant steam train operation. (Alaska Railroad Archives)

Locomotives of the Alaska Central-Alaska Northern included:

No. 1   4-4-0. Class F-1. Portland #499. Built Sept. 1883 for Northern Pacific, Nos. 78-4-270. Purchased by Alaska Central through a dealer. To Alaskan Engineering Commission from Alaska Northern in 1915, No. 10. Retired by AEC in 1920 and scrapped in 1930.

No. 2   4-4-0. Class F-1. Baldwin #5880. Built Oct. 1881 for Northern Pacific Nos. 846-90. Alaska Central, Nov. 15, 1904. Obtained from Alaska Northern by AEC No. 11.

No. 3   4-6-0. Baldwin #11280. Build for Northern Pacific 1890, No. 369. To Port Townsend Southern No. 3; Alaska Central No. 3 to AEC No. 20 from Alaska Northern.

No. 4   4-6-0. Baldwin #9696 in 1889. Ex-Northern Pacific Nos. 374-436. Believed to be locomotive destroyed in fire at Seward in May 1916.

Chapter 8

The Alaska Commissions

The people of Alaska had become discouraged as a result of the continued failure of companies such as the Alaska Central and Alaska Northern, as well as others which had proposed and started railroads from such places as Katalla and Valdez to the interior.

Alaska was pleading for help with the railroads. At the same time Congress, which had become disillusioned by private railroad financing, was unwilling to continue the policy of land grants to pioneer railroads and refused to come to the aid to distressed Alaskan ventures.

The lawmakers, however, deemed it an outrage that a Territory twice the size of Texas should for all practical purposes be without a railroad.

First efforts to get the government to take over the financially plagued Alaska Northern resulted in Walter Fisher, Secretary of the Interior, visiting the Territory in 1911 to find a solution to Alaska's problems. He examined the routes from Valdez, Cordova and Seward and in his report for the year officially recommended that the government purchase the Alaska Northern and complete it to the Yukon River. The Army and the Navy Departments were also interested in the project as a military measure, with coal an all-important factor for the Navy and its ships on patrol in northern waters.

President Howard Taft sent special messages to Congress in Feb. 1912 asking an authorization of $35 million to carry out Secretary Fisher's recommendations. Opponents to government railroads in Alaska, however, had a rider attached to the Alaska Territorial Act on Aug. 24, 1912 creating an Alaska Railroad Commission and appropriating $25,000 for expenses. This provided for examining routes for the government railroad from the coast to the Interior.

The Alaska Railroad Commission (also known as the Taft Commission) as appointed by President Taft, was composed of four men—Major Jay J. Morrow, U.S. Army Corps of Engineers (later Governor of the Panama Canal Zone), chairman; Dr. Alfred H. Brooks, geologist in charge of the Division of Alaska Mineral Resources, vice chairman; Leonard M. Cox, U.S. Navy engineer; and Colin M. Ingersoll, consulting railroad engineer from New York.

The Commisssion submitted a voluminous report to Congress on Jan. 10, 1913 on the advantages and disadvantages of the various routes, but winding up recommending that two railroads be constructed. One was from Cordova by way of Chitina to Fairbanks—the first part being the route of the Copper River & Northwestern. The other from Seward around Cook Inlet to the Iditarod River—part of the route of the Alaska Northern.

Other routes studied, along with brief comments, included the White Pass which was traversed by the White Pass & Yukon Railroad and was almost wholly in Canadian territory. The Chilkoot route, almost adjacent, which was higher and not feasible for railroad development.

Also considered was a route from Pyramid Harbor or Haines up the Chilkat River to the Alsek, over passes some 3,200 feet high and through the flat divide between the White and Tanana basins and then to Fairbanks. This was the longest of all proposed routes and was also in foreign territory for more than half the distance.

Another was from Yakutat Bay to the mouth of the Alsek and then up the Alsek valley to the Pyramid Harbor/Haines route 200 miles from the coast. This, too, passed through Canadian territory, and was not as favorable as the Pyramid Harbor/Haines routing over the same area.

The Copper River Valley route was next considered, with three alternatives. One was from either Cordova or Katalla directly up the river; the second, from Valdez over 1,800-foot high Marshall Pass and down the Tusnuna to the Copper River Valley; the third was from Valdez, over 2,750-foot Thompson Pass and a lesser summit at Ernestine, and thence to the Copper River at a point near Copper Center. Along this route the Copper River and Northwestern Railway had already been constructed to Chitina from Cordova, 132 miles apart. This was the longest of the three, but had no grades to surmount until the divide between the Copper River and the Yukon Basins.

Next was from Seward on Resurrection Bay, over the route started by the Alaska Central and Alaska Northern. This route also presented promise of allow-

The **Alaska Railroad Commission** was created by the Alaska Territorial Act of Aug 24, 1912. Members named of the commission by President Howard Taft, pictured as they arrived in Cordova are standing: Alfred H. Brooks and Leonard M. Cox; seated: John M. Ingersoll and Major J. J. Morrow, chairman. (Seattle Historical Society)

ing for a connection with the great Kuskokwim Basin through one of the passes leading from the headquarters of the Yentna, a tributary of the Susitna. Rainy Pass, about 2,900-feet in elevation, was the most promising.

Upper Cook Inlet is closed by ice during the winter season, but were it not for this fact, a railroad based on some harbor in the inlet might have been considered. West of Cook Inlet high and rugged mountains seem to bar any direct access to the Kuskokwim from the west side. The Iliamna Lake Region offered a possible route from some such terminal point as Iliamna Bay into the Kuskokwim, and from that great valley possibly on into the lower Yukon from which it is separated by only a low watershed.

In 1914 two bills were introduced in Congress, one by Senator Chamberlain of Oregon and providing for $40 million for completion of the road. The other was by House Delegate James Wickersham of Alaska, identical in most respects other than calling for $35 million for construction. The later bill was passed by both House and Senate and approved on March 2, 1914, authorizing the President to "locate, construct and operate a railroad in the Territory of Alaska." The bill also gave the President the authority to select the route.

Less than two months later, on May 2, 1914, Presi-

dent Woodrow Wilson directed Secretary of the Interior Franklin K. Lane to proceed with surveying of routes for the railroads in Alaska. The President appointed the Alaskan Engineering Commisssion under authority of the Interior Secretary. Named to the Commission were William C. Edes, chairman and chief engineer, who had more than 30 years experience in locating and constructing railroads in the West; Lt. (later Col.) Frederick J. Mears of the Army, who had been engaged in railroad building in the West and in Panama; and Thomas Riggs, Jr., who had served as chief surveyor on the Alaska Boundary Commission and who had spent many years in Alaska. He later became governor of the Territory.

An appropriation of $1 million was made by Congress to defray preliminary expenses of the Commission which on May 8, 1914 received instructions to employ assistants, purchase supplies and equipment, and proceed to Alaska at the earliest possible date. On May 22 members of the Commission arrived in Seattle, rented offices and set in motion machinery to accomplish the survey of the routes and study conditions connected with the project. The party left Seattle on May 26 and eleven survey parties under the direction of competent engineers were organized and in the field by the middle of June. The main bases for supplies were established, one at Ship Creek on Knik Arm, Cook Inlet, and the other in Fairbanks.

During the summer of 1914 practically every available route from the Coast to the Tanana and Yukon Rivers was examined and surveys made including examination of the Copper River and Northwestern route, then operating from Cordova to Kennecott and which had been offered for sale to the Government, the route from Valdez parallelling the Valdez-Fairbanks Military Road, and the Alaska Northern route from Seward.

In Feb. 1915 the Commission presented its complete report to the Secretary of Interior, with the remarks that "in presenting this report the Commission has not deemed it necessary or proper to make any recommendation as to the best route to follow. This Commission is essentially an engineering one, organized to handle the subject along technical lines. In selecting the route other questions, besides strictly engineering ones are to be considered."

With all the surveys before him and with the facts of the possibilities and needs of the Territory delineated, President Wilson on April 10, 1915 issued an executive order selecting the Western or Susitna route, commencing at the town of Seward, passing around Turnagain Arm across the Matanuska Valley, up the Susitna Valley, over Broad Pass and then along the Nenana River to the Tanana, across the Tanana and

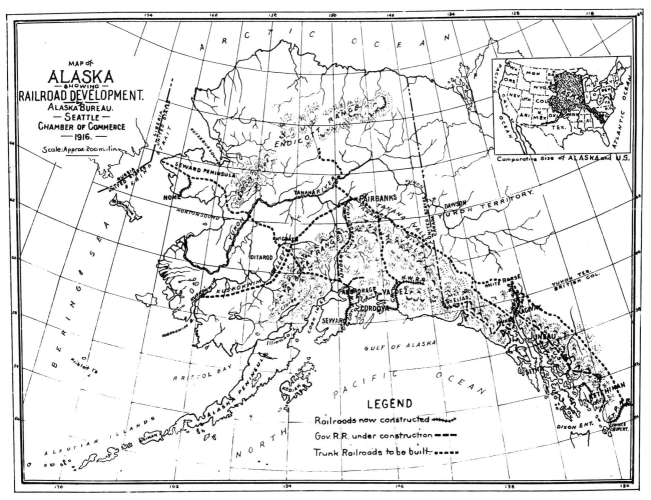

LEGEND
Railroads now constructed
Gov. R.R. under construction
Trunk Railroads to be built

The various railroads planned, under construction or completed by 1916 are shown on the map of Alaska. The map was prepared by the Alaska Bureau of the Seattle Chamber of Commerce prior to the Chamber's trip to Alaska. (Seattle Historical Society)

thence northeasterly to Fairbanks. This called for a railroad of approximately 467 miles in length with a branch line of about 40 miles to the Matanuska coal fields.

The President also authorized the purchase of the Alaska Northern at a price of $1,150,000 set under government appraisal as provided for by the Alaska Railroad Act giving it power of appraisal and condemnation. (Opponents to this route and many others expressed the opinion that President Wilson selected this routing over the Copper River route due to his intense hatred of the Morgan-Guggenheim financial interests). The Canadian owners of the Alaska Northern were asking $6 million, and an investigation by the Commission demonstrated that the Alaska Northern had cost the original owners and builders $5,250,000. The owners claimed that they had $4,125,000 invested in the property including advance work and surveys; and the Interstate Commerce Commission reported total investment in road and equipment of $3,616,800.81 as of June 30, 1912.

The actual payment price of $1,157,339.49 (another government report placed the figure at $1,154,188.48) was slightly below the physical value of the property as established by the engineers of the Commission and as certified to by the valuation experts of the ICC. Either figure came out roughly $16,000 per mile.

Although the government took over the Alaska Northern properties almost immediately, the first installment of $504,188.49 was not paid until Aug. 15, 1915, when litigation on ownership had ceased. The remainder was paid on June 30, 1916, at which time the government came into full possession of the Alaska Northern and its route.

It was not, however, until the completion of the railroad and the driving of the Golden Spike by President Warren G. Harding on Aug. 15, 1923, that the railroad officially became the Alaska Railroad, and the names under which construction had gone ahead and equipment had been marked - "U.S. Government Railroad," and Alaska Northern Railroad - were finally dropped.

Chapter 9

The Alaska Railroad

The decision of President Woodrow Wilson to adopt the Susitna Route for the Government Railroad was made on April 10, 1915, and at the same time, by executive order, the duties of the Alaskan Engineering Commission were extended to include the construction of the proposed railroad.

Engineers and workmen were on the ground and attacking the job of laying out the first construction camp 16 days after the President signed the order designating the route. William C. Edes, chairman of the commission, was designated the chief engineer and placed in general charge of all the commission's activities. The administrative offices were set up in Seward with the head of the various divisions reporting to Edes there.

Frederick Mears was placed in charge of work on the new line from Ship Creek northward. He left Seattle on April 18, arriving in Ship Creek on April 26, and proceeded with the work of construction.

Thomas Riggs Jr. proceeded to Fairbanks and additional surveys and relocations of the line were made between Fairbanks and Broad Pass during the summer. There was no actual construction work done on this section in 1915.

Three days after Mears arrived at the Ship Creek Camp the first spike was driven, on April 29, 1915—not by a high government official as might be expected, but by "Babe" White, whose mother ran the Whitehouse bunkhouse in the construction camp. During the summer 34 miles of line was cleared and graded and by the end of 1915, 20 miles of track had been laid.

Repairs on the Alaska Northern trackage and dock at Seward and building of a new machine shop to replace the one which burned during the summer were the main order of business in the Seward area.

In the construction of a railroad there are two general classes of work. The first includes the clearing of right-of-way, grubbing, grading, excavation, etc., a kind of labor that could be standardized and for which each unit prices could be established. The second covers building of bridges, laying of tracks, building of snowsheds, etc., where no such standardization is possible.

All of the clearing and grading of right-of-way, which started in May 1915, was done by contract on the "station" or "piece work" system. A gang or number of men associated as partners were given a contract for clearing a section at a given price per cubic yard, with each man sharing in the contract. When the work was completed, it was measured and the gang paid at the agreed upon price, each man receiving an individual check for his share.

In this way, each man became a small contractor, and there was no middleman. Contractors were not boarded by the commission, but were allowed to purchase supplies and provisions from the commissary at reasonable prices. For other work ordinary day laborers received about $3 for an eight-hour day and were charged a dollar a day for good board at the construction camp. A hospital was provided for free care, and provisions made to remove ill or injured workers to Seattle for special treatment at government expense.

Rugged living conditions were endured by workmen on the construction of the railroad from 1915 to 1923. Tents without floors, pole bunks covered with wild hay for mattresses and no bedding (you packed your own) were the accommodations available. There was no smiling camp steward to direct the new arrivals to their quarters. New arrivals generally had to provide or build their own.

In some areas log cabins chinked with moss were hastily constructed. Roofs were made of strong poles laid with little pitch or slope, then covered with birch bark, hay and moss, capped with an overall covering of two or three feet of top soil or earth. Door hinges were ingeniously made out of bent nails or leather

Construction workers watch as "Babe" White, daughter of the operator of the Whitehouse bunkhouse at Ship Creek (Anchorage), drives the first spike in the construction of the Government Railroad (Alaska Railroad) on April 29, 1915. (Seattle Historical Society)

This tram, No. 2, was operated by the U.S. Government Railroad in the summer of 1915 after the operation was taken over from Alaska Northern. The location is somewhere along Turnagain Arm. (Clifford Collection)

from old boot tops, and homemade wooden latches held the doors shut. Empty flour sacks covered the openings where windows should have been.

The bunks were made out of poles like honeycomb cells at both ends of the building, similar in arrangement to postoffice boxes. They were usually four feet square and eight feet in depth and were aptly called "muzzle loaders." The extra two feet of depth was for duffel storage. Two coal oil lamps suspended from the ceiling provided the illumination and heat was by a central heating stove. One should not claim to be an Alaska Railroad pioneer unless he had spent at least one night in a "muzzle loading" bunkhouse.

Ship Creek soon developed into a community of 2,000 or more persons and on June 10, 1915, under direction of the General Land Office, a new townsite was surveyed with 1407 lots put up for sale, July 10-17. Citizens soon voted to change the name of the new town to Anchorage. The town was governed by a townsite manager appointed by the commission. Certain restrictions were put on the purchase of lots—

The first new locomotive brought to Alaska for the Alaska Railroad was this Alco-Rogers 0-4-2ST&T purchased by AEC in 1915. The engine was later used for roundhouse switching in Anchorage. It was eventually retired, sold to Bethlehem Steel Co., Seattle, and scrapped in 1947. (Seattle Historical Society)

The land auction at Ship Creek (Anchorage) on July 10, 1915 attracted many of the construction workers working on the U.S. Government Railroad. Lots sold for a minimum of $75 and as high as $1,100, bringing a total of $147,235 for the entire townsite. Certain restrictions were put on the use of the lots including the prohibition of the sale of liquor, gambling or immoral purposes. (Anchorage Historical and Fine Arts Museum—Alaska Railroad Collection.)

One of the two Alco Rogers Saddle-tankers obtained by the Alaska Engineering Commission for the U.S. Government Railroad. Built in 1915 and 1917 the 0-4-2ST&T were used in construction of the Railroad and carried on the list of locomotives as No. 1 and No. 5, although neither were so marked. (Anchorage Historical and Fine Arts Museum—Alaska Railroad Collection)

prohibiting their use for the sale of liquor, gambling or immoral purposes. Non-compliance with these restrictions resulted in forfeiture of the lots—a far cry from the use of many of these same lots today. Lots sold for a minimum of $75 to as high as $1,100 for a total of $147,235 for the entire townsite, a record for such government sales at the time.

The first business established in the town of Anchorage was the Montana Cafe.

The Anchorage sale was followed by a similar sale at Seward, Sept. 11 and 12, 1915. The lots were sold outright with half the purchase price paid at the time and the balance within one year. There were no restrictions on use of the property.

The Act of March 12, 1914 made mandatory the use of any "machinery, equipment, instruments, material and other property of any sort whatsoever," no longer needed for construction of the Panama Canal. As a result, a representative of the commission went to Panama and arranged for the shipment by chartered vessel of steam shovels, derricks, locomotives, flat cars, structural steel, shop machinery, and other construction and railroad equipment.

At the time the French started work on the Panama Railroad and the digging of the canal, they used five-foot gauge track and equipment. The Alaska Railroad used standard gauge—4 feet, 8½ inches—so it was necessary to convert the locomotives acquired from the Isthmian Canal Commission by installing extra wide steel tires on the wheels. This was estimated to cost $775 for each locomotive. The 24 Mogul M-1, 2-6-0 locomotives available had been purchased from the American Locomotive Co., in 1906 at a cost of $11,000 each. A total of 18 were eventually acquired by the AEC.

The commission also acquired at least six narrow gauge locomotives from the Isthmian Commission for construction and mine use. A total of 22 of these little saddle-tankers, built by H.K. Porter Co., Davenport Locomotive Co., and the Vulcan Works, were declared surplus and eventually disposed of. They were originally purchased at prices ranging from $2,950 to $3,163 each. One of the little Porter 0-4-0 saddle-tankers is now on display in front of the Alaska Railroad offices in Anchorage, and a Davenport is on display at Palmer.

Conversion of freight and flat cars was carried out at a cost of approximately $28.50 each. The equipment was made available at no cost to the Alaskan Commission other than transportation and modification.

The first summer also saw the government operate light gas motor-car equipment over the first 34 miles of track from Seward, charging passengers 12½ cents a mile and freight service was available at 1½ cents per pound for the entire distance.

The Government Railroad got its feet wet in river navigation in 1916 when the Alaskan Engineering Commission built docks and various terminal facilities on the Tanana River at the native village of Tortella, almost immediately renamed Nenana. Until 1920 materials were brought in through St. Michaels and Whitehorse for construction of the railroad between McKinley Park and Fairbanks. Vessels operated by Northern Commercial Co. and American Yukon Navigation Co. handled this cargo.

Following withdrawal in 1921 of service below Fort Yukon by the American Yukon Navigation Co., which had purchased the Northern Commercial Co. river lines and various independents to become the only operator on the river, service became so chaotic that immediate action was necessary to assure some semblance of service to out-of-the-way points and to prevent collapse of the entire economy of the river.

The only service available was by two small stern-wheelers and two barges operated and maintained by the Army Transport Service to serve Forts Egbert, Hamlin and Gibbon as well as the Military Telegraph Service along the Tanana and Yukon Rivers. The War Department discontinued this service when it abandoned all installations in Alaska except for Chilkoot Barracks at Haines, a small detachment at Anchorage, and a few Signal Corps locations.

This equipment was turned over to the Government Railroad by executive order in the fall of 1922. In May 1923 the Interior Department established a passenger, mail and freight service between Nenana and Holy Cross, a distance of 642 miles. In 1925 the route was extended to Marshall, 132 miles below Holy Cross and in 1946 to Circle and the following year to Fort Yukon.

During the following years the original equipment was replaced. A rehabilitated vessel (steamer Alice) was put into operation in 1929 and retired in 1953. The steamer Nenana, built at Nenana in 1932, was acquired in 1933. Other vessels used included the Yukon and the Barry K, which were retired in 1946 and 1947 respectively. Various other barges were purchased and later retired. In the years 1947 and 1951 various steel barges were built by the railroad at Nenana. In 1953 motor vessels Tanana and Yukon and Barges OB-2 and OB-3 were acquired. These hulls were of modern design for river service and met the demands of a difficult service without failure.

On March 1, 1955 the Alaska Railroad awarded a contract to the B. and R. Tug and Barge Co. to operate the river transportation system on the Tanana

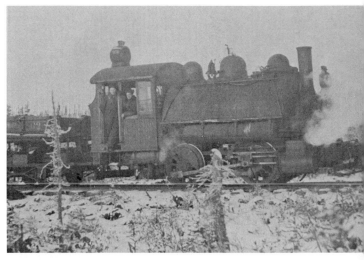

This is also one of the two Alco-Rogers used by the U.S. Government Railroad during the construction period. The engines were numbered No. 1 and No. 5 although such numbers do not show in photographs. (Clifford Collection)

This Alco-Brooks 2-8-2 No. 31 was obtained by the Alaska Railroad after service by the Buffalo & Susquahana, Pittsburg & West Virginia and Southern Iron & Equipment Co. Built in 1903 it was obtained by the Alaska Railroad in 1927 and retired during the 1930s. (Clifford Collection.)

and Yukon Rivers. B. & R. in turn transferred interest to the Yutana Barge Lines, Inc., which since has been conducted as a private enterprise. The railroad's last sternwheeler, the Nenana, was declared surplus and turned over to the Fairbanks Chamber of Commerce in 1956 and now is a tourist attraction at Alaskaland.

The last of the sternwheelers operated by the Alaska Railroad was the Nenana which was put in service in 1933 and retired and turned over to the Fairbanks Chamber of Commerce in 1956. The vessel is now on display at Alaskaland in Fairbanks (Western Airlines)

Concurrent with the building of dock facilities at Nenana a construction camp was established there and in Aug. 1916 the first lots were sold, bringing in $129,705. On Oct. 24, 1916 Mrs. Emma Duke drove the first spike when trackage was commenced on the Fairbanks division. She was the first white woman to reach the settlement at Nenana when the trading post was established in 1906 by her husband, James Duke.

In the spring of 1916 active work on the rebuilding of the Alaska Northern continued with work consisting of the rebuilding of bridges, elimination of high trestles by fills, improvement in alignment and some slight reduction in grades. Seventy-five thousand new ties were laid.

By Sept. 1916, a total of 3,582 workers were on the job, including 300 imported from Seattle for special tasks. During the year 60 miles of main line track and 100 miles of grades were completed, and the right-of-way cleared for a total of 230 miles. Work progressed on rebuilding the old Alaska Northern trackage and work headed south from Fairbanks was making good progress.

The first two passenger coaches for the railroad arrived in Anchorage on Sept. 23, 1916.

The year 1917 was one of problems for the railroad. The U.S. went to war and material and labor costs jumped. Much controversy centered over the fact that the headquarters of the railroad was moved from Seward, which originally had been designated as the permanent headquarters for the railroad, to Anchorage.

The year also saw the narrow gauge Tanana Valley Railroad purchased for $300,000 and the branch line to the Matanuska coal fields completed. A Chamber of Commerce had been organized in Anchorage and in one of its bulletins, apparently attempting to bring new people to town, it printed a listing of wages paid at the time. Unskilled labor earned 50 cents an hour, or $4.00 a day; cooks made $100 to $125 per month plus board; locomotive engineers made $204 per month; and steam shovel engineers $210 per month —the highest scale.

By the end of the year 121 miles of road was in operation, and a year later this had been extended to

One of 18 American Locomotive Co. 2-6-0s built in 1906 to five-foot gauge for the Isthmus Canal Commission for the building of the Panama Canal. Shipped to Alaska for use on the U.S. Government (Alaska) Railroad was this one, No. 285. Converted to standard gauge by adding wide wheel treads, these locomotive were used into the 1930s. (Clifford Collection)

168 miles. The average monthly number of workers in 1917 was 4,466, but dropped to 2,550 in 1918 due to many able-bodied men going to war.

During 1919 little work was done on the railroad until late summer due to lack of appropriations from Congress. Some work was done on both the Northern and Southern Division lines, but by the end of the year there was still a gap of 122 miles between the two divisions. A general administrative reorganization to become effective at the end of the year was set up.

Following his return from service in France, Colonel Frederick Mears, formerly in charge of railroad construction with headquarters in Anchorage, was appointed chairman and chief engineer for the Alaskan Engineering Commission. He succeeded William C. Edes, chairman since its organization in 1914. Edes was appointed consulting engineer with headquarters in Washington D.C. and retired in 1920.

Shortly after Colonel Mears' appointment, monies began to flow from Congress and work was resumed on the construction of the railroad.

In 1920, for the first time since construction started, there was ample funding available in advance for the summer working season. Also the year marked the successful mining of coal for use of the railroad at

Eska, with the average cost per ton being $6.00. Some 32,276 tons were mined.

On Nov. 20, 1920 the City of Anchorage was incorporated and the operation and maintenance of the city was turned over to local authorities on Dec. 1, 1920. By the end of the year the gap between the Northern and Southern Divisions was closed to 84 miles for steel and 50 miles for grading, and the 31.9 miles of narrow gauge trackage of the Tanana Valley Railroad had been supplemented by 48.5 miles of narrow gauge track, temporarily laid on standard gauge roadbed to carry the rails to the Tanana River.

Dining car service was in full operation during 1920 with lobster, combination, tuna, Alaska salmon salads at $1.00 per portion; fried or baked halibut $1.00; mountain trout with bacon $1.25; roast leg of pork $1.25; prime rib of beef $1.50; chili con carne 75 cents. No service for less than 20 cents and pie was 20 cents; cold drinks 25 cents; coffee a dime; and tea 25 cents.

Nov. 1921 saw the Northern and Southern Divisions of the railroad as such abolished, and all divisions changed to departments.

One of the more difficult construction projects involved in the building of the railroad, the Hurricane

One of the several narrow gauge saddle-tankers obtained by the Alaska Engineering Commission from the Isthmus Canal Commission in 1917 and turned over to various coal mine operations in the Matanuska Valley is seen in operation. Bearing No. 22, this little Davenport does not appear on the AEC roster but is a sister locomotive to No. 5 which is on display at Palmer. (Clifford Collection)

G. LINE No 22. A.E.C. G 601 P.S. HUNT

A former Panama Canal Railroad 2-6-0 built to 5-foot gauge being used as a work locomotive during the construction of the U.S. Government (Alaska) Railroad. Built by American Locomotive Co. in 1906, the engines were converted to standard gauge by adding wide steel treads to the wheels. No. 225 was retired and scraped in 1936. (Anchorage Historical & Fine Arts Museum—Alaska Railroad Collection.)

One of several locomotives acquired from the Panama Railroad, No. 605, upon completion of the building of the canal. The 2-6-0 locomotives were built by Alco-Brooks in 1905-06 to 5-foot gauge and converted for use on Alaska's standard gauge by adding wide steel treads to the wheels. Such can be seen on the drivers of No. 605. (Anchorage historical and Fine Arts Museum—Alaska Railroad Collection)

Work nears completion on the Hurricane Gulch bridge at Mile 285 of the Alaska Railroad as this photo was taken on Aug. 8, 1921. The bridge was complete a week later and the first official train crossed the structure three days later. (Clifford Collection)

Gulch bridge, a marvel in engineering, was completed in 1921. Construction was by the American Bridge Co. (one of the rare occasions where work was turned over to an outside contracting firm). A construction camp was set up at Mile 285 in May 1920 for preliminary clearing and grading with actual construction work starting in March 1921. Two hinged spandrel arch spans 384 feet in length each, were constructed for the total overall span of 918 feet 2 inches. Work was completed on Aug. 15, 1921 with a work train testing the span on that date. The first passenger train crossed the span on Aug. 18, 1921.

With trackage, except that over the Tanana River completed, the following winter saw narrow gauge rails laid on the ice and passengers and freight carried across the river for transfer to standard gauge trains at the south bank. The narrow gauge rails were removed from the river on April 19 and for a short time transfers

were made by team. All transferring was discontinued on May 1 and boats were used to cross the river starting on May 9.

A contract was awarded to the American Bridge Co. to construct the Tanana River bridge and on June 15, 1922 all narrow gauge trackage was replaced by standard gauge. This was accomplished by adding a third rail on the section between Happy and Fairbanks, permitting narrow gauge trains as well as standard gauge equipment over this section. The third rail was used until 1930 when service to Chatanika was terminated.

The bridge over the Tanana was completed on Feb. 27, 1923, with a 700-foot span, the second largest truss bridge in the country.

On Sunday, July 15, 1923, President Warren G. Harding drove the Golden Spike connecting 471 miles of railroad from Seward to Fairbanks, with the ceremonies held at the north end of the Nenana bridge. The official party included the First Lady, Mrs. Harding; Secretary of Interior, Hubert Work; Secretary of Commerce, Herbert Hoover; Secretary of Agriculture, Henry Wallace; Alaska Governor, Scott C. Bone, and many others. Absent was Colonel Frederick Mears, who had been chairman of the Alaskan Engineering Commission during the final years of construction, but who had returned to the Army for a short tour of duty at the time of the ceremonies. Thomas Riggs Jr., another member of the commission, had resigned in 1918 to become governor of the Territory.

To start the ceremonies, Gov. Scott Bone carefully inserted the golden spike in a hole prepared for it and the President tapped it lightly. The golden spike was then removed and an iron spike substituted. The President missed it twice and then finally drove it home. The Alaska Railroad was officially completed and the Alaskan Engineering Commission went out of business as did the designation Government Railroad.

The golden spike ceremonies were "repeated" on the 50th Anniversary of the completion of the railroad. One of the special guests at that time was Sam Chiamis a retired "professional spike driver." Chiamis was at North Nenana when President Harding took part in the initial ceremonies and watched the President drive the final spike of the railroad Chiamis had helped build to that point.

At the Anniversary ceremony Chiamis placed the duplicate "golden" spike in place for the driving by John W. Ingram, chief of the Federal Railroad Administration, representing President Richard Nixon at the ceremonies.

This is the first regular train to cross the Hurricane Gulch Bridge on the Alaska Railroad. The date was Aug. 18, 1921. The bridge was constructed by the American Bridge Co., one of the few instances where work on the Alaska Railroad was turned over to an outside contracting firm. Work on the 918 foot 2 inch span was started in March 1921 and completed on Aug. 15, 1921. The two hinged sprandel arch spans 384 feet. (Clifford Collection)

President Warren G. Harding came a great distance to drive the golden spike marking the completion of the U.S. Government (Alaska Railroad). The ceremony took place at Nenana on July 15, 1923 with a host of dignitaries on hand. (Alaska Railroad Archives)

The Alaska Railroad marked the completion of 50 years of service by re-enacting the golden spike ceremony at Nenana on July 15, 1973. Those invited to the ceremony were presented with this Golden Spike Plaque. (Clifford Collection)

Actually there were two "official golden spikes" driven on the Alaska Railroad. One spike is now owned by the Southern California Arms Collectors Association. This spike was presented to Colonel Mears by the City of Anchorage for his work as chairman of the Alaskan Engineering Commission. He designed and built the Alaska Railroad and served as the railroad's general manager from 1919 to 1923. Reportedly this spike was "driven" on completion of the Seward-Anchorage section of the railroad on Sept. 10, 1918.

The second golden spike was the one driven by President Harding at Nenana on completion of the railroad. This spike is on display in the Harding Museum Home at Marion, Ohio.

The California owned spike was returned to Alaska for the 1967 Centennial and was on display at A-67 in Fairbanks—improperly described as the spike which President Harding drove at Nenana.

Track was laid across the frozen Tanana River during the winter of 1921 to tie together the southern standard gauge and northern narrow gauge sections of the Alaska Railroad. Narrow gauge locomotive No. 151, purchased by the AEC for use on the Tanana Valley section, and No. 6, one of the little saddle tankers now on display in Anchorage, are seen testing the river ice. (Anchorage Historical and Fine Arts Museum-Alaska Railroad Collection)

A gold-plated spike was used on the July 15, 1973 reenactment ceremonies.

The years from 1924 to 1945 were difficult ones for the Alaska Railroad. Though the line was officially completed, it had been pioneered through and much of the construction was temporary. Through the years repeated recommendations of the general managers that sufficient funds be appropriated to improve the condition of the railroad by constructing permanent structures and finishing partly completed work were to no avail. Budgets were slashed or ignored. At first some improvements and repairs were made only as needed to keep the railroad in operation.

The true purpose of the Alaska Railroad—to aid in the development of the territory of Alaska—was forgotten. The annual operating deficit that had to be made good became a red flag to the Appropriations Committees. Putting the railroad on a paying basis was the goal and all else was ignored. The railroad was forced to use outmoded equipment, at times do without needed supplies and necessary maintenance, yet there was an annual deficit until 1938.

The original construction appropriation was $35 million. The railroad had cost $70 million, partially caused by high prices during and after World War I. No one charged that there was fraudulent waste of funds, no shrewd promotor made a million or even a dollar. Every cent was properly accounted for.

After completion, however, the first investigator arrived. After a hurried 36-hour visit he declared that the railroad was a failure and the country in which it was built was worthless and money spent constructing it wasted. He advocated the tearing up of the rails and the junking of the whole project.

The colonization of the Matanuska Valley, a movement sponsored by the Federal Emergency Relief Administration and later turned over to the Alaska Rural Rehabilitation Corporation, brought more than 200 colonists with families to the Palmer area and gave additional travel impetus to the the railroad. Another boost came as a result of the building of the Mt. McKinley Park Hotel which was turned over to the railroad by the National Park Service on Dec. 8, 1938 and which was completed and opened for business on June 1, 1939.

In 1941 the United States was on the threshold of World War II and the Alaska Railroad was ill prepared for the burden of increased tonnage imposed by the preparation for war. Instead of a seasonal operation, the railroad was faced with the problem of carrying more tonnage every month than it had previously carried in its peak months. Total tonnage rose from 157,000 in fiscal year 1939 to 627,000 tons in 1944.

As a World War II measure, in order to safeguard the flow of military supplies, equipment and personnel from tidewater to Anchorage and Fairbanks, a branch

General Simon B. Buckner leads a group of military and railroad dignitaries after "holing through" on the secret Portage-Whittier tunnel constructed during World War II. Work on the project, completed in the spring of 1943, was made necessary to make Whittier a safe wartime port protected from the Japanese. The 14,410-foot tunnel was dedicated to Anton Anderson, chief engineer of construction, in December 1976. (Anchorage Historical and Fine Arts Museum—Alaska Railroad Collection)

Remainders of World War II are these former troop carriers now on display at the Alaska Transportation Museum at Palmer. (Western Airlines)

called the Whittier Cut-Off was constructed in 1942-1943 under the supervision of the U.S. Army Corps of Engineers. This part of the mainline extended from Whittier on Passage Canal, Prince William Sound, to Portage Station. This new line was 12.4 miles long and included two tunnels through the mountains, one 13,090 feet long and the other 4,910 feet in length. The construction of the cut-off shortened the distance from tidewater to Fairbanks by 51.5 miles and gave the railroad two terminal ports where connections were made with ocean vessels—Seward and Whittier. A branch line was also constructed from the terminus in Fairbanks to Ladd Field.

Due to loss of personnel to the Armed forces and to the construction industry in Alaska and elsewhere during the early days of the War, outside assistance was necessary for the railroad to perform its mission of transporting military supplies. The 714th Railroad Operating Batallion was assigned to the Alaska Railroad in 1943. The battalion departed from Camp Clayborne, La., on March 14, 1943 and moved onto the railroad on April 3, 1943. The unit was commanded by Lt. Col. Herbert S. Huron, who was later succeeded by Lt. Col. W. Hastedt.

The 714th was on the railroad for more than 24 months, augmenting the civilian personnel in all departments. The unit was relieved on May 7, 1945 and departed for the Lower 48 three days later.

Very little difficulty was experienced in integrating the members of the military with the regular employees and the two groups worked side-by-side for the two-year period. It was not uncommon for an engine crew to consist of one civilian and one enlisted man.

Probably one of the most unusual days in the history of the Railroad was Feb. 24, 1944, when a moose delayed five trains for a total of four hours and 40 minutes in the area of Curry and Mile 255. The first train was delayed for an hour and one-half before the moose allowed it to pass. A short time later the same moose stood off a rotary snowplow crew for more than two hours and 40 minutes before he was felled by a bullet. Three more trains were thrown off schedule and held on siding awaiting the two delayed trains.

An extremely stubborn animal, the moose prefers using the snow-free railroad tracks day or night. The railroad still has the problem of coaxing the moose off the right-of-way and is still ignominiously unsuccessful, systems and many, many words later.

Among the approaches tried at one time or another are oscillating lights, high-pitched whistles, hot steam, fuses, rocket pistols, aluminum sheeted bridges, snow balls and a shot of hot coffee from the pots of certain railroad cooks.

One improvision which failed miserably, were turnouts along the track through the snowbanks. Section men and bulldozer operators sliced turnouts and "parking lots" at 45 degree angles which would, on the surface, appear to be enticing no end to the entry of the moose. Moose, however, just didn't give a Tinker's damn for the turnouts, and Alaska Railroad locomotives still carry the nickname of "Moose Goosers."

Meanwhile trains still chug into stations hours late and the obstinate moose, who choose to challenge the right-of-way with 2,000-ton trains are still joining all the other little mooses that tried the same ridiculous trick 20 years ago.

In 1954, one stunt was found to work. A big moose was discovered sound asleep on the track and an exasperated brakemen walked up and placed a flare under his tail. The brakeman lit the flare and hopped back on the train. Needless to say, the moose left the tracks pronto and headed for the nearest snowbank. After publicizing this incident, the ARR received so many letter of protest from animal lovers that orders were issued to use the red flares only for standard purposes.

The winter kill of moose by the Alaska Railroad has been cut back considerably in recent years by the turning off of the oscillating light on the locomotives when approaching a moose. The animals apparently are hypnotized by the light and refuse to move.

Following the war, rehabilitation and reorganization of the railroad began, including the replacing of 70-pound rails with those of 115-pound gauge. The railroad's first streamliner, the AuRoRa, made its shakedown run to Palmer on Oct. 16, 1947 and formal service was inaugurated to Mt. McKinley on Alaska Day, Oct. 18, 1947. The year also marked completion of $9.5 million in new terminal facilities in Anchorage and Fairbanks.

On Jan. 15, 1951 one of the most disastrous blazes in the history of the railroad destroyed the Anchorage machine shop and coach shed, and along with it records of equipment and maintenance since the railroad was organized.

The longest freight train in the history of the railroad, 108 cars loaded with 5,200 tons of freight, and powered by five diesels, three on the head and two cut 60 cars back, made its way from Whittier to Anchorage on June 25, 1951. During the months of May and June of that year a total of 270,000 tons of freight was handled—also a record. On Aug. 31 the railroad had its biggest payday with 6,200 paychecks totaling $1,350,000 being handed out.

This little Porter 0-4-0ST saw service on several railroads during its long and busy life. Built in 1899 it was with North American Transfer and Trading Co. in Vancouver, B.C.; the Northern Light, Power, Coal and Transportation Co., Dawson City, Y.T.; the Tanana (Valley) Mines and eventually the Alaska Engineering Commission, the U.S. Government Railroad, and the Alaska Railroad. The little workhorse on a Tanana Valley trestle, was retired in 1930 and is now on display at Alaskaland in Fairbanks.

A special Alaska Railroad train provided transportation to the Hatcher Pass area for the filming of "The Cheechakos" by the Alaska Moving Picture Corp. Filmed in 1923, "The Cheechakos" was the first motion picture made in Alaska by an Alaskan company. Prints of the film are still available and are often shown at gatherings of Alaska sourdoughs in many parts of the country. (Anchorage Historical and Fine Arts Museum—Alaska Railroad collection)

A scenic attraction no longer seen. An Alaska Railroad train on the famous "Loop" with snow covered mountains in the background. Riding the Loop, which was constructed by the Alaska Central and Alaska Northern crews, was quite a thrill as in its later years the wooden structure began to sag and terror was added to the thrill and beauty of crossing the structure as it swayed in the wind. At the time of the building of the railroad the Loop was necessary because of the nearness of the Bartlett Glacier, which since has receeded nearly a mile. The Loop, between Mile 47.5 and Mile 50.8 was eliminated in a 1951 improvement plan. (Anchorage Historical and Fine Arts Museum— Alaska Railroad Collection)

The scenic, but costly "Loop," constructed by the Alaska Central and Alaska Northern between Miles 47.5 and 50.8, was eliminated in a $1 million improvement program during the fall of 1951. A golden spike was driven to mark the occasion, which cut 1.1 miles off the Seward-Anchorage run. This also resulted in the elimination of five bridges, a heated tunnel—to keep out the ice—and a snow shed, thus saving $36,000 in maintenance costs each year.

The new grade curved close to the base of the snubbed and muddy nose of the Bartlett Glacier. The relocation was completed over ground that 30 years earlier had been covered with 75 to 100 feet of ice. The Bartlett Glacier had retreated nearly a mile in 30 years, exposing a hillside that permitted a track location that would have been impossible when the right-of-way was first laid out.

The loop until 1920, when it was redesigned, was a thrilling adventure to ride. As it aged the wooden structure started to sag. Terror was added to the thrill and beauty of a crossing as the structure would sway with the winds. At times the swaying would become so great that the engines would jump the track and have to be put back on with crowbars.

The post-war rehabilitation program cost $75 million and on Nov. 17, 1952 ceremonies and dedication of a monument at the Anchorage headquarters of the railroad marked the occasion.

Up until 1953 all of the general managers had been federally appointed, their expertise having been gained in military railroading. With the first Republican Administration in 23 years came a change.

Presidents of U.S. railroads and officials of the Association of American Railroads were asked to sub-

Repairs on the "Loop" carried on in the winter by Alaska Railroad workers. The Loop was one of the most interesting attractions on the Alaska Railroad in the early days. (Anchorage Historical and Fine Arts Museum—Alaska Railroad Collection)

mit names of likely candidates for the job. In this way, for eight years Alaska became a training ground for private stateside railroad companies. The system worked well inasmuch as it lifted the railroad out of the area of local politics and provincialism.

General manager of the Alaska Railroad and dates of their appointment have been:

Lee H. Landis	Oct. 1, 1923
Noel W. Smith	Dec. 19, 1924
Colonel Otto F. Ohlson	Aug. 1, 1928
(reappointed)	Aug. 12, 1943
Colonel John P. Johnson	Jan. 1, 1946
Frank E. Kalbaugh	Sept. 1, 1953
Reginald N. Whitman	April 16, 1955
John H. Lloyd	Aug. 16, 1956
Robert H. Anderson	Aug. 16, 1958
Donald J. Smith	Sept. 21, 1960
John E. Manley	March 1, 1962
Walter S. Johnson	Jan. 1, 1972
William Dorcy	Apr. 1, 1976
Stephen A. Ditmeyer (interim)	July 4, 1979
Frank H. Jones	Jan. 30, 1980

Alaska Railroad steam locomotive shops in Anchorage. It was here that the various steam locomotives operated by the Alaska Railroad were rebuilt, modified and repaired. (Anchorage Historical and Fine Arts Museum—Alaska Railroad Collection.)

One of the major branches of the Alaska Railroad which was first put in service in Aug. 1916, was closed down in May 1968 when the military facilities at Elmendorf and Richardson changed from coal to oil.

The line ran from the main line at Matanuska Junction, some 26 miles north of Anchorage through Palmer and up the Matanuska River to the Sutton Y and the Eska and Evans Jones Coal Co. mines.

There were also other mines in the area such as the Buffalo Coal Mine and Premier Coal Co. properties, which had been served by three-foot narrow gauge track and Davenport 0-4-0T locomotives obtained from the Panama Canal project.

The Jones Co., one of the largest in the Matanuska Valley, also had some equipment of its own, the first of which was put into operation in Aug. 1936. All were battery powered mine-type locomotives.

Included among the equipment disposed of with the closing of the facilities were:

Mine Locomotives

No.1 0-4-0 General Electric #12126, purchased new Aug. 1936. Five-ton, battery powered. 3.5 mph. 85 volt.

No.2 0-4-0 General Electric #9976, built 1925, purchased by EJC 1936. Five-ton, battery powered. 3.5 mph.

No.3 0-4-0 Westinghouse-Whitcombe #80217. Ten-ton battery. Built April 1947 for U.S. Treasury Department as 60 cm gauge for USSR. Never shipped.

No.4 0-4-0 Mancha #2352 Titon A. Three-and-one-half ton. Battery.

No.5 0-4-0 General Electric #15830. Buiilt June 1942 for Alaska Railroad for use at Eska and sold to EJC. Six-ton, 85 volt, battery. 4 mph. Sold to Klondike Cement Co.

No.6 0-4-0 General Electric #15829. built June 1942 for Alaska Railroad for use at Eska and sold to EJC. Six-ton, 85 volt, battery. 4 mph.

No.7 0-4-0 scrapped.

No.8 0-4-0 Westinghouse-Whitcombe #89216. Ten-ton. Battery. Built for U.S. Treasury Department April 1947 for USSR. Never shipped. Sold to Klondike Cement Co., Anchorage.

No.9 0-4-0 Westinghouse-Whitcombe #80219. Ten-ton. Battery. Built for U.S. Treasury Department April 1947 for USSR. Never shipped. Sold to Klondike Cement Co., Anchorage.

Premier Mine No. 5., one of a half dozen Davenport 0-4-0 narrow gauge saddle-tankers obtained by the Alaska Railroad from the Panama Canal. It was used in the railroad's coal mining operations and is now on display at Palmer. (Clifford Collection)

Carried on the Alaska Engineering Commission roster as No. 4, this 0-4-0ST American is seen with the Isthmus Canal Commission No. 19 still painted on one of the domes. This locomotive was shipped to Alaska, carried over the White Pass & Yukon Route and then shipped down the Yukon River to Nenana. It was later stripped and the boiler used as a water tank at Nenana. (Clifford Collection.)

Earthquake and tidal wave damage to Alaska Railroad facilities from the Good Friday 1964 Alaska earthquake. Damage to railroad in Southcentral Alaska ran into the millions of dollars. (Anchorage Historical and Fine Arts Museum—Alaska Railroad collection)

Tracks of the Alaska Railroad disappeared into the waters of Turnagain Arm near Portage following the earthquake of March 27, 1964, which did millions of dollars of damage to the ARR. In many areas the land mass dropped 15 to 20 feet and in other areas it rose out of the nearby waters about the same amount. (Clifford Collection.)

Other equipment also included 45 wooden ore cars and 79 metal ore cars and miscellaneous other gear.

The Alaska Railroad became a full-fledged bureau in the Department of Interior and in Oct. 1966 Congress established the Department of Transportation and within the new department is the Federal Railroad Administration which has the responsibility of operating the Alaska Railraod.

Steam locomotives were retired from the Alaska Railroad in November 1956, although No. 557 was kept on standby basis for another ten years. In 1966 it was finally sold to Monte Holm of Moses Lake, Wa., where he operates it as a hobby over some 900 feet of track.

Disaster hit the Alaska Railroad, and most of Southcentral Alaska at 5:36 p.m. on Good Friday, March 27, 1964 when the great earthquake with a Richter magnitude of 8.4 to 8.6 took its toll.

The quake released twice as much energy as the 1906 earthquake which wrecked San Francisco and was felt on land over an area of almost half a million square miles.

For the Alaska Railroad, that three and one-half minute disaster cost some $27 million in rebuilding sections of track twisted like pretzels, other sections and the entire dock facilities at Seward slid into Resurrection Bay, waves ruptured two tank farms which resulted in widespread fire as they spread the conflagration.

Rails to nowhere following the earthquake and tidal wave of Good Friday, 1964 in Alaska. This is part of the Seward waterfront, where damage was extensive. Overall damage ran into millions of dollars. (Anchorage Historical and Fine Arts Museum—Alaska Railroad collection.)

In other areas, waves hit standing freight cars so hard that the flanges on their wheels ripped the rails loose, popping spikes out of ties. Alaska Railroad inspectors found ties still in place not moved an inch with little other than the spike holes to indicate that they once were a railroad track.

The entire town of Portage was lowered so that the tracks were under water at high tide. In the 185 miles from Seward to the Matanuska Valley most of the bridges buckled, in short were "cambered from compression."

But there was one bright spot in the whole picture—the technological advance which has changed the whole pattern of maintenance. Gone was the crack all-woman crew section crew from Cantwell, gone the gandy dancer, his hand tools and reliance on brawn. Earth-moving equipment, power shovels, tie tampers, caterpillar tractors for spreading ballast, inserted ties and laying rails enabled eight section men to accomplish the same amount of track work that 80 men were able to handle some 15 years previous.

Service north from Anchorage to Fairbanks was restored in about a week. In about three weeks trains were rolling again to Whittier—on a slow wheel basis. In all, about 186 miles of the total 536 were damaged, 110 bridges weakened, with 71 needing immediate repairs before use.

In 1969 President Nixon proposed the selling of the Alaska Railroad to cut down on government expenditures, but nothing ever came of it. During past years other efforts have been made to sell the railroad, valued at more than $100 million, but there has been no interest on the part of private owners. The Alaska Railroad was withdrawn from the market in 1975.

With the building of the trans-Alaska oil pipline, a 10.2 mile extension from the City of Fairbanks to the Fairbanks International Airport was constructed at a cost of $800,000 in the spring of 1972.

In 1975 officials representing the Alaska and Canadian railroads, U.S. and Canadian government transportation officials, and othersmet with proposals to extend the Alaska Highway to connect with the Canadian system.

That same year the railroad, finding itself short of equipment as a result of pipeline construction, purchased three new 3000 hp locomotives and borrowed 12 similar locomotives from the U.S. Army.

The Alaska Railroad is no Toonerville Trolley, although it does offer services not found on any other railroad. It is a messenger service, a grocery delivery service, a hunter taxi service, a riverboat company, a scenic tour and Izaak Walton guide, pointing out the best streams in the area.

Often one sees the engineer deliver groceries to people along the track on the more remote sections of the line. He delivers notes into town or on to other mileposts and other residents. The train stops anywhere on the line for hunters and fishermen—and will stop at the same point days later to pick them up with their bag or catch.

That's the Alaska Railroad.

Alaska Railroad locomotive No. 610, one of the 2-6-0 "600" built in 1905-06 by Alco-Brooks as 5-foot gauge for use on the Panama Railroad during construction of the Canal. They were converted to standard gauge before being shipped north by adding extra wide steel treads to the wheels at a cost of approximately $775 per engine. They arrived in Alaska in 1923 and were put into service at that time. (Anchorage Historical and Fine Arts Museum—Alaska Railroad Collection)

Alaska Railroad Locomotives

Narrow Gauge

No. 1	0-4-0ST H. K. Porter #1792. 3/1899. Ex-North American Transfer and Trading Co., Vancouver, B.C.; Northern Light, Power, and Transportation Co., Dawson City, Y.T.; Tanana Mines (Tanana Valley) No.1, July 1905 Alaskan Engineering Commission, 1917. Retired 1930 and on display at Alaskaland.
No. 1	0-4-0ST. Early records indicate this was a Vulcan, built in 1910 by Vulcan Iron Works. Ex-Isthmus Canal Commission No.20. AEC No.1, 1917. (See Note 1).
No. 4	0-4-0ST. Early records indicate this was an American. Ex-Isthmus Canal Commission No. 19. AEC No.4, 1917. Shipped by way of White Pass & Yukon and Yukon river to Nenana. Partly stripped and boiler used as water tank at Nenana. (See Note 1).
No. 6-1	0-4-0ST. Davenport #764. 10/1907. Ex-Isthmus Canal Commission No.802. AEC No.6, 1917. Partly stripped and boiler used as a compressor reservoir. Converted to standard gauge about 1930 and used as shop switcher. During 1947 renumbered No.1 and placed on display at Alaska Railroad general offices, Anchorage. (See Note 1).
Nos. 20-21	0-4-0ST. Davenport Locomotive Works, 1908. Ex-Isthmus Canal Commission. AEC 1917. Leased to coal operators on Moose Creek branch. (See Note 1).
No. 50	4-4-0 Baldwin #4294. 3/1878. Ex-Olympic & Tenino RR, later Olympia and Chehalis Valley No. 1, "F. H. Quimette"; Columbia & Puget Sound No. 10, 1890; White Pass & Yukon No. 4, 1898; rebuilt in 1900 and renumbered No. 54; Tanana Mines (Valley) No. 50, 1905. AEC (Alaska Railroad) No. 50, 1917. Scrapped 1930.
No. 51	2-6-0. Brooks #578. 1881. Ex-Kansas Central Ry. No. 8; Union Pacific No. 102, 1885; Columbia & Western No. 3; Utah & Northern; Columbia and Western (Trail tramway) No. 3; Canadian Pacific; White Pass & Yukon No. 65, 1900; Tanana Mines (Valley) No. 51, 1906. AEC No. 51, 1917. Scrapped by Alaska Railroad 1930.
No. 52	2-6-0. Baldwin #10880. 5/1890. Ex-Alberta Railway & Coal Co., No. 12; Tanana Mines (Valley) No. 52; AEC No. 52, 1917. Used on Chatanika Branch. Scrapped 1930.
No. 151	2-8-2. Consolidated type. Purchased by AEC from logging road in Seattle in 1917. Retired 1921. Scrapped 1936.
No. 152	4-6-0 Baldwin #53296. 6/1920. Purchased by AEC for Tanana Valley 1920. Used on Chatanika Branch. Retired 1932. To U.S. Army No. 152, 1942, for use on White Pass & Yukon; Lathrop Transportation Corps. Depot, Calif.; Davidson Scrap Metals Co., Stockton, Calif.; Antelope & Western Ry., No. 3, Roseville, Calif; Camino, Cable & Northern, Camino, Calif. CC&N ceased operation in 1974 and disposed of locomotive to unknown operation in Pennsylvania.
No. 830	0-6-0ST. H. K. Porter. 1910. Ex-Isthmus Canal Commission No. 830. AEC 1917. No. 830 (See Note).

Note

The Alaskan Engineering Commission obtained 9 of these small dinkeys. Numbers in the early days in not a matter of record. The locomotives, obtained from the Panama Canal with the Panama numbers included a Vulcan No. 20, American No. 19, Davenport No. 802, and Porters Nos. 823, 824, 830, 833, 851, and one with no number. Nos. 823, 824 and 833 were never uncrated and did not see service on the railroad.

Alaska Railroad locomotive No. 151 heads a train moving freight and pasengers across the Nenana River ice during the winter of 1921. The ice crossing tied together the northern and southern sections, prior to the completion of the bridge at Nenana. (Alaska Railroad Archives)

This little Davenport 0-4-0ST built in 1907 now bears the Alaska Railroad No. 1 and is on display at the Anchorage headquarters for the railroad. It is the former Isthmus Canal Commission No. 802, brought to Alaska in 1917 by the AEC as No. 6. It was converted from narrow gauge to standard gauge in 1930 and used as a shop switcher. Following rebuilding and reconstruction of the ARR after World War II it was renumbered No. 1 and put on display. (Western Airlines)

Standard Gauge

No. 1   0-4-2 ST&T. Alco-Rogers #47317. 7/1915. Purchased from American Locomotive Co. in 1915. Later used for roundhouse switching in Anchorage. To Bethlehem Steel Co., Seattle, 1947 for scrapping.

No. 5   0-4-2 ST&T Alco-Rogers #56438. 11/1917. Purchased by AEC for Alaska Railroad in 1917. Sent to Nenana by way of White Pass & Yukon to Dawson and then down the Yukon to Tanana, then to Nenana where it was assembled.

No. 10   4-4-0 Portland #499. Built for Northern Pacific. Ex-Alaska Central No. 1. Obtained by AEC from Alaska Northern No. 1. Retired by Alaska Railroad and stored at Seward Scrapped in 1930.

No. 11   4-4-0 Baldwin #5880. 10/1881. Ex-Northern Pacific Nos. 846-90; Alaska Central, 10/1904. AEC No. 11 from Alaska Northern. Stored for period in back of roundhouse in Anchorage. Believed scrapped.

No. 20   4-6-0. Baldwin #11280. Ex-Northern Pacific; Alaska Northern, 1915. AEC 1917. Leased to Healy River Coal Corp. Recommended for scrapping in 1924 and scrapped in 1930.

No. 21   4-6-0. Alco Rhode Island. Ex-Climax Lumber Co. Used as stationary boiler at Curry.

No. 31   2-8-2 Alco-Brooks #27796. 7/1903. Ex-Buffalo & Susquahana No. 118; Pittsburg & West Virginia No. 118; Southern Iron & Equipment No. 2137, 1923-24; Alaska Railroad and rebuilt from 2-8-0 to 2-8-2 and shipped to ARR and placed in service as No. 31 Nov. 1927. Retired in 1930s.

No. 101   2-8-0. Alco Rhode Island #44600. 11/1907. Ex-Copper River & Northwestern No. 23. Alaska Railroad 1940. Sold for srap to Bethlehem Steel Co., Seattle, 1947.

——   2-8-2. Brooks #55491. 11/1915. Copper River & Northwestern No. 71. ARR 1940. Reported never used due to poor condition.

——   2-6-0. Brooks #46183 5/1909. Copper River & Northwestern No. 101. ARR 1940. Reported never used due to poor condition.

Nos. 200 series   2-6-0 American Locomotive Co., 1906. Built as 5-foot gauge for Panama RR during construction of Panama Canal. Converted to standard 4' 8½" gauge prior to shipping north by applying wide tread on wheels. Panama Nos. 101-124. Retired June 30, 1913. Shipped to Alaska in 1915 and 1916.

No.		
208	Alco #39099	Scrapped 1930
221	#39112	Scrapped 1936
224	#39115	
225	#39116	Scrapped 1936
239	#39150	Rebuilt 0-6-0, scrapped
242	#39152	Scrapped 1930
247	#39158	Scrapped 1930
264	#39175	
265	#39176	Scrapped 1930
266	#39177	
270	#39181	Scrapped, Beth Stl, 1947
272	#39183	Scrapped Beth Stl, 1947
275	#39816	Scrapped 1930
277	#39188	
278	#39189	
280	#39191	
285	#39196	Scrapped Beth Stl, 1947
287	#39198	Scrapped Beth Stl, 1947

No. 301	0-6-0 Alco-Manchester #39530 Northern Pacific No. 1042 to Alaska RR 2/1943. Scrapped Bethlehem Steel, Seattle, 1947.				
No. 300 series	0-6-0 Lima for U.S. Army and acquired by ARR from Army as surplus.				
	No. 310	#8390	2/1944	USA No. 4056	Retired 4/54
	311	#8402		USA No. 4068	To N&PL No. 56
		Alaska RR roster 1953. Retired 4/54			
	312	#8407	12/1943	USA No. 4073	Retired 4/54
	313	#8406	2/1944	USA No. 4072	Retired 4/54
	314	#8408	2/1944	USA No. 4074	
	315	#8391	2/1944	USA No. 4057	Retired 4/54
	316	#8379 or #8392	2/1944	USA No.4054	Retired 4/54
	317	#8393	2/1944	USA No. 4059	Retired 4/54
	318	#8392	2/1944	USA No. 4004	Retired 4/54
	319	#8383	1/1944	USA No. 4049	Retired 4/54
No. 500 series	2-8-0 Lima. Renumbered 400 series by ARR. Acquired from U.S. Army.				
	501-401	#7879	2/1942	USA No. 6998	Sold to F. C. deLargero in Spain through American Aid Mission, Jan. 1958.
	502-402	#7880	2/1942	USA No. 6999	Sold to F. C. deLargero in Spain, Jan 1958.
	503-403	#7881	3/1942	USA No. 6986 to US Corps of Engineers No. 10, to Alaska Railroad.	
	504-404	#7877	3/1942	USA No. 6996	
	505-405	#7875	2/1942	USA No. 6994	Sold to F. C. deLargero Spain Jan 1958.
	506-406	#7876	2/1942	USA No. 6995	Sold to F. C. deLargero Spain, Jan 1958.

No. 315 was one of the "300" series of locomotives acquired by the Alaska Railroad from the military and then shipped to Spain in 1958 for use by F.C. de Largero. The transfer was through the American Aid Mission. Giant cranes were used to hoist the locomotives aboard ship. (Anchorage Historical and Fine Arts Museum—Alaska Railroad Collection)

Locomotive No. 312 was one of several Lima 0-6-0's obtained from the U.S. Army surplus during 1944 and retired in the mid-50's. Most were used for switchers. (Anchorage Historical and Fine Arts Museum—Alaska Railroad Collection)

ARR No. 502 was one of the "500" series Lima 2-8-0 locomotives acquired by the Alaska Railroad from the U.S. Army in 1942. They were renumbered in the 400s after being put into service. Many of these locomotives went to Spain following retirement from the Alaska Railroad. (Anchorage Historical and Fine Arts Museum—Alaska Railroad Collection)

Locomotive No. 551, first of the Baldwin 2-8-0's acquired from the Army by the Alaska Railroad in 1943. The locomotive was one of the standard 'Gypsy Rose Lee' type—stripped down for action. These locomotives were retired in 1956. (Anchorage Historical and Fine Arts Museum—Alaska Railroad Collection)

Nos. 550 series	2-8-0 Baldwin. Built for U.S. Army. Nos. 551-556 acquired by ARR direct from Army 9/10/43. Others acquired surplus. All standard Army "Gypsy Rose Lee."			
	551	#69636	6/1943	USA No. 2379	Retired 11/56
	552	#68637	6/1943	USA No. 2380	Sold to F. C. deLargero Spain, Jan. 1958.
	553	#69638	6/1943	USA No. 2381	Wrecked 1943 in head-on collision with ARR No. 901. Scrapped.
	554	#69639	5/1943	USA 2392	Retired 11/56 and sold to F. C. deLargero, Spain, Jan 1958.
	555	#69654	8/1943	USA 2626	Retired 4/54
	556	#69655	8/1943	USA No. 2627	Retired 11/56 and donated to City of Anchorage for display.
	557	#70480	12/1944	USA No. 3523	Sold to Michelson Steel, Everett, Wn. To Monte Holm, Moses Lake, Wa. Used for tourist attraction. Last steam locomotive in service on Alaska Railroad.
	558	#70478	12/1944	USA No. 3521	Sold to F. C. deLargero in Spain 1/58.
	559	#70449	12/1944	USA No. 3522	Retired 4/54. Sold to F. C. deLargero, Spain, 1/58.
	560	#70637	12/1944	USA No. 3410	Retired 4/54. Sold to F. C. deLargero, Spain, 1/58.
	561	#70366	12/1944	USA No. 3409	Retired 11/56
	562	Alco-Schen. #70431	11/42	USA No. 1600	Retired 11/56

Alaska Railroad No. 562, the last of the "550" series obtained by the Alaska Railroad. The 2-8-0 engine was built in 1942 by Alco and acquired by the ARR as surplus from the military following World War II. No. 562 was retired in 1956 and is shown with a small snowplow replacing the cowcatcher. (Anchorage Historical and Fine Arts Museum—Alaska Railroad Collection)

Locomotive No. 556, a Bladwin 2-8-0 acquired from the U.S. Army in 1943 and retired in Novembver 1956, was one of the last of the steamers to be used on the Alaska Railroad. A sister locomotive, No. 557, was retained an additional number of years as a backup for use during flood conditions and was the last steamer on the ARR. No. 556 Was donated to the City of Anchorage and is on display in a downtown park. (Western Airlines)

The last steam locomotive in service on the Alaska Railroad was No. 557, retired in 1956 but retained by the railroad because it could pull trains through water which diesels could not do. Oftimes tracks were flooded during spring runoff. The locomotive was acquired by Monte Holm of Moses Lake, Wa., in 1966. No 556, a sister locomotive, is on display in Anchorage. (Anchorage Historical and Fine Arts Museum—Alaska Railroad Collection)

Alaska Railroad locomotive No. 556, one of the last steamers to see service on the railroad, with a passenger train. No. 556 was obtained from the U.S. Army in 1943 and retired from service in 1956. The Baldwin 2-8-0 is now on display in the Anchorage city park. (Anchorage Historical and Fine Arts Museum—Alaska Railroad Collection)

Locomotive No. 701 was the first of the "700" series engines acquired by the Alaska Railroad in 1927. Most of these Baldwin 2-8-2's were retired in 1954 and many of them were shipped ot F.C. de Largero in Spain in 1958. (Anchorage Historical and Fine Arts Museum—Alaska Railroad Collection)

This locomotive might be termed one of the tough-luck engines on the Alaska Railroad. This Baldwin 4-8-2 was built in 1932. It was wrecked in 1942 when it hit a slide between Potter and Indian. Rebuilt it was wrecked again in 1950-51 and never rebuilt. (Anchorage Historical and Fine Arts Museum—Alaska Railroad Collection.)

No. 600 series	2-6-0 Alco-Brooks originally built 5' gauge for use on Panama RR. Converted to standard gauge before shipment to Alaska. Acquired by Alaska Railroad (AEC) in Jan. 1923.			
	601	#39122	4/1906	Rebuilt with 54" drivers. Unsuccessful.
	605	#39126	4/1905	
	606	#39127	4/1906	Scrapped Beth. Steel, Seattle 1947
	610	#39131	4/1906	
	614	#39135	4/1906	Wrecked 3/32. To Beth. Steel, Seattle, 1947, scrapped.
	618	#39137	4/1906	Carried President Harding to Nenana for Golden Spike ceremony marking completion of Alaska RR.
	620	#39141	4/1906	Wrecked 2/38.

No. 701 2-8-2 Baldwin #59605 10/1926 To ARR in 1927. Retired 4/54. To F. C. deLargero, Spain, 1/58.

No. 702 2-8-2 Baldwin #59606 10/1926 To ARR in 1927. Retired 4/54. To F. C. deLargero, Spain, 1/58.

No. 703 2-8-2 Baldwin #60689 12/1928. To ARR 1929. Retired 4/54. To F. C. deLargero, Spain, 1/58.

No. 751 2-8-2 Alco-Schen. #46856 1909 or 1910 Northern Pacific No. 1676. To ARR 2/1942, to Beth. Steel, Seattle, 1947.

No. 752 2-8-2 Alco-Schen. #46872 1910 Northern Pacific No. 1692. To ARR 2/43. To Beth. Steel, 1947.

No. 801 4-8-2 Baldwin #61736 5/1932. Wrecked 1942 when hit slide between Potter and Indian. Rebuilt and wrecked again 1950-51. Never rebuilt.

No. 802 4-8-2 Baldwin #64366 7/1942. Arrived Alaska knocked-down and assembled in Anchorage.

No. 901 4-6-2 Baldwin #62515 12/1940. To F. C. deLargero, Spain, 1958.

No. 902 4-6-2 Baldwin #70336. 6/1945. Last steam locomotive delivered to Alaska Railroad, Sept. 1942.

No. 16 2-8-2 Baldwin 1929. Ex-Comox Lumber Co., Canada to Western Railway Assoc. Leased and operated by Alaska Railroad during summer of 1967 for Centennial Celebration. Ran from Anchorage depot to Anchorage International Airport.

Alaska Railroad Diesels

	Mfg.	Mfg No.	Yr. Mfg.	To ARR	Notes
No. 1000	Alco GE	#71319	1944	1944	First diesel acquired by Alaska. Now on display at State Transportation museum, Palmer.
No. 1001	Alco GE	#71320	1944	1944	
No. 1002	Alco GE	#70659	1943	1949	Ex-USA No. 8038. ARR No. 1055. Retired 1965.
No. 1010	Alco GE	#70662	1943	1947	Ex-USA No. 8041. Retired 1965.
No. 1011	Alco GE	#70663	1943	1947	Ex-USA No. 8051. Renumbered ARR No. 1075. Retired 1964.
No. 1012	Alco GE	#70664	1943	1947	Ex-USA No. 8043. ARR No. 1077. Retired 1965
No. 1013	Alco GE	#70665	1943	1947	Ex-USA No. 8044. Retired 1965.
No. 1014	Alco GE	#70666	1943	1947	Ex-USA No. 8045. Retired 1964.
No. 1015	Alco GE	#70656	1943	1948	Ex-USA No. 8035. ARR No. 1065. Retired 1972.
No. 1016	Alco GE	#70647	1942	1947	Ex-USA No. 8026. ARR No. 1067. Retired 1965.
No. 1017	Alco GE	#72157	1945	1950	Ex-USA No. 8664. Retired 1965.
No. 1018	Alco GE	#70672	1943	1949	Ex-USA No. 8048. Retired 1965.
No. 1019	Alco GE	#70674	1942	1950	Ex-USA No. 8053 ARR No. 1078. Retired 1964.
No. 1021	Alco GE	#69567	1941	1950	Ex-CMStP&P No. 1678, USA No. 8002. ARR 1054. Retired 1963.
No. 1026	Alco GE	#70663	1943	1949	Ex-USA No. 8042. Retired 1971.
No. 1027	Alco GE	#70670	1943	1948	Ex-USA No. 8049. To Mate 1.
No. 1028	Alco GE	#70640	1942	1950	Ex-USA No. 8019. Retired 1964.
No. 1029	Alco GE	#70650	1942	1950	Ex-USA No. 8020. Retired 1964.
No. 1030	Alco GE	#70641	1942	1950	Ex-USA No. 8023. Retired 1964. Scrapped 1967.
No. 1031	Alco GE	#69424	1941	1950	Ex-R1 No. 748, USA No. 8005. Retired 1964.
No. 1032	Alco GE	#70645	1942	1951	Ex-USA No. 8024. To USATC 1956; TVA 39, Grahamville, KY.
No. 1033	Alco GE	#70660	1943	1951	Ex-USA No. 8039. To USATC 1956; TVA 38, Stevenson, ALA.
No. 1034	Alco GE	#69427	1941	1951	Ex-A&STAB, 902 USA No. 8011. To USATC 1956; DOT 013. Pueblo.
No. 1035	Alco GE	#70634	1942	1951	Ex-USA No. 8013. To USATC 1956; TVA 43, Kingston, TENN.
No. 1036	Alco GE	#72143	1945	1951	Ex-USA No. 8650. To USATC 1956; TVA 36, Stevenson, ALA.
No. 1041	Alco GE	#69570	1941	1951	Ex-CRI&P No. 747, USA No. 8004. To USATC 1956; DOT 011, Pueblo.
No. 1042	Alco GE	#69425	1941	1951	Ex-CRI&P No. 749, USA No. 8006. To USATC 1956; TVA 8006 Muscle Shoals, ALA.
No. 1043	Alco GE	#69568	1941	1951	Ex-CMStP&P No. 1679, USA No. 8003. To USATC 1956; DOT 8003. Destroyed in Test.

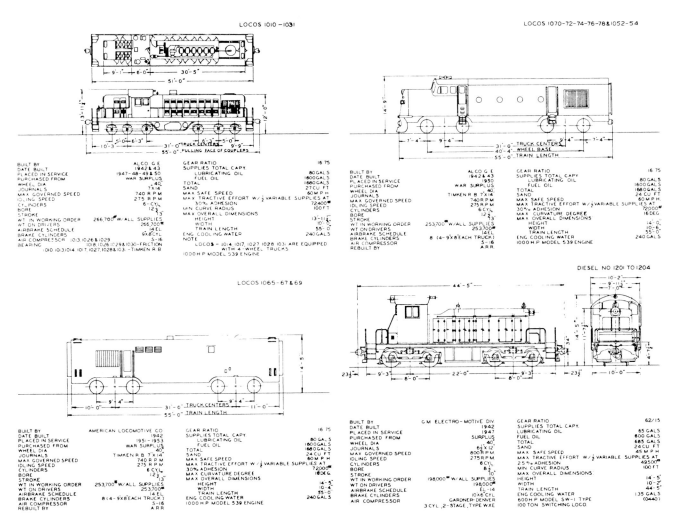

Diagrams of the various 1000 series, 1200 series and 2500 series diesel electric locomotives on the Alaska Railroad. (Anchorage Historical and Fine Arts Museum—Alaska Railroad Collection)

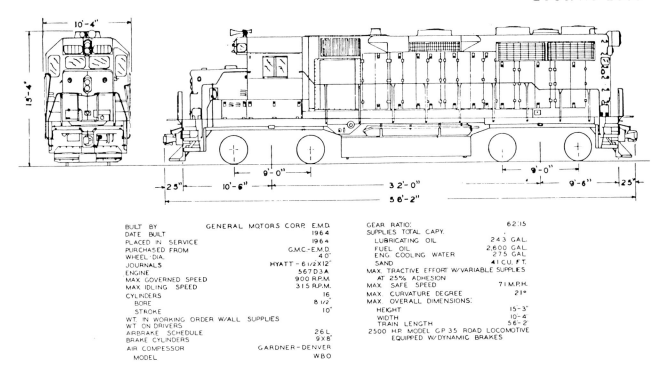

The first diesel on the Alaska Railroad was No. 1000 an Alco-GE which was purchased new in 1944. The locomotive was retired and is on display at the Transportation Museum in Palmer. (Western Airlines)

No. 1050	Alco GE	#70661	1943	1947	Ex-USA No. 8040. Retired 1963.
No. 1051	Alco GE	#70675	1943	1947	Ex-USA No. 8054. Retired 1964.
No. 1052	Alco GE	#70676	1943	1950	Ex-USA No. 8055. Retired 1963.
No. 1053	Alco GE	#70642	1943	1950	Ex-USA 8021. ARR No. 1089. Retired 1965.
No. 1054	Alco GE	#70678	1943	1950	Ex-USA No. 8002. APR No. 1021. Retired 1964.
No. 1055		(See No. 1002)			
No. 1057	Alco GE	#69993	1942	1950	Ex-USA No. 8001, NYS&W No. 223. ARR No. 1085. Retired 1963.
No. 1065		(See No. 1015)			
No. 1067		(See No. 1016)			
No. 1069		(See No. 1021)			
No. 1070	Alco GE	#70668	1943	1949	Ex-USA No. 8047. Retired 1970.
No. 1072	Alco GE	#70673	1943	1950	Ex-USA No. 8052. Retired 1972.
No. 1074	Alco GE	#70657	1943	1950	Ex-USA No. 8036. Retired 1966.
No. 1075		(See No.1011)			
No. 1076	Alco GE	#70667	1943	1950	Ex-USA No. 8046. Retired 1970.
No. 1077		(See No. 1012)			
No. 1078		(See No. 1019)			
No. 1085		(See No. 1057)			
No. 1087		(See No. 1054)			
No. 1089		(See No. 1053)			

Two of Alaska Railroad's "retiring" steamers along side one of the new diesels, No. 1001 which arrived in 1944. The two steamers are of the "200 series," 2-6-0 American Locomotive Co. engines built in 1906 to 5-foot gauge for use on the Panama Canal and then converted to standard gauge for use on the Alaska Railroad. (Anchorage Historical and Fine Arts Museum—Alaska Railroad Collection.)

Decked out in Alaska Railroad colors is the ex-U.S. Army Alco G.E. diesel No. 8040, renumbered No. 1050 by the ARR. The Alaska Railroad acquired the locomotives following World War II and used them into the mid-1960's (Anchorage historical and Fine Arts Museum—Alaska Railroad Collection.)

No. 1100	Porter	#7459	1943	1947	Ex-USA No. 7157, Nevada Ord. Depot. To Sherwood Templeton Co. No. 7438.
No. 1101	Porter	#7439	1943	1947	Ex-USA No. 7168, Navajo Ord. Depot. Retired 1954.
No. 1102	Porter	#7392	1942	1947	Ex-USA No. 7033, Sierra Ord. Depot. Retired 1954.
No. 1103	Porter	#7405	1942	1947	Ex-USA No. 7034, Toledo Ord. Depot. To Dewey Cement Co. No.7034.
No. 1104	Porter	#7425	1942	1947	Ex-USA No. 7024, San Jasiste Ord. Depot. Retired 1954.
No. 1105	Porter	#7404	1942	1947	Ex-USA No. 7150, Toledo Ord. Works To Greenville Mfg. Co.
No. 1106	Porter	#7317	1942	1947	Ex-USA No. 7187, Jefferson Proving Grounds No. 1. Retired 1954.
No. 1107	Porter	#7318	1942	1947	Ex-USA No. 7188, Jefferson Proving Grounds No. 2. Retired 1954.
No. 1201	E.M.D.	#2000	1942	1947	Ex-USA No. 7003. Retired 1957. To Prescott Equipment Co., Seattle 1967.
No. 1202	E.M.D.	#2001	1942	1947	Ex-USA No. 7004. Retired 1957. To Prescott Equipment Co., Seattle1967.
No. 1203	E.M.D.	#1990	1942	1947	Ex-USA No. 7001. Retired 1957.
No. 1204	E.M.D.	#2012	1942	1947	Ex-USA No. 7002. Retired 1957.

One of the series of FMD diesel-electrics obtained by the Alaska Railroad in 1953 is this one, shown ready to depart on a passenger run on the Anchorage-Fairbanks link of the ARR. (Anchorage Historical and Fine Arts Museum—Alaska Railroad Collection.)

One of several diesel electrics purchased from the Denver & Rio Grande in 1970 is ARR No. 1526, pictured along side of No. 2502 an FMD built in 1965. (Anchorage Historical and Fine Arts Museum—Alaska Railroad Collection)

No. 1300	Baldwin	#71745	1945	1949	Ex-USA V-1801, Oakland Army Terminal. Retired 1957. Scrapped 1967.
No. 1500	E.M.D. F-7		1952	1952	
No. 1501	E.M.D. F-7		1952	1952	Retired 1962
No. 1502	E.M.D. F-7		1952	1952	
No. 1503	E.M.D. F-7		1952	1952	
No. 1504	E.M.D. F-7		1952	1952	
No. 1505	E.M.D. F-7		1952	1952	
No. 1506	E.M.D. F-7		1953	1953	
No. 1507	E.M.D. F-7		1953	1953	
No. 1508	E.M.D. F-7		1953	1953	
No. 1510	E.M.D. F-7		1953	1953	
No. 1512	E.M.D. F-7		1953	1953	
No. 1514	E.M.D. F-7		1953	1953	
No. 1515	E.M.D. F-7B	#9550	1950		
No. 1516	E.M.D. F-7A	#8015	1948		
No. 1517	E.M.D. F-7B	#5868	1949		
No. 1518	E.M.D. F-7A	#8513	1949		
No. 1519	E.M.D. F-7B	#16537	1952		
No. 1520	E.M.D. F-7A	#16519	1952		
No. 1521	E.M.D. F-7B	#16540	1952		
No. 1522	E.M.D. F-7A	#16526	1952		
No. 1523	E.M.D. F-7B	#16342	1952		
No. 1524	E.M.D. F-7A	#5866	1959		
No. 1525	E.M.D. F-7B	#11416	1950		
No. 1526	E.M.D. F-7A	#16522	1952		
No. 1528	E.M.D. F-7A	#16520	1952		
No. 1530	E.M.D. F-7A	#11406	1950		
No. 1532	E.M.D. F-7A	#11408	1950		
No. 1821	E.M.D. GP-7		1951	1959	(leased), 1964 acquired from Army.
No. 1825	E.M.D. GP-7		1951	1959	(leased), 1964 acquired from Army.

No. 1826	E.M.D. GP-7	1951	1959	(leased), 1964 acquired from Army.
No. 1827	E.M.D. GP-7	1951	1959	(leased), 1964 acquired from Army.
No. 1828	E.M.D. GP-7	1951	1964	(leased), 1964 acquired from Army.
No. 1830	E.M.D. GP-7	1951	1959	(leased), 1964 acquired from Army.
No. 1831	E.M.D. GP-7	1951	1959	(leased), 1964 acquired from Army.
No. 1834	E.M.D. GP-7	1951	1959	(leased), 1964 acquired from Army.
No. 1836	E.M.D. GP-7	1951	1959	(leased), 1964 acquired from Army.
No. 1837	E.M.D. GP-7	1951	1959	(leased), 1964 acquired from Army.
No. 1838	E.M.D. GP-7	1951	1959	(leased), 1964 acquired from Army.
No. 1839	E.M.D. GP-7	1951	1959	(leased), 1964 acquired from Army.
No. 2000	E.M.D. GP-30	1963		
No. 2501	E.M.D. GP-35	1964		
No. 2503	E.M.D. GP-35	1964		
No. 7107	Alco SW-2	1943	1955	(leased from Army) destroyed in quake.
No. 7109	Alco SW-2	1943	1955	(leased from Army)
No. 7112	Alco SW-2	1943	1955	(leased from Army)
No. 7123	Alco SW-2	1943	1955	(leased from Army)
No. 1809	E.M.D. MRS-1	1952	1952	(leased from Army) returned 1955.

All locomotives 0-4-4-0
F-7A&B Frt locos.
FP-7 Frt. & Pass. locos
SW-2 Switcher

GP-7 General purpose
GP-30 Road
GP-35 Road

Roundhouse Switchers

No. 50	0-4-0	25-ton	150 H.P.	GE 27501	Built 1944	Retired 1956
No. 51	0-4-0	25-ton	150 H.P.	GE 13146	Built 1941	Retired 1956
No. 60	0-4-0	20-ton	Whitcomb Gas Mechanical #13182			
No. 61	0-4-0	20-ton	Whitcomb Gas Mechanical #13179			

Motorrailers and Trailers

211—14 passgr.   214—32 passgr.   303 Trailer—56 passgr.
212—42 passgr.   215—24 passgr.   3-4 Trailer—60 passgr.
213—40 passgr.   216—34 passgr.
All since retired from service.

Note

A fire in the shops of the Alaska Railroad in Jan. 1951 destroyed all mechanical records of the railroad. This listing of locomotives has been compiled from records at the National Archives—the most complete available, plus duplicates of parts of previous records, newsmedia reports, interviews with ARR personnel, the two-volume picture history of the Alaska Railroad, "The Alaska Railroad" by Bernadine M. Prince, and the Moose Gooser, publication of the Alaska-Yukon Railroad Historical Society. Special mention should be made for the help from Louise Bremmer, administrative assistant to the General Manager of the Alaska Railroad, for making records available to the author.

One of the many diesels obtained from the military by the
Alaska Railroad was this one which went into service in the
original olive drab and without an Alaska Railroad number.
Later, as time allowed, these locomotives were rebuilt in the
ARR shops, painted in Alaska Railroad colors and given
numbers. (Anchorage Historical and Fine Arts Museum—
Alaska Railroad Collection)

This is just one of several "war surplus" steam locomotives
acquired by the Alaska Railroad from the military and then
shipped to Spain in 1958 for use by F.C. de Largero. The
transfer was through the American Aid Mission. Giant cranes
were used to hoist the locomotives aboard ship. (Anchorage
Historical and Fine Arts Museum—Alaska Railroad
Collection)

Route map of the Alaska Railroad. The track runs from
Seward on Resurrection Bay on the South to Eielson AFB,
east of Fairbanks on the North. Also shown is the Whittier
cutoff from Portage. (Clifford Collection)

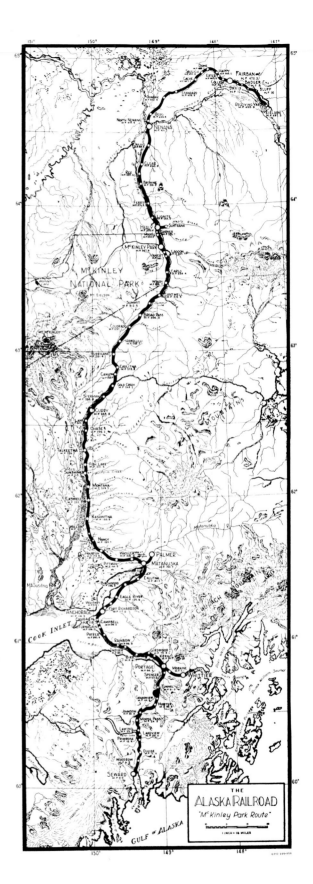

THE
ALASKA RAILROAD
"McKinley Park Route"

1 INCH = 16 MILES

This narrow gauge motor tram was used on the Alaska Railroad between Nenana and Fairbanks during early days of the operation. (Clifford Collection)

Alaska Railroad motorrailer No. 215, a 24-passenger used on shorter runs and during periods of light traffic. All of the motorrailers have been retired from service. (Anchorage Historical and Fine Arts Museum—Alaska Railroad Collection)

Rail bus "Ice Worm" of the Alaska Railroad. The vehicle was brought to Alaska and used to carry passengers between Whittier and Portage in 1965-66. The bus was operated by the owners of a sportman's lodge in Whittier and operated on a regular schedule hauling passengers to their facility. The bus was later taken over by the Alaska Railroad (Western Airlines)

Alaska Railroad passenger train with Mt. McKinley in the background. The ARR operates on a regular schedule between Anchorage and Fairbanks and is one of the favored tourist attractions in the 49th State. (Anchorage Historical and Fine Arts Museum—Alaska Railroad Collection)

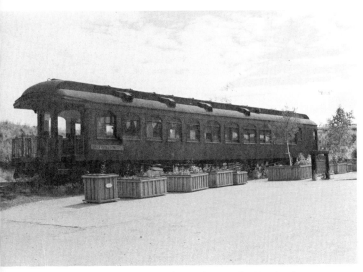

The "Denali," President Warren G. Harding's private car when he was in Alaska for the Golden Spike ceremony at Nenana on the Alaska Railroad in June 1923. The car is now on display at Alaskaland in Fairbanks. (Western Airlines.)

One of the first switching locomotives obtained by the Alaska Railroad is this Lima 2-6-0 being unloaded at Whittier. The engines were obtained as surplus from the military in 1947. (Anchorage Historical and Fine Arts Museum— Alaska Railroad Collection)

Well deserved retirement has been earned by this little Porter which saw service for more than a quarter century on several different railroads. On many it carried No. 1, including the Tanana Valley and U.S. Government (Alaska Railroad). Now on display at Alaskaland in Fairbanks, the narrow gauge engine was built in 1899. (H. Clifford)

Chapter 10

Tanana Mines (Valley) Railroad

A little, unmarked Porter 0-4-0 wood-burning saddle-tank locomotive located in the far corner of Alaskaland (Fairbanks) is the only physical reminder of a 45-mile narrow gauge railroad which operated in the Fairbanks area for a period of 12 years—1905 to 1917 —until taken over by the Alaskan Railraod Commission to become part of the government-owned Alaska Railroad.

The Tanana Mines Railroad was organized and incorporated in 1904 under the laws of the State of Maine by Falcon Joslin, an enterprising Fairbanks attorney who had been extremely successful in Dawson City and was a former president of the Bering River Coal & Oil Company Railroad. He planned to build a railroad from a point on the Tanana River near the town of Chena to a point on the Yukon River near the town of Circle City, with branch lines to Fairbanks and the mines in the Fairbanks District.

Financed by New York and Chicago business interests, the TMRR (which was changed to the Tanana Valley Railroad in 1907) was part of an overall plan to expand a route to Circle City and Dawson City, with a 600-mile link to Nome. Another line was to go up the Tanana Valley across the Yukon Boundary and south down the Chilkat River to a point on Lynn Canal near Haines. This route would pass through what was believed to be 800 miles of rich gold and copper country.

Gold was in its heyday in Fairbanks when the narrow guage Tanana (Mines) Valley Railroad started operating from Chena to Chatanika. This photograph shows the ceremony in which the golden spike was driven. (University of Alaska Archives—Terry Cole Collection)

The TVRR was built in two stages. In 1905 the road was put in from Chena to Gilmore on Pedro Creek, with a spur of 4.7 miles to Fairbanks which started operation in September 1905. The next year this 26 miles of line was considerably improved. In 1907 the six-month working season brought extension of the TVRR to Chatanika.

The obstacles overcome by Joslin and his associates were considerable. Land near Chena was low and subject to periodic floods. Trestle bridges up to 600 feet in length were required over the creeks. Spruce was at hand in suitable quantity and quality for ties and trestles, but the 30-pound rails and equipment had to be transported as much as 6,000 miles and handled as many as eleven times. Six flat cars intended for the TVRR wound up at the bottom of the Yukon River. Laborers were paid $7.50 a day and as many as 200 men were employed at times during construction.

Offices and shops for the line were first located at Chena, where the tracks ran down Front Street for two-thirds of a mile by warehouses and docks. There were terminal grounds at Chena Junction, Fairbanks and Gilmore. The amount of money spent on surveys,

preliminary work, actual construction and equipment amounted to $815,969.05. When the TVRR was built in the summer of 1905, a gold spike ceremony took place. Federal District Judge James Wickersham made the principle speech of the day. The road was built without any government subsidy except for a five-year dispensation from the federal tax of $100 a year for each mile of track.

During the riverboat months, usually the last of May to early October, the Tanana Valley Railroad moved people and goods out of the port of Chena, as the town was located directly on the Tanana River. In other seasons trains picked up express and passengers arriving in Fairbanks over a sledge stage route from Valdez on Prince William Sound.

As Chena started to decline, Fairbanks became the dominant city in the Interior and operations were transferred to Garden Isle in Fairbanks in 1915.

Early equipment consisted of four locomotives, four passenger coaches and thirty freight cars. Included were the little Porter 0-4-0 saddle-tanker which had been obtained from the Northern Light, Power, Coal and Transportation Co., near Dawson City, and

Tanana Valley R. R.

TIME CARD

Effective Sept. 16, 1912.

Leave Fairbanks .... 8:30 am.
" Ester Siding .... 8:45 am.
" McNeer .... 9:20 am.
" Carlson .... 9:30 am.
" Fox ....10:05 am.
" Gilmore ....10:30 am.
" Ridgetop ....11:30 am.
" Olnes ....12:05 pm.
" Little Eldorado .....12:25 pm.
Arrive Chatanika ....12:40 pm.

Returning.

Leave Chatanika .... 1:20 pm.
" Little Eldorado ..... 1:30 pm.
" Olnes .... 1:45 pm.
" Ridgetop ....2:15 pm.
" Gilmore ....3:05 pm.
" Fox .... 3:20 pm.
" Carlson .... 3:40 pm.
" McNeer .... 3:50 pm.
" Ester Siding .... 4:15 pm.
Arrive Fairbanks .... 4:35pm.

CHENA TRAIN.

Leave Fairbanks ....5:05 pm.
Arrive Chena ....5:40 pm.

Returning.

Leave Chena ....7:00 am.
Arrive Fairbanks ....7:35 am.

Motor car leaves Fairbanks for Gilmore at 10:30 am. and 4:05 pm.

Returning leaves Gilmore at 7:55 am. and 12:05 pm.

Parker's Auto connects with trains and electric car at Ester Siding for Ester City.

McLean's Stage connects with trains at Gilmore for Fairbanks Creek on Mondays, Wednesdays and Friday.

Stage connects at Chatanika for Cleary City.

C. W. JOYNT,
General Manager.

The little Porter 0-4-0 acquired by the Tanana Valley from the Northern Lights, Power, Coal and Transportation Co., of Dawson City, prepares to depart from a station in the Fairbanks area with its train of one passenger car. The little narrow gauge locomotive was the TVRR No. 1 and also carried the same number for the Alaska Engineering Commission. The locomotive is now on display at Alaskaland, Fairbanks. (Clifford Collection.)

Tanana Valley Railroad Baldwin 4-4-0 with snowplow attached serving as a work train locomotive at a gravel pit near Fairbanks. The Baldwin was built in 1878 for the Olympia and Tenino Railway and served with several other railroads, including the White Pass & Yukon before being acquired by the TVRR. The little narrow gauge was later acquired by the Alaska Engineering Commission and was scrapped in 1930.

Tanana Valley Railroad "time card" for Sept. 16, 1912 as published in a Fairbanks newspaper of the period. The scheduled listed daily service between Fairbanks and Chatanika as well as Fairbanks and Chena. There was also twice daily motor car service between Fairbanks and Gilmore. Stage connections with the various trains are also listed. (Clifford Collection.)

Tanana Valley Railroad Company

Time Table No. 13. Effective 12:01 a. m., May 10, 1909.

This Company reserves the right to vary from this Time Table at Pleasure

Chena and Fairbanks

North Bound Daily.		South Bound Daily.
No 7 Mixed		No. 8 Mixed
Lv. 7:00 a. m.	.................Chena.................	Ar. 7:00 p. m.
Lv. 7:25 a. m.	..............Junction..............	Lv. 6:25 p. m.
Ar. 7:50 a. m.	..............Fairbanks..............	Lv. 6:00 p. m.

Fairbanks, Gilmore and Chatanika.

NORTH BOUND				SOUTH BOUND		
NO. 1 Mixed Daily	NO. 3 Goldstream Special Daily	NO. 5 Chatanika Passenger Daily		NO. 6 Fairbanks Passenger Daily	NO. 4 Goldstream Special Daily	NO. 2 Mixed Daily
A. M.	A. M.	P. M.		A. M.	P. M.	P. M.
9:30 Lv	11:00 Lv	3:40 Lv	...... Fairbanks	10:00 Ar	2:30 Ar	5:30 Ar
9:45 M	11:15 Lv	3:55 Lv	..... Junction ....M	9:45 Lv	2:15 Lv	5:10 Lv
9:50 Lv	11:20 Lv	4:00 Lv	...... Ester	9:40 Lv	2:10 Lv	5:00 Lv
10:25 Lv	11:50 Lv	4:30 M	....Big Eldorado ...	9:10 Lv	1:40 Lv	4:30 M
11:00 Lv	12:20pm	4:55 Lv	.... Fox	8:45 Lv	1:10 Lv	3:50 Lv
11:20 Lv	12:30 Ar	5:10 Lv	.... Gilmore	8:30 Lv	1:00 Lv	3:35 Lv
12:10pm		5:55 Lv	......Ridgetop	7:50 Lv		2:50 Lv
12:40 Lv		6:20 Lv	.... Olnes	7:25 Lv		2:20 Lv
1:00 Lv		6:35 Lv	..Little Eldorado	7:10 Lv		2:00 Lv
1:10 Ar		6:45 Ar	..... Chatanika	7:00 Lv		1:50 Lv

North bound Trains have right of track over South bound Trains.

FALCON JOSLIN, President.   A. P. TYSON, Gen. Mgr.

Passengers holding tickets to points beyond Gilmore on trains No. 1 and 3 may stop over at Fox or Gilmore to train No. 5 on date of sale only; and passengers on train No. 6 holding tickets to Fairbanks may stop off at Fox or Gilmore until train No. 4 or No. 2 on date of sale only.

Tanana Valley Railroad Time Table No. 13 as published in a Fairbanks newspaper. The schedule was effective May 10, 1909 and listed three trains daily in each direction between Fairbanks, Gilmore and Chatanika. Below the Tanana Valley schedule is a notice of service on the White Pass & Yukon Route for those contemplating a trip outside. (Clifford Collection.)

A Tanana Valley train makes its way across one of the slough in the Fairbanks area. The locomotive is believed to be the former White Pass & Yukon Baldwin No. 4 and 54 acquired by the TVR in 1905. (University of Alaska Archives—Erskine Collection)

A Tanana Valley train makes its way over Ridgetop during the winter with the help of a booster locomotive in the rear. Oftimes trains were stranded in the snows in this area and crews had to be rescued by dog team. (University of Washington Historical Library—Northwest Collection)

barged down the river to Fairbanks, arriving on July 4, 1905.

The second locomotive, a Baldwin 4-4-0, built in 1878, was obtained from the White Pass & Yukon Railroad in 1905.

A Brooks 2-6-0 was also obtained from the White Pass & Yukon (No. 65) in 1906, and became the TVRR No. 51.

The Tanana Mines also obtained a Baldwin 2-6-0 built in May 1890 from the Alberta Railway & Coal Co. (No. 12) and became the Tanana No. 52 and was also acquired by the Alaskan Engineering Commission (Government Railroad) and later scrapped.

Like other early-day railroads, the TVRR had its problems. In the spring, Goldstream, one of many creeks in the area, overflowed its banks and the railroad tracks as well. With several feet of water on the Goldstream Flats, it was necessary for the brakemen to don hip boots, climb out on the cowcatcher with a pike pole and then wade through the water, checking to feel that the tracks were not off and down the embankment. There were times when the force of the water running across the tracks floated the ties and rails out of position so that the train couldn't progress.

Another problem was complying with Interstate Commerce Commission regulations regarding the transportation of explosives. The ICC rules required that a 10-car spacing be maintained between the car carrying dynamite and the car carrying the explosive caps. Sometimes this was a problem, as there were not that many cars available to make up a train. Such could cause some railroads trouble—but not the Tanana Valley. They loaded the dynamite in the last car, and handed the caps to one of the passengers to hold in his lap with instructions that when the train stopped at the station where the dynamite was to be unloaded, he was to hand the package to the conductor for delivery. (The railroad had not "loaded" the caps on the train in violation of ICC regulations.)

Oftimes trains in the winter became stranded in the drifting snow on the north side of Ridgetop. One time such happened and it was necessary to send out a dog team to rescue the passengers and crew. The train itself was not seen back in Fairbanks for more than two weeks.

Two locomotives of the Tanana Valley Railroad are snowed in on the north side of the notorious Ridgetop. Oftimes it was necessary to send out dog teams to rescue the passengers and trains were not seen back in Fairbanks for a couple of weeks. (Clifford Collection.)

The little Porter 0-4-0 saddle-tanker, first on the Tanana (Mines) Valley Railroad, makes its way through the muskeg on the old Chatanika run. The little No. 1 locomotive is now on display at Alaskaland in Fairbanks. (University of Alaska Archives—Charles Bunnel Collection.)

At the height of operations the TVRR operated twice daily service in both directions between Fairbanks and Chena, and in addition a gasoline autocar operated twice daily between Fairbanks and Fox. Passenger and freight totals depended on the mining activity, with a tops in passengers being in the mid-and high-50 thousands in 1909 and 1910 and as low as the mid-20 thousands in 1914. In 1900 approximately 16,000 tons of freight was carried, which dropped more than one-third by 1914. Passenger revenue was 13 cents per passenger mile and freight was 58 cents per ton mile, compard with $3.00 for teams prior to inauguration of service by the Tanana Valley.

Shortly after the line was extended into Fairbanks, plans were made to extend the line to the Sourdough mining district along what is now the Richardson Highway, but a pole trestle built across the Chena River during the winter of 1906-07 was washed out in the spring and the tracks never went further than the Weeks Field area.

These tracks, however, did not go to waste. They were used to haul firewood from Weeks Field storage area for Northern Commercial Co.'s power plant, and supplies for the machine shop on Third and Barnette Streets. The only passengers this line carried were company employees who rode the train to the annual Fourth of July picnic held in the log storage area— which was empty at that time of year following a winter's use of logs. This service was discontinued in 1924 when the steam plant converted to coal.

Fairbanks, by this time, was reporting steady growth and in five years, what had been a tent city now had 5,000 inhabitants and the usual amenities of community life. There were a book store, two hospitals (St. Joseph's and St. Matthew's), a green house, and two fortune tellers (Mlles. Melbourne and Zelpha). A reader of Fairbanks papers in 1908 could learn that the Tanana Valley Railroad would handle livestock by special arrangements only, but that empty beer kegs and soda bottles would be carried free; that ice and roller rinks and moving pictures were advertising for customers; that "not a single good location can be found for rent and there is a lively demand among those desiring to buy cabins." If one were musically inclined, Sunday concerts featured such original compositions as "Toast to the Brides of Fairbanks," and "St. Fairbanks Tickle." Feature stories spoke of increase in the use of cigarettes, and "How It Feels to Fly an Aeroplane."

Gas-car service continued between Chena and Fairbanks until 1917. The cars were manufactured by the Beech Manufacturing Co. in New York, which also made battery-operated vehicles for the Edison Company.

From the standpoint of investment the Tanana Valley never proved a financial success, though it was able to meet expenses and pay interest on its indebtedness of $660,000. Operating expenses were about 62 percent of gross earnings. It must not be overlooked that, although not a money maker, the service of the

Tanana Valley to the gold creeks was important. Weekdays the railroad brought passengers, fuel and supplies. Sometimes on Sundays and holidays excursions were offered at bargain rates to sightseers.

The Government Railroad brought changes to the Tanana Valley. In 1917 the line was first leased and then sold to the government. Considering the bad state of the roadbed and age of the equipment, the sale price of $300,000 seemed fair to all concerned.

Under government operation the roadbed was improved, and a temporary narrow gauge line built to the Tanana. Pending construction of a bridge across the river, freight was brought across by ferry in the summer and by sledge and laying of narrow gauge tracks on the ice for trains in the winter. Upon completion of the Alaska Railroad and the construction of a bridge across the river in 1923 the Nenana-Fairbanks section was converted to standard gauge.

In the early 1920s the College Electric Car Service was started to the Alaska Agricultural College and the School of Mines, which opened in 1922. In 1931 the College-Fairbanks narrow gauge track was ripped out, and the Beech Cars replaced by larger Brill Gas-Electric cars, which resembled present day railroad coaches rather than the trolley-like Beech vehicles.

Five years later commuter service by rail was discontinued between College and Fairbanks and the Brill cars were sent to Matanuska Valley, near Palmer, and used for transportation between Palmer and Anchorage until the 1950s. Track from College was extended to the Eielson AF base for military cargo use, and continues to be used today.

In Aug. 1930 the narrow gauge operation to Chatanika was discontinued and the rails removed and little remains today to indicate where the line once ran.

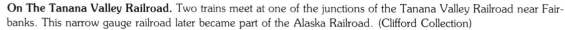

On The Tanana Valley Railroad. Two trains meet at one of the junctions of the Tanana Valley Railroad near Fairbanks. This narrow gauge railroad later became part of the Alaska Railroad. (Clifford Collection)

Tanana (Mines) Valley Railroad No. 50 Baldwin 4-4-0 locomotive in action in the Fairbanks area on a work train project. The locomotive was built for the Olympia and Tenino and later saw service on the White Pass & Yukon before being obtained by the TVR in 1905. (University of Alaska Archives—Bunnell Collection)

Tanana (Mines) Valley locomotives.

No. 1   0-4-0 H. K. Porter, Pittsburg, Pa., #1792. 3/1899. Ex-North American Transfer & Trading Co., Vancouver, B.C.; Northern Light, Power, Coal and Transportation Co., Dawson City, Y.T.; Tanana Mines No. 1, July 1905 to Alaskan Engineering Commission, 1917. Retired in 1930 and on display at Alaskaland, Fairbanks.

No. 50.   4-4-0. Baldwin #4294. 3/1878. Built for Olympia and Tenino Ry., later Olympia & Chehalis Valley No. 1, "E.H. Quimette"; Columbia & Puget Sound No. 10, 1890; White Pass & Yukon No. 4, 1898; rebuilt in 1900 and renumbered No. 54; Tanana Mines No. 50, 1905 to Alaskan Engineering Commission No. 50, 1917. Scrapped 1930.

No. 51   2-6-0. Brooks #578. 1881. Ex-Kansas Central Ry., No. 8; Union Pacific No. 102, 1885; Columbia and Western No. 3; Utah and Northern; Columbia & Western (Trail Tramway) No. 3; Canadian Pacific; White Pass & Yukon No. 65, 1900. Tanana Mines No. 51, 1906 to Alaskan Engineering Commission No. 51, 1917. Scrapped 1930.

No. 52   2-6-0. Baldwin #10880. 5/1890. Built for Alberta Railway and Coal Co., No. 12. Tanana Mines No. 52 to AEC No. 52, 1917. Scrapped 1930.

No. 151   2-8-0. Consolidated type. Purchased by Alaskan Engineering Commission from logging railroad in Seattle, 1917. Retired 1921. Scrapped 1936.

No. 152   4-6-0. Baldwin #53296 6/1920. Purchased new by Alaskan Engineering Commission. Retired 1932. U.S. Army No. 152, 1942 for use on White Pass & Yukon; Lathrop Transportation Corps Depot, Calif.; Davidson Scrap Metals Co., Stockton, Calif., Antelope & Western Ry., No. 3, Roseville, Calif.; Camino, Cable & Northern, Camino, Calif.; CC&N ceased operation in 1974 and disposed of locomotive to unknown operation in Pennsylvania.

Although never listed on the Tanana (Mines) Valley roster, the following locomotive was used over TVR trackage by the Alaskan Railroad Commission.

No. 6   0-4-0ST. Davenport #764. 12/1907. Built 36" gauge for Isthmus Canal Commission No. 802; Alaskan Engineering Commission 1917; converted to standard gauge 1930 and used as shop switcher. Renumbered No. 1, 1947 and placed on display at Alaska Railroad headquarters in Anchorage.

Chapter 11

Yakutat & Southern

Probably the only railroad in the world that operated on a tide-table rather than a timetable was the Yakutat & Southern, which served the Yakutat area for more than 60 years.

This unusual, and sometimes unbelievable railroad, was first conceived in 1903 when F.S. Stimson of Seattle and some associates incorporated the Stimson Lumber Co. and the Yakutat & Southern Railroad, with the announced intention of operating a salmon cannery, sawmill, railroad and general store.

They did all four, but the railroad and sawmill came first. The railroad to haul timber and the latter to cut it into lumber to build the rest of the facilities. The sawmill had a capacity of 36,000 board feet a day and an adjacent planing mill could turn out 5,000 feet a day. As the cannery got into operation in 1904, the sawmill turned out shocks for the wooden cases in which the cans were packed.

Yakutat is a fishing village on Yakutat Bay, at the extreme northwest corner of the Alaska Panhandle, about 350 miles southeast of Anchorage. A majority of the some 250 inhabitants are Tlingit Indians.

The Russians established a colony on Yakutat Bay in 1795, but it was wiped out by Indians a few years later. Settlers finally came back, but until World War II Yakutat was one of the most isolated areas in the Territory, being reached only by boat. The War brought a paved airport runway and now Yakutat is served by regular air service. A road connecting the community with the Alaska Highway, some 60 miles away, is planned.

There was some placer mining in the Yakutat area in the 1880s. In 1888 the Swedish Mission Con-venance established a mission there and soon afterward a couple of salteries were built to pack both salmon and herring. The first real industrial development began in 1903 when the Stimson group incorporated the lumber company and the railroad.

The original Stimson company carried on the operation for a number of years, then it was taken over by Gorman & Company, which had a number of salmon cannneries in Southeast Alaska. In 1913 the operation was sold to Libby, McNeill and Libby, and in 1951 Bellingham Canning Co. took over.

The Yakutat & Southern trackage, which started on the cannery wharf and ended eleven miles away in the brush on an uninhabited river bank, was standard gauge with 40-pound rails. The tide-table operation was made necessary when operations changed to the hauling of fish rather than lumber, and it was only when the tide was high on the Situk River that fishermen could unload their boats and skiffs from the train and fish scows could be brought alongside the track to load fish for the cannery.

Passengers and their effects were carried free. There were no tickets—one just got aboard a wooden, open-platform Hollingsworth-built combination coach and baggage car, providing he or she had the nerve to ride.

At one time there was a seven-mile branch to Lost River, but this was abandoned when an automobile road took its place. In the early years there was talk of extending the railroad southward on the coastal plain to the mouth of the Alsek River at Dry Bay—crossing the Situk, the Ahrnklin, the Dangerous, the Itallo, the Akwe and the Ustay Rivers on the way—but nothing came of it. Some say that the formidable number of bridges necessary for such a route was the main deterrant.

The original motive power on the Yakutat & Southern was a Heisler geared locomotive that was believed to have been discarded by the New York Elevated Railroad when it was electrified. The Heisler (No. 1) proved unsuited for the needs of the Y&S and was scrapped with its bell going to the mess hall to call workers to their meals, and various parts finding other uses in the operation over the years.

A 2-6-2 Lima Prairie locomotive built in 1907 was acquired from the Lima Works in 1913. It was retired in 1949 following World War II in an economic move as it required two tons of coal on a round-trip to the Situk River.

The Lima was succeeded by a make-shift, jack-type gas engine using the wheels of the old Heisler. The bell from the Lima went to one of the Alaska Steamship freighters serving the Yakutat area.

Other stock at the time included flat cars, some gon-dola cars and a pair of Plymouth switch engines—also of unknown history.

At one time a Packard flanged-wheel sedan was used. Later the line's rolling stock consisted of a Chevrolet truck with flanged wheels and a big box on the back, plus a home-made buggy-type gondola car. A hand car was also available for use by berry pickers and picnic parties.

Since operations ceased in the mid-1960s, the Lima locomotive, on three occasions—twice by gift and once by purchase—has belonged to the Alaska-Yukon Chapter of the National Railway Historical Society, but failure to move the 26-ton locomotive from cannery properties has resulted in it being involved in various legal entanglements as the cannery moved through many hands and in 1972 was involved in bankruptcy court in Seattle.

Plans have also been announced for the reconstruction of some of the trackage and the restoring of the Lima as a tourist attraction in the area. This program, too, is somewhat up in the air.

This Lima locomotive, built in 1907 and acquired in 1913, was the second locomotive to see service on the Yakutat & Southern. The engine was retired in 1949 after seeing heavy service during World War II. It is stored in the remains of the old engine house at Yakutat. (University of Alaska Archives—McCracken Collection)

It's a long way from the elevated rails of New York City to the banks of the Situk River near Yakutat in Alaska, but this little Heisler saw duty at both places. It was the first locomotive on the Yakutat & Southern, being acquired in 1904. The railroad started operating that year and continued service for more than a half century. (John Cobb Collection, University of Washington Library)

Yakutat & Southern Equipment.

No. 1   0-4-2 Heisler No. 1092. Believed to have been built for New York Elevated Railroad. Yakutat & Southern in 1903. Boiler and cab scrapped. Running gear converted to box cab and diesel motor. Still in engine house.

No. 2   2-6-2 Lima No. 1057. Built 8/1907. Y & S 1913. Stored in engine house in Yakutat.
Two Plymouth gas switch engine.
One 1930 Packard sedan with flanged wheels.
One 1949 Chevrolet truck with flanged wheels.
One open end combine built by Hollingsworth of Wilmington, Del.

When it became uneconomical to operate steam locomotives on the Yakutat & Southern they were replaced with trucks with flanged wheels. One of several such trucks is seen as it pulls a "fish car" between the cannery and the loading area on the Situk River. The trains hauled fish from the river landing to the cannery and personnel and supplies from the cannery area to the fish boats along the River. (University of Alaska Archives—McCracken Collection.)

Chapter 12

Valdez and the
Keystone Canyon Caper

The late 1800s and early 1900s brought a rush of proposed railroad builders to the open ports and harbors of Prince William Sound with visions of instant wealth if they could bring together the rich copper deposits which had been discovered in the Copper River Valley, the coal at Bering River, and the variety of other minerals in the Tanana and Yukon River Valleys.

Feasible rights-of-way were few in this section of Alaska, with its precipitous grades over rocky mountain passes, blanketed with deep snows fully half of the year.

About this same time the 55th Congress came to the aid of those attempting to construct railroads by the passing of the Transportation Act of 1898. The Act, which was passed on May 14, agreed with stipulations to grant franchises, only to "railroads, duly organized, under law." Land for rights-of-way and terminals, and timber and stone for construction were made available. A tax of $100 per year for each operating mile was levied against the railroads.

As a result, more than a dozen embryo railroads were proposed to run from Valdez and from nearby Port Valdez on Valdez Arm, up the Lower River Valley, through the narrow confines of Keystone Canyon and then over to the Copper River Valley and on to the Interior. This resulted in much confusion as records, reports, and the like were sadly inadequate in those early days.

There were only two practical routes by which a railroad could be constructed into the Interior from the Valdez area. The routes were identical for a distance of about 27 miles, extending up the Lowe River Valley as far as Heiden Canyon. From there one route led

through Marshall Pass, at an elevation of 1,756 feet, and down the Tusnuna River to its junction with the Copper River, 54 miles from Valdez, and thence to the Interior. The other route crossed Thompson Pass at an elevation of 2,700 feet, and a minor summit at Ernestine Pass, reaching the Copper River Valley some 100 miles from Valdez.

Of the many roads proposed over these routes, only four carried out any work of consequence, other than possibly preliminary surveys. They were the Valdez, Copper River and Tanana Railroad Co., the Copper River and Northwestern Railway Co., the Valdez-Yukon Railroad Co., and the Alaska Home Railroad Co.

Among those which did little more than try to raise money by selling stock was the Alaska Central Railroad Co. of Arizona (not to be confused with the Alaska Central which started construction at Seward and later became the Alaska Northern and eventually the present-day Alaska Railroad). This company planned to build from Prince William Sound to the Yukon River near the boundary between Alaska and British North America, a distance of 330 miles. Papers were filed with the Government Land Office in May 1898.

In 1899 a group of Iowa businessmen founded the Copper River and Yukon Railroad Co. to build a railroad and telegraph line from Valdez to the Klondike with a branch line from some point east of Mantasta Pass down some stream to the Yukon River of the Canadian border. This group sought 50-year rights and a government subsidy of $16,000 a mile through application made in Congress by Rep. Curtis of Iowa.

This is the way the town of Valdez looked shortly after the turn-of-the-century when such railroads as the Copper River and Northwestern, Valdez-Yukon, and the Alaska Home centered their activities in this Alaskan port. Today, despite never having a successful railroad, Valdez is a thriving seaport community and the southern terminus of the trans-Alaska oil pipeline. (University of Washington Library, Northwest Collection photo)

In Feb. 1900 the Akron, Sterling and Northern Railroad Co. of Colorado, filed to build from Valdez Bay via Marshall Pass to Eagle City, a distance of 409.42 miles, according to survey. This group proposed certain branches to reach into the coal, copper and other mineral fields.

The great Trans-Alaska Railroad Co., (one of three companies carrying this or similar names) came into the news in 1901 with plans for a land route direct to the door of Siberia. The southern terminus, as planned by Captain John Healy, well known for his Klondike activities, was to be at Valdez. The line would pierce the valley of the Copper and Tanana Rivers, then go westward at the junction of the Tanana and the Yukon to the Bering Straits, via Norton Sound, to Port Clarence and the Nome country. The total distance was approximately 1,200 miles, with the proposal that the route tap the Canadian border at desireable pockets. English capital was proposed for the all-American route, modeled after the financing of the White Pass and Yukon Railroad.

The Trans-Alaska as such never got much further than the planning stage, running into financial dif-

ficulties. It was revised in 1903 as the Valdez and Copper River Railroad, with much less ambitious plans, but this also ran in fund raising problems and fell by the wayside.

Another railroad which possibly came closer to being built than many of the others was the Valdez-Eagle (City) Railroad. This line was headed by Captain J.R. DeLamar of New York, who had acquired a large number of mining properties along the proposed route. He announced that they had obtained the services of Michael J. Heney, the White Pass & Yukon builder.

The Valdez-Eagle was to run from Valdez through central Alaska to Eagle City, with a proposed extension from Eagle City to the Klondike, also making it an all-American route to Dawson City. Financing was to be by London Loan, Mortgage and Trust Co., with capitilization at $15 million. One of the major promoters of this company was Frank Bradshaw of Los Angeles.

One of the more ambitious projects was that of the Alaska, Copper River and Yukon Railroad Co., which not only planned a rail link between a point on Prince

Grading and track laying crew of the Valdez-Yukon Railroad. Work on the right-of-way started in August 1906 and extended several miles up the Lowe River to Keystone Canyon. Like many of the other early day companies the Valdez-Yukon withdrew activites in the Valdez area, being the last to go. (Clifford Collection.)

The first, and only, locomotive on the Valdez-Yukon Railroad was this 4-6-0 Rogers purchased from the Southern Pacific Railroad. The engine was later sold to the Copper River & Northwestern Railroad and became their No. 50, first and one of the busiest obtained by Mike Heney's operation. (Clifford Collection.)

William Sound and the Yukon River in the vicinity of Eagle City, but also proposed to operate a steamship line between Seattle and Prince William Sound and to operate smelters and refineries and do a general mining business in Alaska.

Capitalization was $25 million, with the railroad system alone to cost in the neighborhood of $10 million. The entire amount was to be subscribed by Eastern U.S. and European financiers. Articles of incorporation were filed in Washington State in 1902 by F.D. Bannister, Alfred B. Iles and C.L. Parker. From the terminal on the Sound, the line would run through Mantasta Pass on the Yukon, touching the stream somewhere near Eagle.

Early in 1902 an Alaska land grant right-of-way was filed with the U.S. Congress for the Alaska Gulf and Yukon Railway Co., by Rep. Jenkins of Wisconsin to build a railroad to Eagle City. The land grant was to consist of alternate sections of 10 miles in width on each side of the track. Mineral rights were to be available to the company upon completion of the railroad.

In the late summer of 1902 the Valdez, Copper River and Yukon Railroad Co. was incorporated with capitalization of $23 million to operate a railroad through the Copper River Valley and central Alaska from Valdez to Eagle City and Dawson on the Yukon River. The road was to be 380 to 400 miles in length. At the same time the Angelo-American Construction Co. was formed and capitalized at $3 million to handle construction of the railroad. Both organizations were incorporated under the laws of New Jersey. Manager of construction and one of the prime movers on the project was F.C. Jelm. Plans called for construction of 40 miles the first year and completion of the entire route in two and one-half years.

At about this same time promotional work was being done on the Pacific and Yukon Railroad Co. by D.A. McKenzie. Like so many others, it never actually came into being and soon dropped from sight.

In mid-summer 1903 the Valdez and Copper River Railway Co. announced that it had secured financing and that contracts for construction had been let to James F. McDonald and John Hays Hammond, contractors. The contract called for the road to be built in 14 months and the promoters put $1 million in funds to the credit of the construction firm. The project attracted some attention as McDonald had a reputation as a railroad builder in Columbia and other South American countries, and Hammond was a mining engineer and promoter of South African projects. Like so many others, however, the Y&CRR Co. died on the vine.

In April 1904 papers were filed with the Government Land Office by the Valdez, Marshall Pass and Northern Railroad Co. of New Jersey (formerly the Valdez and Northern Railroad Co.) to build from Valdez to Eagle City, with the route and distance not listed.

On Jan. 31, 1905 a bill was introduced in Congress creating the Alaska Railroad (not to be confused with the Alaska Railroad as it exists today) authorizing the company to layout, locate, construct, furnish, maintain and enjoy a continuous railroad, telegraph and telephone lines from a point on the Gulf of Alaska thence northward to a point on the Yukon River near Eagle. Preliminary surveys of the various routes had been made by Judge D.A. McKenzie and a party which packed in to the Copper River Valley, went down the river to its mouth and then on to Valdez and other points on Valdez Bay in search of a terminal location.

These reports cover the various organizations which did little more than promotion and paper work in the way of building a railroad in Alaska.

More active, but not any more successful was the Valdez, Copper River and Tanana Railroad Co., which early in 1903 proposed a steel highway from Valdez to the American Yukon River, by way of the Tanana diggings. This road was promoted by A.B. Iles (who had been active in the Alaska, Copper River and Yukon Railroad Co.) and Portland, Ore., capitalists. They also were the first to attempt to raise local Valdez money to support construction and were successful in obtaining subscription totaling $75,000 based on contributions of portions of the total for each five miles of railway constructed. In May 1903 Iles secured a permit from the town council to allow construction along Front Street, and the company completed a dock and a 1,300-foot long connecting trestle. George F. Baldwin was the company's chief engineer and the preliminary survey of the first 35 miles of the route was completed.

The Valdez, Copper River and Tanana Railroad was also the first to announce that a locomotive and two rail cars were being brought to Valdez. No record is available to determine that the equipment actually arrived. The firm also let a contract for the building of the first five miles of road, which apparently was never completed.

First proposed in 1905, the Valdez-Yukon Railroad actually started contruction under the direction of Colonel A.W. Swartz with the driving of the first spike on Aug. 16, 1906 at its terminal site, about a mile west of Valdez. Grading was completed for a distance of several miles up the Lowe River, to the mouth of Keystone Canyon. The Valdez-Yukon also brought a locomotive to Valdez, a Rogers 4-6-0 manufacturer's #2858, built in 1881 for the Southern Pacific. The engine bore several SP numbers, including No. 187, 1665 and 2098. The Valdez-Yukon was the last of the early companies to leave the Valdez area, and when

construction finally stopped on the V-Y the locomotive was sold to the Copper River Railway as its No. 50, first to be owned and operated by that line out of Cordova.

Initial references of the Copper River and Northwestern Railway Co. are a bit confusing as records show that the company was chartered on May 16, 1905 under the laws of Nevada.

The Sitka Alaskan of July 8, 1905 carried news of the incorporation of the Copper River and Northwestern Railway Co. in Washington State by Monty Thomsen, formerly of Spokane; John Rosene, an Indianapolis barber who hit it rich at Dawson City; and others. Capital stock was shown at $250,000 of which $5,000 was reported subscribed. The story also stated that the principal place of business would be Seattle, but that the chief office would be in Carson City, Nev., where the State Agent and Transfer Syndicate Inc., was named as agent.

In 1905 the Copper River and Northwestern applied for the right-of-way under the Railway Act of Congress of 1898. The company was financed by the Guggenheim family, which was active in Alaska and the Yukon mining circles and already had been accused of high-handed treatment of smaller railroad and mining interests.

In compliance with the Act, the CR&NW filed a description of the tracts of land needed to build a railroad from a point west of Valdez to and through Keystone Canyon to the interior of Alaska. On Jan. 17, 1906 the application was approved by the Secretary of the Interior.

The original Copper River route survey had been made by George C. Hazelette, who had come to Alaska with a survey party to find a feasible railway route from tidewater to Eagle on the Yukon. This party made two surveys, one up the Copper River Valley, the other from Valdez by way of the military trail over the range. Joining at what now is Willow Creek, these two routes became identical and continued north to the Tanana through the richest mineral belt in the territory.

Because of the obvious great engineering difficulties involved by way of the Copper River Valley, the Valdez route was determined to be the most practical and was the one recorded by the company in Washington. Work was started on schedule under direction of Hazelette, with John Rosene also active in the program.

During the time the CR&NW was active in the Valdez area it completed about one third of the grading necessary between Port Valdez and Valdez, and then nothing else in the area until reaching

Local citizens took pride in volunteering to work with pick and shovels in grading the first mile of roadway for H.D. Reynolds' Alaska Home Railroad on Aug. 13, 1907. Headquarters for the project were set up in the church building in the background. (Clifton Valdez Museum photo)

The Copper River & Northwestern Railroad cut in Keystone Canyon where Alaska Home Railroad employees did battle with Guggenheim employees, protecting CR&NW properties and the tunnel excavated in the Canyon. This was the only access to the interior over this route. The tent which served as headquarters for Deputy Marshall Edward Hasey is seen in the background. The "battle" resulted in a least one death, with several wounded. (Clifford Collection.)

This tunnel, a few hundred feet in length, was the center of the gun battle between Guggenheim employees protecting Copper River & Northwestern Railroad property and workers on the Alaska Home Railroad. Today a historic marker along the highway marks the spot and gives a brief description of the melee which took place on Sept. 27, 1907. (H. Clifford.)

Keystone Canyon. Through Keystone about 25 per cent of the necessary grading was completed, including 100 feet of tunnel, at a cost of $85,000, but no work was undertaken beyond the Canyon. It was obvious that the Copper River intended to stake its claim to the route through its work in the narrow canyon. The company, however, had failed to comply with the Railway Act which specified that twenty miles of roadbed must be constructed within one year.

In the meanwhile, M.J. Heney had contacted the Guggenheim interests in New York with the intention of selling them on construction of the railway through the Copper River Valley.

It was during this period also, that the Alaska Syndicate was formed as a partnership by the Guggenheims and the New York financial house of J.P. Morgan & Co., along with the Havemeyer finacial interests, and Kuhn, Loeb & Company. The agreement was signed in July 1906 and one of the first changes brought about by the pact was the ordering of another survey of the Copper River route - as a result of Mike Heney's prodding.

One of the most promising and respected railroad engineers in the East, M.K. Rogers, was called upon to make the survey. He made a casual survey of the Valdez and Copper River routes, and then proceeded on his own to Katalla in the coal district. Rogers' report to the New York interests was enthusiastically in favor of Katalla as a base of construction and his report was adapted and a million dollars advanced by the combined Guggenheim-Morgan interests for construction from this point.

In early August Rogers announced in Valdez that the CR&NW proposed to move its operations to Katalla, much to the disappointment of the Valdez residents. Depression and gloom settled over the city.

By 1907 Valdez had lost out, although the Copper River maintained guards - or a skeleton staff - at Keystone Canyon.

A new, bright light appeared however, in the person of Henry Derr Reynolds, who had a proposition for the people of Valdez. Plans for the Home Railroad Co., also known as the Alaska Home Railroad, were formulated in Valdez on Aug. 9, 1907. A meeting of all the townsfolk was called for McKinley Hall the following evening, chairmanned by ex-governor John C. Brady.

Both men were well known to the residents of Valdez from previous business deals and when the meeting was over, Reynolds had raised $106,000 in contributions ranging from $1 to $10,000 from citizens of the community.

Thus began one of the most bizarre episodes in Alaskan history, an effort of bold planning, visionary dreams, stirring adventure—and tragedy. An episode that was to have political impact on the territory for years to come.

Reynold's plan called for the building of a railroad to the summit of the coast range, a distance of 34 miles in 90 days, from which passengers and materials would be transferred to the government trail for transportation to the Interior. The road would be a narrow gauge line, constructed with 30-pound rails. Power would be electricity, generated by nearby waterfalls. The project would be capitalized at $10,000 per mile of completed road. Shares would be sold at $1.00 per share, to be full paid and non-assessable.

There would be no construction profits, no graft, no incompetence. There would be no free passes for travelers, no rebates. No promotion shares would be issued. No bonds or other indebtedness. It would be in the peoples' interest, of Alaska, by Alaska, for Alaska.

Headquarters was established in an old church. The next day a survey was made for the Valdez terminals. Warehouses, wharf and a sawmill were acquired and on Aug. 12 engineers began the actual survey of the route. At the same time the company received a ninety-nine year franchise from the Valdez City Council giving the Alaska Home Railroad exclusive use of the city's streets and alleys. The first shovelfull of earth was turned by Ex-Gov. Brady on Aug. 13 and the citizens of the town graded the first mile of the right-of-way. Antonelle and Nelson of Seattle, were named contractors for the project.

Some other events were taking place. On Aug. 19 a branch of the Reynolds Bank was established in Valdez to facilitate the financing of the road. The next day Reynolds acquired a major interest in many of the business establishments in the town, including the Valdez Prospector, the newspaper. Stock subscriptions were increased and in late August Reynolds arrived in Seattle, set up headquarters and acquired additional properties, such as the Boulder-Alaska Copper Co., LaTouch-Alaska Copper Co., Reynolds-Alaska Coal Co., Alaska Coast Copper Co., the Alaska Coast Steamship Co., all with the Alaska Development Co., capitalized at $3,000,000 as the foundation of the structure, and with H.D. Reynolds as president.

On Aug. 29 the railroad established offices in New York, and was incorporated in the State of Washington for $10,000,000. The company filed with the Office of Land Management in early September for a permit to build from Valdez through Keystone Canyon.

Meanwhile on Sept. 14 the first railroad equipment arrived in Valdez on the Steamer Jeannie including the Home Railroad's first locomotive, cars and rails.

As the week progressed, it was necessary for Alaska Home survey crews to enter Keystone Canyon, where the CR&NW crews continued to occupy the right-of-way. Warnings were issued against the Alaska Home crews about trespassing, and a confrontation was in the offing.

This, according to many, was the key to the Reynolds plan, in addition to his stock selling efforts. The "ace" up his financial sleeve was that he had

Local citizens gathered at the railroad's terminal site in Valdez for the driving of the first spike of the Valdez-Yukon Railroad on Aug. 16, 1906. The line brought in a locomotive and graded and laid considerable track up the Lowe River before abandoning the project. Colonel A. W. Swartz, well known in railroad circles, was in charge of construction for the Valdez-Yukon and drove the first spike. (Clifford Collection.)

It was a big day in Valdez when Mrs. Blamey Stevens, wife of the chief engineer of the Alaska Home Railroad, took the throttle to start this little saddle-tanker over the first mile of rails on Oct. 4, 1907. Little Valdez Cameron, first white child born in Valdez, was at the whistle. It was Alaska Home Railroad's Day of Glory. (Clifton Museum photo.)

planned his survey along the previous one of the Guggenheim-Morgan organization, where there was room for only one such railroad. Some day, the Syndicate with all its money, would pay him a substantial sum to "lay off" rather than institute legal proceedings with the ensuing delays, and then for a life of luxury in Boston, his old home.

His treacherous scheme, however, was conceived too late and his offer met with a flat refusal. The CR&NW already had become deeply involved in the Katalla operation and for all practical purposes given up on Valdez. In a last desperate attempt, he sent his construction gangs into the disputed territory.

Thus the scene was set for the Battle of Keystone Canyon. On Sept. 25 Reynolds' men forced the issue. A work party of from 150 to 200 men set out from town to establish construction camps in and beyond the Canyon.

Two Deputy U.S. Marshalls, Ed C. Hasey and Duncan Dixon, in the pay of the Syndicate, were stationed in the Canyon to safeguard the threatened Guggenheim camp and a rock barricade had been erected half-way across the grade. A white tent was also pitched by the barrier to serve as headquarters for the group.

The Home Railroad crew approached the barrier, carrying work tools and no other arms. There was at first some good natured bantering between the two work forces, as friend recognized friend across the line. General foreman William Koch, riding a stallion, headed the Home forces, and William O'Neill was in charge of the CR&NW group. O'Neill is reported to have come forward from behind the barrier and was seized by some of the advancing men.

Ed Hasey, who was known to be quick tempered and who recently had been transferred to Valdez from Ketchikan where he was found innocent of killing a man who resisted arrest, fired shots into the air, demanding O'Neill's release. Such however was not forthcoming. The Home forces were egged on by the railroad counsel, Charles E. Ingersoll from Juneau. He told them the rival company no longer had any right to Keystone Canyon as their right-of-way permit had expired.

The Home workers were confused. They had been told that there would be no violence; that Dixon and Hasey were Deputy U.S. Marshalls, pledged to keep the peace. It was unthinkable that their friends across the line would fire upon unarmed men.

Such, however was not the case. Perhaps the shots reverberating off the cliffs above, caused Hasey to believe that the Home forces were returning the fire, William Quitsch, newly hired by the Syndicate to assist as a watchman, later so testified when he gave detailed information on the incident.

The advancing workers still thought that perhaps the shots were only a warning, but when some of their companions collapsed, they knew that they were under fire. Their immediate reaction was to flee. They turned and stormed down the narrow canyon. The

shots continued - five to seven in all. Five took effect. As the wounded fell, some of their friends stopped to render assistance. Others fled down the grade.

The town of Valdez erupted in rage when the wounded were carried in. Chris Olsen had a bullet hole through his body near the heart. Others were hit in the limbs. Threats of reprisals swept through Valdez, but the U.S. Marshall and a few troops from nearby Fort Liscum restored order.

Meanwhile Fred Reinhardt, wounded in the thigh, died as a result of his wound, and Olsen, apparently the most seriously wounded of the five, disappeared from Valdez, never to be seen again.

Hasey was indicted on five counts of intent to kill. Because feelings ran so high in Valdez, a change of venue to Juneau was granted and the trial set for sometime in March 1908.

Meanwhile work on the Home railroad continued with renewed vigor. Reynolds in Seattle, stated that Alaska Home had complied with the law in every respect and that it had been the policy of the company not to antagonize the Guggenheims. He characterized the shooting of peaceful men as the work of common assassins.

The first rails were laid on Oct. 4 by Alaska Home crews and the first train ran that same day. Mrs. Blamey Stevens, wife of the chief engineer for the

Enthusiasm ran so high that citizens brought their own picks and shovels to start work on the grading of the right-of-way for the Alaska Home Railroad in Valdez. Despite the enthusiastic sendoff, the project was soon to come to a tragic end and scores of Valdez citizens were to lose their life savings. (Clifton Valdez Museum photo.)

Mayor T.C. Quinn took over the throttle from Mrs. Blamey Stevens as the first locomotive carried its first passengers on the Alaska Home Railroad on Oct. 4, 1907. Approximately one mile of track had been laid by this time. (University of Alaska Archives, Valdez Cameron Henry Collection photo)

railroad, was at the throttle, and little Valdez Cameron was on the whistle cord. This was the railroad's Day of Glory.

Work on the Alaska Home Railroad ceased on Oct. 10 and hundreds of penniless workers were walking the streets, carrying time checks unhonored, and with no prospects of their being cashed. The City of Valdez provided emergency food and housing until a ship could remove them - fortunately to other railroad jobs in Alaska. Gov. William B. Hoggatt ordered all saloons closed. The Reynolds bank closed its doors. Collapse of the railroad was blamed on its inability to sell stock.

The workers were owed some $30,000, local merchants another $20,000 and liabilities in Seattle were estimated at $75,000, besides bank liabilities estimated at $85,000. Everything belonging to Reynolds was attached, although he was able to sell the Alaska Coast Transportation Co. to Tacoma interests before it was taken over.

Shortly thereafter Reynolds was seen boarding a train in Tacoma headed East. The law caught up with him the next spring and he was tried and convicted of using the mail to defraud and sent to prison.

Charges and counter-charges of bribery, threats, and tampering flew during the trial of Hasey. On the initial charges involving Reinhardt and Olsen he was acquited, but then the government charged him with wounding of two other men and he was found guilty and eventually served 18 months in prison.

In the meantime, an English syndicate obtained an option on the Valdez-Yukon Railroad and on a couple of copper properties, but soon thereafter worked on the V-Y ceased and the equipment went to the Copper River and Northwestern Railway.

It was not until the advent of the trans-Alaska oil pipeline that Valdez again became a major transportation center, and at present Valdez has a "railroad" in the form of two Alaska Railroad five-tonners #7324 and #7249 working on the dock there.

Chapter 13

Katalla, Where the Rails Meet the Sails

Promoted as the "Coming Metropolis of Alaska, Where the Rails Meet The Sails," Katalla became the center of Prince William Sound railroad construction activity following the demise of Valdez as the key point, and as such it became a typical boom town, springing up overnight and composed mainly of saloons, dance halls and gambling dens.

During the next few years almost as many railroad companies as showed an interest in Valdez joined in the rush to follow the two leaders, Alaska-Pacific Railway and Terminal Co., and the Copper River and Northwestern Railroad Co., in attempts to reach the rich copper and coal fields from Katalla. Here again, as was the case at Valdez, competing railways of more or less questionable intentions, as well as financial backing, sprang up, willing to "lay down" at any time for a substantial consideration.

The Alaska Pacific Co. was organized and incorporated in Washington State for the purpose of building from Martin Island in Controller Bay to the Yukon River near Eagle City, with certain branch lines. Filing with the Land Office of the Territory of Alaska was on Jan. 23, 1906.

The APR&T Co. was headed by Dr. M.W. Bruner and his operation was often referred to as the Bruner Road. Construction was by the Keystone Construction Co.

The CR&NWRR Co. moved its operations from Valdez at a cost of thousands of dollars as a result of the Guggenheim-Morgan interests tiring of the attempts there, with its slow progress, physical encounters and legal entanglements. They had sent M.K. Rogers, to look the area over, including M.J. Heney's survey from Eyak (Cordova), but their supposed wizard made a decision favoring the Katalla locality as the proper terminal for the project.

Copper River construction was handled by the Katalla Co., headed by Rogers, and the next 12 months constituted the most spectacular spending orgy in the early checkered history of Alaska. More than $2 million dollars was spent in a futile attempt to demonstrate the wonderful virtues of the section, a widely known impossibility to all well-informed Alaskans.

Rogers, as well as Katalla with its treacherous harbor and its well-known gift of kicking up a real one hundred percent storm on short order, both began making history for themselves.

Vessels from the States, heavily loaded with supplies and materials of all kinds, stopped, looked, and listened at the entrance to this tempermental body of water before taking the long chance of shipwreck. It was a case of "get in and get out" just as quickly as possible, if possible. Many a ship—in the process of unloading—had to weigh anchor and head for open water as a violent storm, typical of the locality, hit with unbelieveable suddenness and violence. Others left their anchors buried in the bottom of the harbor, as anchor chains parted from the heavy poundings of a hurricane-like storm.

Lighters were used in attempts to get the goods to shore, but with little success and much expense. On one occasion, and perhaps one that was destined to do much in formulating the decision to eventually abandon Katalla as a terminus for the railroads, was the loss of the winter supply of whiskey, beer and potatoes aboard a barge being towed to shore.

Many ships were lost, including the old gold ship Portland, which had escaped many such storms in the past. Others escaped by the narrowest of margins.

The CR&NW attempted to construct a high-tide rubblestone jetty built from a pile trestle, which advanced into the open seas by use of a revolving piledriver at the head of the trestle. The proposed jetty had a shore arm extending 4,000 feet into the sea in a generally southern direction and from that point 2,000 feet farther in a direction bearing about 30 degrees northeast. Most of the construction was in depths exceeding 30 feet, and a considerable part in depths up to 50 feet and more.

At the same time the company built some eight miles of standard gauge track towards the Bering coal

Construction crews work along the waterfront as work progresses towards building a causeway to one of the outer islands in the Katalla region. Winterstorms, however, washed out all such work and left the area in shambles. It was soon deserted as far as railroad construction was concerned. (University of Washington Library—Northwest Collection)

fields and did some construction work in the direction towards the Copper River.

Survey crews had been sent out as far as Chitina, a distance of 220 miles. The crews reported many bears. One man sat down to eat a pot of beans, and a bear approached. The worker left the beans to climb a tree and the bear followed only to return to devour the beans. The man was reported so scared that it took rescue teams more than six hours to find him. On another occasion a man with a couple of blankets was chased by a brown bear. He dropped the blankets and rushed to the top of a hill, to observe the bear making himself comfortable for the night on the blankets. The man maintained a lonely vigil on top of the hill until morning.

The APR&T Co. also proposed the creation of an artificial harbor. They planned construction of a breakwater on the west side of the Martin Islands. The plan was to build a double trestle, connecting Whale and Fox Islands by a breakwater and to anchor another breakwater on Outer Island, the latter structure to extend 2,150 feet in a northerly direction. The breakwater between the two islands was to be 1,600 feet long in water not exceeding 30 feet in depth. The APR&TCo. also constructed a sawmill to supply ties and timbers, but this was soon put out of operation by winter storms which flooded the mill.

Both artificial harbors left a considerable section unprotected against the winds, and both were subject to rapid filling should there be considerable movement of sand along the coast.

There was great rivalry between the two outfits, and on one occasion the Alaska-Pacific workers dynamited

a trestle and equipment owned by the Guggenheim-Morgan syndicate, and took over the property. An armed counter attack led by Tony de Pascal was successful and he was presented with a $1,000 cash bonus. On another occasion the Guggenheim forces were attempting to lay track over a right-of-way disputed by the A-P Co., which had constructed an immense "go-devil" of railway rails, blocking the way. The "go-devil" operated by powerful machinery, was swung back and forth over the disputed right-of-way, and was operated by armed men behind fortificatons.

A similar $1,000 bonus was offered by the Guggenheims, and this time an Alaskan pioneer worker, Jack McCord, led an armed band of laborers in laying track over the disputed right-of-way—with bullets whizzing over their heads. One worker was killed and 10 seriously wounded. A ship load of soldiers soon restored order.

The Syndicate forces also tangled with M.J. Heney—with less success. He had taken control of narrow Abercrombie Canyon on the Copper River and was doing construction work there for his road from Cordova. Heney's men had mined the area with dynamite and were successful in turning back the "invaders." This may have had something to do with the Guggenheim-Morgans later purchasing his right-of-way and hiring him to construct the railroad up the Copper River for them.

The distance to the copper mines would be approximately the same for both the Alaska-Pacific and Copper River and Northwestern railroads from Katalla. Both lines would follow the Katalla River Valley, go over a low divide to Bering Lake for coal,

Workers for the Katalla Co., builders of the ill-fated Copper River & Northwestern Railroad project at Katalla, are seen at Bruner Crossing as they take a break from their duties to pose for the photographer on July 14, 1909. The Katalla Co. was one of several firms engaged in railroad building in the Katalla area. (Alaska Historical Library)

then around the coastal headlands, along the westerly boundary of the Copper River delta plain. There would be practically no grades, the most difficult being 0.87 percent, and the longest about two miles in length.

After a lengthy and expensive battle with the elements, the Guggenheim-Morgan forces called Rogers to New York for a conference, along with E.C. Hawkins, who had been called in to do another survey; and M.J. Heney, who had started work on the Copper River Railway out of Cordova.

Following the conference, it was announced in the fall of 1907 that the Copper River & Northwestern Railway Co. would make its temporary headquarters in Cordova until a breakwater was built at Katalla. The Katalla Co. office force was moved to Seattle. Shortly thereafter, checks issued by the Alaska Pacific Railway and Terminal Co. were returned from the banks, spelling the end of that operation also.

Following a further announcement by Hawkins that "work on the Copper River line from Katalla had been suspended, one of the reasons being the financial stringency in the States," the CR&NW locomotives at Katalla were moved to Cordova.

Other railroad companies entered the competition. The Catalla and Carbon Mountain Railroad Co., of Washington, filed in Nov. 1907 to build from the mouth of the Bering River at Controller Bay, up the river 21.87 miles to the coal fields. Three surveys were filed in Juneau, one Oct. 2, 1909; another Aug. 21, 1909 and the third on Dec. 20, 1907. The company was organized by Clark Davis and retained the old spelling of Catalla.

Plans called for the building of a three and one-half mile trestle over the flats to a dockside location on a deeper channel. The road was to run from the far end of the coal fields to the water.

The Kush-Ta-Ka Southern Railroad Co., was

The aftermath of a winter storm in the Katalla area left wreckage such as this. One of the little saddle-tanker locomotives (No. 5) used in construction is mired in the mud. The trackage on which it rested has almost totally disappeared. Such were the winter storms in Katalla. (Alaska Historical Library)

another, filing a survey Feb. 15, 1909 to connect the Copper River and Northwestern to the coal fields. The firm was headed by Charles F. Munday and was surveyed by J.L. McPherson, to run to the claims of Michael Heney and his brother Patrick A. Heney. The Kush-Ta-Ka route included a trestle to Kanak Island for its docksite. The line to Lake Kush-Ta-Ka route included a trestle to Kanak Island for its docksite. The line to Lake Kush-Ta-Ka, going up the west side of the lake.

The Bering River Railroad Co., of Washington filed in March 1908 to build from Kayak Island across Controller Bay and up the Bering River to Clear Creek, a distance of 27.2 miles. Surveys were also filed March 12, 1909 and March 25, 1909. The proposed Bering River route was similar to that of the Kush-Ta-Ka line, but upon reaching the lake went to the east side rather than the west. C.J. Smith was president of the Bering River Railroad and H.L. Hawkins the locating engineer.

One railroad, the Katalla Coal Company Railroad—also known as the Goose City Railroad—did reach the coal fields and operated for several years from Goose City, up past Katalla to a point nine miles inland. The little narrow gauge operated from the early 1900s until it was closed down when the government withdrew entry to the coal

fields following the Ballinger-Pinchot controversy. Also, the company encountered difficulties in shipping coal and other materials from Katalla. The firm had proposed to build a smelter for copper at Katalla with the CR&NW to build a spur line from Mile 39 on the main line to the smelter location.

About this same time the Pacific Coal and Oil Co., headed by Falcon Joslin, who later was to build the Tanana Mines Railroad at Fairbanks; and George Hazelette, who started the original Copper River railroad project at Valdez, announced plans to build their own railroad from Katalla to the coal fields in the Bering Lake area, to handle coal and oil shipments. Known as the "English Company" the firm stated that there was good harbor possibilities at nearby Chilkat and that they planned to build a dock there to ship their products.

Obtaining additional financing the Katalla Company moved its staff back to Katalla and resurveyed a line to the coal fields, about 25 feet above the original survey along the waterfront, hoping to avoid the high water disasters that had plaged them before. The Alaska Pacific Railroad obtained new financing and was granted a one-year extension to complete the necessary franchise work, being required to complete 20 miles of roadway prior to March 18, 1908.

Another firm in the field was the Controller Bay and Navigation Co., incorporated under the laws of New Jersey to build from Controller Bay to the coal fields. Filings were made Dec. 10, 1910 with a capitalization of $500,000.

This firm, however, along with the Katalla Company and the Alaska Pacific failed in their efforts to get major construction projects started.

A latecomer, and one that at a time gave every indication of being a successful operation was the Alaska Anthracite Coal and Railway Co., which was organized in Seattle on April 19, 1909, to build from tidewater on Controller Bay to the Bering River coal fields.

It was not until late in 1915, however, that actual work started on the project. A construction camp was set up on the east bank of the Bering River where there was a good landing for barges. A sawmill was erected and bunkhouses and shops built. This line too, was located at what was known as Goose City, and its planned route followed closely the line surveyed by the Catalla and Carbon Mountain Railroad Co.

Actual construction began in 1916 and continued in 1917 with 17 miles of standard gauge track layed. Three 40-ton flat cars were brought in along with a 16-ton 0-4-0 locomotive.

The track ran from Goose City across the flat and swampy ground as far as the coal land holdings of the Alaska Petroleum and Coal Company. Some $2 million was spent in construction with about 80 percent of the line completed, but left to build were the difficult parts—a six and one-half mile branch line to the Alaska Coke and Coal Co., and the nine miles of road from the Goose City site to Controller Bay where a deep water wharf was needed.

In 1921 the company was reorganized by Seattle interests with John A. Campbell as president and the name changed to the Alaska Anthracite Railroad. Twenty-year bonds, bearing interest of six percent were authorized in the amount of $1.5 million, but these failed to sell and a couple of years later the firm went into receivership.

Firms involved in the Alaska Anthracite project included the Alaska Petroleum and Gas Co., of Seattle; the Alaska Coke and Coal Co., of Portland, Ore.; and the Alaska Pacific Coast Co., a Washington and New York firm.

July 15, 1925 saw a new organization take over under the leadership of N.W. Quigg of Los Angeles, with plans to raise $1.5 million to complete the railroad, wharf and other facilities. Unfortunately nothing came of this scheme and no further work was ever done on the Alaska Anthracite Railroad. Remains of Goose City and the line across the flats and through the grass—along with some equipment sinking in the marsh—are still there.

For all intents and purposes railroading in Katalla was dead. Oil, however, kept a limited amount of activity in the area, with a total of 44 wells eventually being drilled. The first was drilled by the Alaska Steam Coal and Petroleum Co. at Controller Bay. This venture was abandoned when the drill tool became stuck in the hole and the rig was moved to a second location on the claims leased from the Alaska Development Co., which earlier under direction of T.A. Hamilton, had surveyed for a railroad from the coal oil springs and coal beds to the Yukon River. The coal oil springs were located near the shore of Bering Haven Bay between Cape Suckling and Cape Martin, near the mouth of the Copper River. Surveyors reported the proposed railroad route feasible and easy from the deposits up to the Copper River where the Chitina empties into the same, thence across the Copper River to where the Delta River empties into the Tanana, and then across the latter and on to the junction of Minook Creek and the Yukon River. This never developed, however.

The second well, drilled in 1902 encountered shows at 250 feet and a large flow of oil at 360 feet. It was Alaska's first producing well. Because of the issuance of a Federal ban on oil claims in 1910 that lasted until the passage of the Leasing Act of 1920, Katalla was Alaska's only patented oil field. Again, however, shipping was a big problem.

Activity at Katalla was revived and the field overhauled in 1924 with a regular marketing station established in Cordova. The Chilkat Oil Co. at Katalla shut down its operations in Dec. 1933 when the boiler house for the refinery burned.

That spelled the end of Katalla as an energy producing center—until perhaps the revival of interest due to the Gulf of Alaska activity.

Just about every high tide brought flood waters into Katalla during the height of the winter storms. Stumps and other debris were afloat in the center of town. Such storms, and lack of a suitable harbor soon ended attempts to build a railroad from the coast to the interior from this location. (Alaska Historical Library)

Chapter 14

Copper River and Northwestern Railroad

Just as it was gold that resulted in the building of the White Pass and Yukon Railroad, it was copper in the Wrangell Mountains that brought about the construction of the Copper River and Northwestern Railroad.

Michael J. Heney, who had successfully conquered the White Pass in the building of the railway considered "impossible to build" from Skagway to Whitehorse, was living a life of leisure in the East—much against his style and better judgment. He watched with interest the development of Alaska, its growth, its becoming a territory rather than a district, and finally the finding of rich copper deposits in the Wrangells, plus oil and coal in the Katalla region.

These, and the announcements of plans for the building of a dozen or so railroads to bring these rich resources together and to the United States proper, coupled with the urging of Samuel H. Graves, president of the White Pass, once again brought the "Irish Prince" into action.

In 1904 he made the first move. He journeyed to London and once again secured the financial backing of his old partners, the Close Brothers. He studied the routes from Valdez to the copper discoveries, and decided that they were not suitable for railroad construction. He visited Katalla and decided that the harbor there was unsuitable for the handling of steamships which would be necessary to bring in supplies and to take out oil, coal and copper.

He and his engineers, Sam Murchison and H.L. Hawkins, studied the route of the Copper River from the Wrangells to Prince William Sound, and decided that a water level route was the most feasible. There were problems with this route, he determined, such as the blocking of the Copper River by the Miles and Childs Glaciers some 50 miles from the coast, and the

building of a roadbed through Abercrombie Canyon where the stone walls rose almost straight up to the sky, and where the water currents were so strong and treacherous that no man could live should he fall into them; and the crossing of the treacherous mud flats at the mouth of the river.

Other engineers determined these obstacles impossible to overcome. Heney thought otherwise. He filed his survey and started to prepare for his assault on the Copper River. Previously the Alaska Syndicate, had acquired a majority of the copper claims in the Kennecott and Bonanza regions, and was determined to build a railroad to bring the ore out.

The Alaska Syndicate was formed in 1906 by J.P. Morgan and Company and the Messrs. M. Guggenheim and Sons, and others for the development of copper holdings. The Syndicate soon purchased interests in the Bonanza Copper Mines and the Northwestern Commercial Co., and became involved in subsidiary interests because the corporation owned the Northwest Steamship Company. The Northwest Fisheries which owned 12 of the 40 canneries operating in Alaska and put up one-eighth of the fish pack. The Northwestern Railroad Company was another of the early purchases of the Syndicate with all of the stock being acquired. After six years of experimentation with routes from Valez and Katalla, it became known as the Copper River and Northwestern.

The steamship interest was merged with the formerly independent Alaska Steamship Company, taking that name, and becoming the strongest of the few public and private lines operating in northern waters. The trust also signed an option in 1907 looking to the development of coal claims which Clarence Cunningham and his associates were pushing to patent.

Mike Heney, builder of the Copper River and Northwestern as well as the White Pass and Yukon railroads (right) with one of the backers of the Copper River project taken during the height of construction on the CR&NW (Clifford Collection)

Difficulties developed in the Valdez area, and once again the Syndicate sent an engineer to Alaska to survey a route. This time it was M.R. Rogers, one of the nation's top railroad engineers. He surveyed both the Copper River and Valdez routes and then proceeded to Katalla on the coast, just a few miles away from the newly discovered Bering coal fields. Rogers' report to New York was highly in favor of building from this point, and at the same time tap the rich coal fields. His report was duly accepted and he was put in charge of construction of a railroad from the port of Katalla.

These efforts proved disastrous as Katalla was on a wild and unprotected coast, open to the full sweep of terrible winter seas. The first big winter storm whipped out the wharf and artificial breakwater, which were essential to the scheme. A wire to New York appraised the backers of the problems, and another conference was called at which J.P. Morgan is reported to have slammed the table with his fist and declared, "Whatever the route, we've got to bring the copper and the coal together!"

Meanwhile M.J. Heney began planning construction of the Copper River Railroad on April 1, 1906, at the site which had everything essential to the building and operation of a railroad — an abundance of level ground, a rare occurrence on this rocky shoreline, together with an excellent land-locked harbor of deep waters. Nothing else was needed, but men and money, and he had both.

Heney had previously purchased this freak piece of ground, together with its substantial and commodious buildings — the property of an abandoned cannery with a large dock — through a middleman, a close personal friend, for a moderate sum. Had it been known that this was to be the terminal of a $20 million plus railroad, the price would have soared considerably.

The natives and Swede fishermen were greatly surprised one day in the early spring of 1906 when a large ocean-going steamer arrived at Eyak and unloaded scores of workers with their equipment and bed rolls, hundreds of tons of building materials, railroad equipment, and horses.

Heney's plan called for a standard gauge line from Eyak (renamed Cordova by Heney after he took possession of the town) up the Copper River with a branch line to the much-discussed Bering River coal field back of Katalla at Mile 32; a hundred miles further a branch up into the mountains to the freak Bonanza mine, some 200 miles from salt water; and then on to the Interior to tap the vast bodies of coal in the Matanuska Valley, with an overall slight grade.

The Ballinger-Pinchot affair, withdrawing coal, oil and timber by the federal government, prevented the fulfillment of these hopes.

Although the fisheries interests were subsequently disposed of to the Booth Company, stock in the Beatson Copper mines was added to the combined holdings of the Syndicate in 1910.

With these interests the Syndicate sent engineers into the area to survey the various routes available. One was George Cheever Hazelette, who was sent to find a feasible route from tidewater to Eagle on the Yukon. His party made two surveys — one up the Copper River Valley; the other from Valdez by way of the military trail over the range. Joining at what is now Willow Creek, the two routes became identical and continued north to the Tanana River, through the richest mineral belt in the area.

Because of the belief that it was impossible to overcome the engineering difficulties of the lower Copper River route, the Valdez Trail was determined to be the most practical route and was so recommended when the two surveys were sent east.

The Valdez route was duly recorded and filed with the proper departments in Washington and the Copper River survey was tucked away in an obscure office in New York and promptly forgotten.

This is Eyak as it looked in 1906 at the time the town was purchased by Mike Heney to build the Copper River and Northwestern Railroad. The fish cannery tramway, used by the Alaska Packers Association which owned the town prior to Heney's purchase, runs down the street at the left. This part of the town became known as "Old Town" when the community was enlarged and renamed Cordova (University of Washington Historical Library—Northwest Collection)

On Aug. 8, 1906 the first spike was driven on the curved causeway leading away from the waterfront. A steamer pulled alongside the dock on Sept. 5 and unloaded the first locomotive.

No sooner had the first spike been driven by Heney workmen than the Guggenheim-Morgan interests became very interested. If an engineer of Heney's reputation thought that the river could be bridged, then it meant that the coal and copper could be brought together with one rail line up the Copper River, as it was a natural route, and they moved to lay out their own route.

Another engineer, E.C. Hawkins, who had been chief engineer for the White Pass construction, was called in by the Syndicate to make a survey. He determined that if copper and coal were to be brought together, the route up the Copper River was the most logical one.

The Guggenheim-Morgan group was determined to lay out their own route up the river. They were met in the narrow confines of Abercrombe Canyon by Heney's crews who warned them that the entire canyon was loaded with dynamite preparatory to blasting and that they entered the canyon at their own peril. It was well known that Heney did not bluff. He fully intended to hold Abercrombie Canyon against any and all comers. The Guggenheim-Morgans knew the game was up and began to negotiate to buy the route.

Heney was called to New York to discuss the deal and turned the operation over to Sam Murchison, his

145

Copper River and Northwestern Railroad rails extend out on the ocean dock at Cordova where a couple of steamers load and load at the water terminus of the railroad. Cordova was the former town of Eyak, purchased by Mike Heney as a base of operations for construction of the CR&NWRR. (University of Alaska Archives)

chief assistant. Construction labor was short in Alaska in those days, and pirating from other operations was a way of business. Only a "faked" case of small pox developed by a trusted employee of Heney's by use of a liberal massage of Oleum Tiglit, commonly known as Croton Oil, prevented the pirating of much needed laborers from the Copper River operation. The "small pox" case resulted in the quarantining of the town, prohibiting an expected steamer from landing, and prevented the pirated workers, who had quit the Copper River operation, from leaving town. After idleness running into days and even weeks, the

workers returned to their jobs with the CR&NW, and the labor pirate begged for a "passport" to leave and return to his home base at Seward. Instead, he was offered a job on one of the work gangs, but he promptly refused. Eventually he made his way out of town, never to return.

Heney's trip was successful, resulting in his sale of the Copper River Railway — which by this time had reached some five miles out of town — to the Guggenheim-Morgan combine at a handsome profit to himself and his backers, the Close Brothers.

Work was suspended on the operation as the Syndicate continued to concentrate its efforts on the Katalla project, and Heney spent the summer relaxing and cruising on the Yukon River.

Things went from bad to worse at Katalla, however, and as winter came a factor in the Syndicate's decision to give up on the project was a report made to them by Captain "Dynamite Johnny" O'Brien, one of the most capable and best known of the captains in Alaska service. He battled high seas and a severe winter storm at anchorage for eleven days, trying to get inside the Katalla breakwater to unload his ship, the Seward. After losing two anchors, and endangering the ship, heavily laden with construction materials, O'Brien headed for the sheltered harbor at Cordova and unloaded without incident.

The Guggenheims had wasted five years and millions of dollars and were no closer than they were the first day they came to Alaska. Heney was given the contract for the continuation of construction up the Copper River. E.C. Hawkins was named chief engineer. The same two had combined their skills to successfully construct the White Pass & Yukon Railroad against tremendous odds.

Others on the Copper River staff included Alfred Williams, assistant chief engineer; H.L. Hawkins, one of the original surveyors with Heney and F.A. Hansen, J.C. Surrey and C.E. Wingate, locating engineers. J.R. Van Cleve was superintendent of the operating department; M.E. Smith, chief surgeon; and A.C. O'Neill, superintendent of bridge construc-

Most of the work on the Copper River and Northwestern Railroad, as well as other construction projects of the period, was performed largely by hand labor. On rare occasions steam power such as this shovel was used. The steam shovel is clearing the right of way at Camp 6, Mile 22 on the CC&NWR. (Seattle Historical Society)

Bridge or trestle building on the Copper River flats in August 1908. This was the quick way to get across the flats. Later, after rails had been laid, train loads of gravel were dumped along the right-of-way as ballast. (Clifford Collection)

tion—which proved to be one of the most important tasks in the entire operation.

Heney's assistants were Sam Murchison, superintendent; A.W. Shields, storekeeper; and Dr. F.S. Whiting, surgeon.

Heney, along with his brother Pat, formed a partnership with the Seattle Sand and Gravel Co., to insure continued flow of supplies for the building of the railroad. Pat remained in Seattle, and handled that end of the project.

Work was done under contract and the sale of his already constructed five miles of railroad, plus certain commissary concessions, spurred Heney on to beat his White Pass record. Time was the essential thing. Under their permits from the government, the Syndicate had five years to complete the railroad, and it had lost much time at Valdez and Katalla.

In places track was laid on ice and snow over frozen ground—grading could follow later. Anything to beat time was the rule, just safe enough to carry the work trains over the line was all that was required.

The first obstacle was the tremendous Copper River flats, with miles of quicksand and mud, and prohibitive costs in trestleing. Heney let Dame Nature do her part, by first freezing this immense bog into solid foundation, upon which he later built his road bed fortified by thousands of carloads of heavy ballast, which withstood the spring thaw and remained as a permanent support, thus obviating the great cost of piling.

The single-line track was laid on ties of native timber to standard gauge with 70-pound steel from Cordova to Chitina, and 60-pound rails from Chitina to Kennecott.

Heney's smooth-running organization was soon functioning automatically, and tremendous progress followed. Men were strung along the grade for miles, where at varying intervals, miniature cities of tents sprang up like mushrooms. Alaska's virgin soil was now receiving a very wholesome baptism of dynamite, and heavy detonations broke the previous stillness, night and day. Machine shops and round houses soon appeared at headquarters, and miles of steel rails crept further and further into the wilderness, where giant locomotives creaked and labored at the head of long, heavily-laden construction trains.

As construction work preceeded up the Copper River, the chief of one of the Indian tribes threatened to bring suit against the company. He claimed the noise and whistle of the engines scared the game from the forest and the fish from the river, and that his tribe would be in danger of starving. The suit, however, was never filed.

At the peak of construction about 6,000 men were working on the project. About 15 percent of the 196 miles of track was on bridges or trestles. There were 129 bridges in the 131 miles between Cordova and Chitina, and five major steel bridges into which went 20 million pounds of steel.

The first major bridge at Mile 27 was 1,300 feet long and the second a mile further on was 560 feet in length. These two were completed in the summer of 1909 at a cost of $560,000. Next came the "hot cake" bridge at mile 34, 525 feet in length. Then at Mile 47 was the most famous of them all — the Miles Glacier cantilever bridge which was to become known as the "Million Dollar Bridge" although it actually cost about a million and a half. Some 18,000 cubic yards of concrete went into its two abutments and three cassions, and five million pounds of steel was required for its 1,550 feet of length. Construction, however, was not all that simple. With Heney busy with the actual construction of the railroad, wooden trestles, and the like, the three largest steel bridges were constructed with A.C. O'Neill, stellar American bridge building engineer, in charge.

The task was a complicated one with the bridge required to stand the impact of a thousand-ton iceberg, flood waters, and the like. O'Neill had introduced the novel feature of armoring his piers for the bridge at Sheridan Glacier with sharp steel faces, which were

The first locomotive, No. 50, on the Copper River and Northwestern Railroad was acquired from the defunct Valdez-Yukon and is seen with a work train on the flats out of Cordova. Construction crews built trestles and then filled them in with gravel to maintain a roadbed across the flats. Dump cars such as these were a new construction item for the period. (Seattle Historical Society)

designed to catch and shatter the ice before it strikes the cement pier.

When construction reached the bridge site, Heney had to devise ways to work around it, as the bridge would not be completed for two years. Ferries, barges, runabouts, and a small sternwheeler operated on the river in the summer. In winter ingenious sledges were devised. In fall and spring a few supplies could cross by cable trolley. To work the glacier area, a steamship was freighted piecemeal from Valdez and assembled on the upper river. Heney was everywhere, seeing to the thousands of minute details, distributing supplies, handling men and mules, and ever spurring the work on.

Construction of the bridge at the meeting of the Miles and Childs Glaciers saw Chevaux-de-frise of cement and steel set a short distance upstream from each pier. Three cement piers and two bulkheads were necessary to form the foundations for the great steel structure, which spanned the river at a height

above the surface to allow ample space underneath for passing icebergs. Cassions were sunk fifty to sixty feet from river bed to bedrock to construct the piers.

The three piers were completed late in the fall of 1909 after more than a year of work. The steel work was to be put in place during the depth of winter while the ice was solidly frozen. Obviously no false work could withstand the battery of the bergs for a single hour, so it was necessary to drive piles through the seven feet of motionless ice and into the river bed 40 feet below.

Difficulties in the eastern mills and winter storms delayed the delivery of steel two months. The first of it did not leave Seattle until March 17, 1910. Another two months would certainly find the ice moving in the river — and the possible loss of a million dollars worth of work which would go out with it. Up until March 23 it looked as if a delay of a whole year was inevitable. On April 5, however, the last piece for the first two spans was on the ground and checked. A single piece found

Falsework holding the No. 3 span of the Miles Glacier bridge in place. The spring break-up on the Copper River came only minutes after the bridge span had been safely and securely placed on the piers—thus averting a disaster which would have cost the builders of the Copper River and Northwest Railroad a year's work and hundreds of thousands of dollars. (Washington State Historical Society)

River, forty feet below the surface. The ice was a solid sheet seven feet thick and it was borne on a twelve knot current. Into it the forest of piles was solidly frozen.

When the rising water began suddenly to lift the ice and with it the 450 feet of falsework on which the third span was being put together, there was a preliminary emergency of some consequence. It might easily be but an hour or two's work for a resistless river to wreck the whole span that way. The emergency had to be met, as scores of others had been met before.

Steam from every available engine was driven into small feed pipes and every man in camp was put to work to steam-melt or chop the seven feet of ice to clear the piles. The holes were kept open through the day and night of a bitter cold and hundreds of cross-pieces unbolted and shifted while the river rose 21 feet.

Then began the movement downstream. At first it was but an inch a day; then three or four inches. The melting and chopping went on almost unceasingly, then the ice made its heaviest charge. A line was taken. The falsework was 15 inches out of line.

Anchorages were hastely built into the ice above the bridges and they were heavy anchorages. Block and tackle was rigged to them and while a gang thawed and chopped the ice around the piles in the maddest

missing later would have spelled ruin. With less than six weeks of time even possibly available, only enough bridge workers obtainable to make a single shift, and abominable weather conditions, the work of putting together more than 1,100 feet of heavy steel bridge was begun.

Despite rain, sleet and storms that raged about half of the time and the alternative of bitter cold and sharp thaws, the first two spans were put into place without too many problems. The first span of 400 feet was completed on April 16 in a total of ten and one half days; the second span of 300 feet went up in six days was completed by April 24. Work on the third span of 450 feet was started on May 6 and with it many problems which came within minutes of destroying the entire structure.

The pocket diary of E.C. Hawkins, under a date of May 14, 1910 carries the following entry:

"The falsework under the third span of the bridge was moved out fifteen inches by the ice and had to be put back." That was all. However, it set the groundwork for one of the most spine-tingling construction efforts ever.

The third span of the Miles Glacier bridge was 450 feet long. The falsework consisted of a thousand or more piles, driven deep into the bottom of the Copper

The Miles Glacier bridge, looking upstream towards Childs glacier, as it appeared upon completion in 1910. The bridge was one of the most important links in the building of the Copper River and Northwestern Railroad, with span No. 3 being lowered into place on the concrete piers just minutes before onrushing ice carried away the construction falsework, holding the span in place. (Washington State Historical Society)

The Miles Glacier "million dollar" bridge as it looked at the time it was part of the Copper River and Northwestern Railroad. Construction of the bridge was a masterpiece of the trade at the time. The bridge withstood the pressure of thousands of tons of ice calving off the nearby Miles and Childs glaciers, only to see the earthquake of 1964 cause one span to drop into the river waters. (Anchorage Histoical and Fine Arts Museum)

of races, the whole 450 feet of towering bridge was dragged inch-by-inch back into place.

The rest was a still more furious race with the ice, for it was moving each day more freely. The last bolt of the span was sent home at midnight after an 18-hour day of one shift. The great steam traveler was slid to a temporary resting place on the third pier, blocks were knocked out and the third span settled on its concrete bed.

At 1 a.m. the whole 450 feet of falsework was a chaotic wreck. The river had lost its fight, by less than a single hour. That hour meant a year saved and that year was a fortune.

The now famous "Miles Glacier Bridge" had become a reality — the weakest link of the entire chain had become the strongest — and remained so until the 1964 earthquake loosened one span and allowed one end to drop into the waters below.

Hawkins gave credit to his men as follows:

"They were on the job at seven in the morning, no matter what the weather. They worked without ceasing till the noon whistle blew, then raced each other to the mess tent. A few minutes late they were flying back like an army of squirrels. And there they stayed until eleven or twelve at night, or until flesh and blood could stand no more. It was the most amazing exhibition of loyalty, efficiency and endurance I have ever known."

Hawkins later cited an example of the desire of the men to complete the job. On one occasion a man broke several of his toes and was ordered to the hospital. He stayed there fretting for one day, and next morning was missing. When the seven o'clock whistle blew he was found on the highest steel work, and neither orders nor threats could budge him from his job.

One of the seven little Dickson saddle-tankers used in construction of the Copper River and Northwestern Railroad (No. 3) is pictured along side of one of the newly arrived American Locomotive Co. Rhode Island class 2-8-0's upon the latter's arrival at Cordova. No 20 was one of four such engines acquired by the Copper River in 1908. (Seattle Historical Society)

The Miles Glacier bridge after the March 24, 1964 earthquake. One span of the bridge, which had become an important link in the Copper River Highway, dropped into the river waters. Repairs and improvements on the bridge have been held up by conservation groups. (Alaska Department of Highways)

The copper mill at Kennecott Mines with a flat car on the rail spur in the foreground. The rich Kennecott mines were the main reason for the construction of the Copper River and Northwestern Railroad, to bring the rich ore to sealevel for shipment to Tacoma and other copper refining centers. (Seattle Historical Society)

153

Officials of the Copper River and Northwestern Railroad are pictured at Miles Glacier, Oct. 5, 1908, where the "million dollar bridge" was to be constructed. Building of the bridge took two years and in the meantime means had to be found to transport material and men beyond that point. Left to right are: W.C. Robinson, transportation master who held the same position on the White Pass & Yukon construction project; Dan Hedican, walking boss; Mike J. Heney, builder and contractor for the Copper River as well as the White Pass; J.R. Van Clive, superintendent motive power, Katalla Co.,; Archie Shields, supply; W.L.M. McCune, assistant auditor, Katalla Co.; James English, track superintendent; Sam Murchison, superintendent of construction and Heney's assistant; Dr. F.B. Whiting, chief surgeon who also handled medical chores on the White Pass; Pat O'Brien, bridge superintendent; E.C. Hawkins, chief engineer and another White Passer; and H.R. "Bill" Simpson, steamshovels and snow king. (Seattle Historical Society)

After the ice went out and flood waters subsided, it was not difficult to construct the fourth span of the bridge, as the river channel was free once more. Span No. 4 falsework was completed, and work on the span itself was started on June 10, and completed on June 19, and daily trains were operated across the bridge.

The "Million Dollar Bridge" crossing the Copper River and separating Miles and Child's Glaciers was made famous in Rex Beach's "Iron Trail."

Metro-Goldyn-Mayer filmed part of the "Trail of '98" at Mile 52 just above the bridge, losing three men in Abercrombie Rapids — more than were lost in the actual construction of the bridge or the blasting of the right of way in the mile-high rock cliffs on each side of the canyon.

Other problems were encountered at Baird Glacier when the track was laid over the glacial Moraine, a few

hundred feet back from the glacier itself, and which moved forward with the ice about a foot a day. Gravel by the carload was dumped on the ice, shoveled under the ties and tamped, but for years it was necessary to use long iron bars to move the track back inch-by-inch against the glacier until it was in alignment again.

Abercrombie Canyon presented the task of blasting the roadbed in the side of precipitous bluffs, where the costs ran as much as $200,000 per mile. Similar conditions were also met further up the line where faces of mountains and canyons were literally torn away by tremendous charges of dynamite and powder with one charge alone consisting of 1,000 kegs of black powder and 35 cases of dynamite.

The highest bridge of all was the Kuskulana River bridge, 228 feet above the floor of its gorge and 550

A roadbed begins to appear on the steep walls of Abercrombie Canyon as workers literally blast their way through. Despite the danger, and the treacherous rapids, a legendary terror, no lives were lost in the construction, although in later years when two movies were made in the area, "The Days of '98" and Rex Beach's "Iron Trail," three persons were lost filming "Days of '98." (Washington State Historical Society)

Bridge builders still argue as to which of the two major steel bridges on the Copper River and Northwestern Railroad was the most difficult to construct. The Miles Glacier span was a battle against time and ice. The span over the Kuskulana River Gorge was battle against the winter elememts with blizzards, temperatures of 50 and 60 degrees below zero weather. Acetylene lights had to be used continually, as construction was during the dark winter months, when there was practically no daylight in that part of the world. After a two-month battle against the elements, the work on the 525-foot cantilever bridge over the 238-foot deep chasm was completed on New Year's Day, 1911. (Washington State Historical Society)

Workers blast their way through some of the solid rock in construction of the Copper River and Northwestern Railroad. Work was slow and dangerous. (Washington State Historical Society)

Breaking camp and moving on to a new location was a hectic time for workers on the Copper River and Northwestern Railroad. This photo was taken as workers loaded equipment and materials at Camp Mile 52 to move to another location. (Seattle Historical Society)

feet long. This construction was carried out during the dead of winter. There were days of terrific blizzards, when men could not even stand up, much less work. Temperatures at times dropped to 60 degrees below and it was necessary to heat the heavy chains used in construction to keep them from breaking in the extreme cold. The work was done, however, just as it had been at Miles and Childs Glaciers, and the span across the Kuskulana gorge was completed on Christmas Day, 1910.

The wooden Gilahina River bridge, 890 feet long and 80 to 90 feet high was built in eight days. The longest bridge crossed the Copper River just out of Chitina at Mile 132. It was 2,790 feet long, built in a horseshoe curve which had to be rebuilt every year as ice would take it out with the spring thaw.

Work above Abercrombie Rapids was assisted considerably by powerfully engined river boats which moved food and material through high water and low, struggling up and down the shifting bars of Wood Canyon.

Supplying the upline camps was one of the major problems during the winter months. On one occasion there was a desperate need for coal and other supplies at Tiekel River camp, a distance of 50 miles above Glacier crossing, over which the track had not been kept open during the winter. When the rotary snowplow was started on this stretch under the able direction of "Rotary Bill" Simpson, who had been the hero of many such occasions during the construction of the White Pass and Yukon as well as the Copper River route, extraordinary conditions were discovered. The rains had penetrated the deep snow, packed it and frozen at the bottom so that the entire fifty miles of track was covered with from six inches to two feet of solid ice.

At this combination of ice and snow the rotary was driven. It would stick its nose in, sending the snow flying, for about 15 feet or more. Then it would be discovered to have climbed the ice cap. The next procedure was to pull back again, and when it landed, the wheels were on the ties instead of the rails. While one crew got the heavy plough back on the track, another chopped out the exposed ice, and the entire operation was repeated. It took 31 days of constant work to reach the Tiekel with the rescue train, making an average speed of a mile and one-half every 24 hours. E.C. Hawkins is the authority for this statement that the plough went off the track in this way no less than 1,500 times.

The winter of 1910-11 saw the road driven far up into the Chitina basin, and by the end of Sept. 1910 the railroad had reached Chitina at Mile 131, with a first class roadbed, water grade and slight curvature. From here a branch was constructed 62 miles to Kennecott and was completed on March 29, 1911.

It was not to be that Mike Heney, leader and driver behind this superhuman effort would see the completion of the project that was so dear to his heart and for which he gambled his own fortune — with success.

Returning from one of his numerous trips "outside" Heney was aboard the S.S. Ohio, two days out of Seattle when the vessel struck a submerged rock in Hickish Narrows during the night. He was on the bridge with the Captain at the time, and although the Captain was of the opinion that it would be possible to make the sandy beach nearby in Carter Bay, passengers were aroused and took to the lifeboats. Heney did not think of himself, but of the 20 head of horses he had below being transported to Cordova for work on the railroad. He made every effort to free the animals from the deck below and enable them to swim to the nearby shore. Such was, however, not possible, and he was aboard the vessel when it slowly went under during a calm and moonlight night. Heney was able to free himself and made his way to a group of lifeboats standing by in the distance. Although badly

overloaded, one of the boats came back for him, and unable to take him aboard, towed him to the beach where other survivors and nearby natives and fishermen built fires to warm their bones.

After the rescue Heney did what he could to allieviate distress among the survivors; buying clothes and gear lost in the shipwreck, paying for funerals and for passage home in some cases.

Riverboats played an important role in the construction of the Copper River and Northwestern Railroad as there was no other method to get men and materials up river to the advance surveying and construction camps. One of those little steamers was the Chittyna, a 70-ton vessel, which was moved from Valdez and reassembled on the shores of the Tasnuna. Single heaviest piece was the boiler which weighed 5,700 pounds. (Clifford Collection)

With a picture of the late Michael Heney looking down from a position just above the locomotive headlamp, E.C. Hawkins, chief engineer, and Sam Murchison, superintendent of construction who took over after Heney's death, alternately drove the Copper Spike which marked the completion of the Copper River and Northwestern Railroad on March 29, 1911. The locomotive is the CR&NW's No. 50, the railroad's first and favorite of Mike Heney. (University of Alaska Archives—Raymond McKeown Collection)

He went on to Cordova and worked alongside his men preparing for the last big push to finish the railroad. His health began to fail, and he returned to the States. As the winter and next summer passed, he continued to decline in health. Doctors said it was his heart, weakened by exposure and overwork.

In Alaska his faithful crews continued the work with all of the efficiency he built into his organization. Sam Murchison stepped into Heney's shoes and the work went on. While all this work was going on, Heney's health failed steadily and in Oct. 1910 he developed pneumonia and six months before the railroad was

finished Michael J. Heney died. The wreck of the Ohio had left its mark—Alaska had lost its Napoleon.

Although his men grieved when word of his death reached them, it drove them on to superhuman effort and the Copper River and Northwestern Railroad was completed on March 29, 1911.

Sam Murchison and Erastus C. Hawkins alternately swung the sledges to drive the beautiful hand wrought copper spike, fashioned from native Alaska copper by a blacksmith in the crew. It was presented to S.W. Eccles, president of the CR&NW and sent to New York.

While the spike was being driven, Heney's own little engine, the one he brought to Cordova in the spring of 1906, and affectionally known as "Old No. 50," stood puffing and spewing steam and smoke. Attached to the front of the engine hung the picture of M.J. Heney—the man who had made it all possible.

Not to be forgotten by Heney was Captain Johnny O'Brien who had carried him back and forth many times on various ships which he commanded, and who played an important role in the Syndicate's decision to move their operations from Katalla to Cordova. Heney left Captain O'Brien $150 a month for life, and then gave most of the rest of his fortune to charities.

On April 23, 1911 Cordova celebrated "Copper Day" when the first train of copper ore, approximately 1,200 tons, arrived from the mines and was poured into the holds of the steamship Northwestern, bound for the smelter at Tacoma, Washington.

Like all other infant railroads, the maintenance of the new line was expensive and trying and was virtually a reconstruction of the whole line. Grades had to be raised and relined, more bridges built and some bridges removed as the case might be. The freshly blasted rock was ever sliding to the roadbed. Snowsheds were built so that the trains could operate in comparative safety during the winter months.

Planned were branch lines to the rich Bering River coal fields at Katalla, and also from Chitina to the Matanuska Valley and from Chitina to the Yukon River near Fairbanks. These routes, however, were never constructed — partially due to the withdrawal of the coal, oil and timber by the federal government.

The CR&NW route became one of the prime tourist attractions in Alaska, and thousands of visitors marveled at Miles and Childs Glaciers as well as others. The snowcapped peaks of Mt. Sanford, Mt. Regal, Mt. Wrangell, and Mt. Blackburn reared their heads from 14,000 to 16,000 feet above the level of the river route.

One of the most popular of the scenic tours was known as the Golden Belt Tour. Tourists left the steamer at either Cordova, northbound, or on arrival at Seward. Those leaving the ship at Cordova, made the trip from the coast to Fairbanks in the Interior, over the Copper River and Northwestern Railroad via Childs Glacier, Copper River Canyon, Chitina, and then over the Richardson Trail by automobile to Fairbanks. The return to the coast was made over the Alaska Railroad to Seward, where connection was made with the following steamer to Seattle. Those leaving the steamer at Seward made the trip in reverse. Two other tours were the Circle and Keystone Canyon trips.

An excursion train on the Copper River and Northwestern Railroad at the Miles Glacier bridge. Such excursions were the highlights of a trip to Alaska in the early 1900s with travel to Seward or Cordova by steamer, the Alaska Railroad or the Copper River and Northwestern and the Richardson Highway to Fairbanks, and a return to the coast via either the CR&NWRR or the ARR, depending which had been used northbound. (Seattle Historical Society)

A relief map of the Copper River country shows the various railroad routes from Prince William Sound to the rich interior. The Copper River and Northwestern Railroad is at the right while the Routes from Seward used by Alaska Central, Alaska Northern and eventually the Alaska Railroad are at the left. (Seattle Historical Society)

During the 27 years of operation, millions of tons of ore came down over the tracks and over the Cordova docks, which made this one of the most successful and profitable railroads in Alaska.

At the start of its operation the Copper River and Northwestern had 15 locomotives, 8 passenger cars, 256 freight cars, 4 steam shovels, 2 rotary ploughs, and 1 wrecking crane.

Chitina, a division point on the railroad, was also a transfer point for freight from the railroad to the Interior.

In 1939 the mines were worked out to the point that it was unprofitable and they were closed down and the railroad abandoned with ICC approval in May 1939, except for a 13-mile section out of Cordova which the Army used during World War II. The CR&NWRR was the second longest railroad in Alaska, constructed at a cost of $23,500,000 of which $8,500,000 was spent for labor. The steel for the four magnificent bridges erected in the building of the railroad weighed 20,300,000 pounds at an approximate cost of $2,500,000; the Miles-Childs Glacier Bridge alone accounting for $1,500,000.

An army of 6,000 men worked during the three years of construction.

In 1940 the company sold three locomotives and 30

An ore train outside of Cordova on the Copper River and Northwestern Railroad. The locomotive No. 23 was an American Locomotive Co., Rhode Island class 2-8-0 built in 1907, one of four owned by the CR&NW. (Seattle Historical Society)

freight cars to the Alaska Railroad. Until 1947 light tram cars operated over the rusty rails from Chitina to McCarthy, near Kennecott, a distance of 60 miles.

In 1964 a Washington salvage firm pulled the last rails from the right-of-way, which had been turned back to the federal government, and in recent years, work on turning the route into a highway was undertaken.

The 1964 earthquake saw one section of the bridge fall into the waters of the Copper River, and although some work was done to try to prevent further damage, conservation groups were successful in preventing further work on the highway until an agreement was reached in 1975 which allows repairs to the bridge, but prohibited for three years extension of the road to Chitina or the Richardson Highway, or until Congress has acted on National Park proposals in the area.

Copper River and Northwestern Railroad locomotive No. 20. An American Locomotive Co. 2-8-0 Rhode Island built in 1907, one of four such engines operated by the railroad. (Washington State Historical Society)

Copper River & Northwestern engine roster

No. 1	0-4-0T	Dickson	#41749	1/1907	To Aloha Lumber Co., No. 1 Aloha, Wash.
No. 2	0-4-0T	Dickson	#41750	1/1907	To Willapa Harbor Lumber Co. Mills No. 5; Port of Grays Harbor, Wash., No. 5.
No. 3	0-4-0T	Dickson	#41751	1/1907	
No. 4	0-4-0T	Dickson	#41753	1/1907	
No. 5	0-4-0T	Dickson	#42765	5/1907	
No. 6	0-4-0T	Dickson	#42267	5/1907	
No. 7	0-4-0T	Dickson	#41748	1/1907	

All above are believed to have come from Katalla where they were used by the Copper River & Northwestern and other construction projects, although some reports show only six coming from Katalla.

No. 20	2-8-0	ALCO (Rhode Island)	#44597	11/1907	
No. 21	2-8-0	ALCO (Rhode Island)	#44598	11/1907	
No. 22	2-8-0	ALCO (Rhode Island)	#44599	11/1907	
No. 23	2-8-0	ALCO (Rhode Island)	#44600	11/1907	To Alaska Railroad 1940, No. 101; Bethelem Steel, Seattle, 1947 scrapped.
No. 50	4-6-0	Rogers	#2859	1881	Ex-Southern Pacific No. 187, No. 1665, No. 2098; Valdez-Yukon No. 101, Copper River Railroad No. 50.
No. 51	4-6-0	Baldwin	#11265	10/1890	Ex-Pacific Coast RR No. 4; Port Townsend Southern No. 4.
No. 70	2-8-2	Brooks	#55490	11/1915	To Midland Terminal No. 62; Mexican Northwestern; Chihuhua Pacific.
No. 71	2-8-2	Brooks	#55491	11/1915	To Alaska Railroad 1940 reported never put in service.
No. 72	2-8-2	Brooks	#55492	11/1915	To McCloud River Railroad No. 26.
No. 73	2-8-2	Brooks	#57291	4/1917	Boiler exploded and scrapped.
No. 74	2-8-2	Brooks	#58164	8/1917	To McCloud River Railroad No. 27
No. 75	2-8-2	Brooks			To Midland Terminal No. 63; Mexican Northwestern; Chihuhua Pacific No. 201.
No. 100	2-6-0	Brooks	#46182	5/1909	
No. 101	2-6-0	Brooks	#46183	5/1909	To Alaska Railroad 1940 never put in service.
No. 102	2-6-0	Brooks	#46184	5/1909	

Chapter 15

Wild Goose, Geese, Gooses?

To say that railroad history in Alaska and the Yukon is at times confusing is to put it mildly, what with the lack of records, no building or construction permits, frequent questionable promotional schemes, and the like.

One of those confusing situations, at least to those not knowledgeable about northern geography, is that of the Wild Goose Railroad — or to be more exact, railroads. There were two such. Both on Alaska's Seward Peninsula, within about 60 miles of each other. Both were built by the same man, at about the same time, and to make matters worse, both used some of the same equipment.

One ran from Nome to Anvil Creek. The other from Council City to No. 15 Ophir Creek.

To build such a railroad — or railroads, over the unstable arctic terrain, without proper ballast, is the kind of impossible dream today's construction industry, with all its engineering knowhow, might attempt. But more than 75 years ago, only dreamers attempted such a task. The location was a few miles south of the Arctic Circle, some 2,500 miles northwest of Seattle,

the nearest supply base; and in an area where ocean transportation was available at the most about four months out of the year.

Gold was discovered in the Nome area in Sept. 1898 when a party from the Swedish Mission at Golovin Bay was driven ashore by a summer storm. Erik O. Lindbloom, John Bryntesen and Jefet Lindeborg staked claims at "discovery" in the Anvil Creek area and on Oct. 18 these three and some other newcomers saw the necessity of forming a mining district, which they called Cape Nome.

In less than two years a train rolled into Anvil City, the actual site of the famous strike, something even these daring and audacious first gold miners never would have dreamed possible.

By this time, prospectors were everywhere — on claims along the miles of beach stretching evenly east and west of Nome, and on the streams whose headwaters lie in the peninsula's rugged interior.

The miners needed supplies, and moving materials over the soggy, spongy tundra was expensive and time consuming, costing $200 to $300 a ton. One of

To reach Council City, where rich gold strikes had been made, was the goal of the Council City & Solomon River Railroad in the early 1900s. The gold petered out, however, before the CC&SR reached Council City, although the "second" Wild Goose Railroad operated in the area in 1902-03. This is First Street in Council City as it looked at that time. (University of Alaska Archives—Seppala Collection)

Track laying across the spongy tundra was a real problem in the building of railroads in the Arctic. A construction crew is laying rails on the Wild Goose Railroad (Council City version) during the summer of 1902. (University of Washington Historical Library—Northwest Collection)

those forced to pay these exhorbitant prices was Charles D. Lane, a prominent Nome resident and president of the Wild Goose Mining and Trading Company, which had rich, profitable operations in the Anvil Creek area.

Lane, who had become wealthy from mining enterprises in the California, Idaho and Nevada gold fields, convinced his firm's directors that the building and operating of a railroad to the Anvil Creek area would be a good investment.

Upon receiving approval, Lane lost little time in carrying out his plans. He shifted into high gear in short order. He bought an ocean going steamer and renamed it Charles D. Lane. Onto this ship he loaded the entire cull stock of a Northwest lumber mill, two 15-ton geared Class A Climax narrow gauge locomotives, rails, a dozen eight-wheel flat cars, and other necessary supplies.

No time was lost. As soon as the ship anchored in the Nome roadstead, work started on the railroad.

Crews, under direction of Major William V. Monroe, a former Indian fighter and Civil War veteran who had worked in the building of both the Union Pacific and Southern Pacific lines, started laying cull lumber across the soft squishy tundra for a roadbed. These first crews were followed by rail men. Foot-by-foot on the soggy landscape moved the Wild Goose construction gangs. By July, four miles of road had been completed to Discovery on Lower Anvil Creek. Working late into the season, an additional two and one half miles of track was laid to Anvil Station, on the western slope of Anvil Mountain.

Anvil Creek was highly profitable for the Wild Goose Company as the area alone produced $21 million in gold, and most of the claims were held by the Wild Goose.

The little narrow gauge, operated under Superintendent Frank Shaw, proved profitable too. The fare from Nome to Discovery was fifty cents each way. To the end of the line it was $2 round-trip.

Parades were the thing in boom-town Nome during the height of the gold rush. Members of the Yukon Order of Pioneers heads the Fourth of July, 1901 parade through the business section of town. It was at this time that the railroads such as the Wild Goose, had their most prosperous years. (University of Washington Historical Library—Northwest Collection)

Freight was two cents a pound. Cost of construction had been $5,000 per mile, but by the end of the first summer income was more than nine times the cost of construction and equipment. The little railroad became known as the "Paystreak Express."

Trains did not operate during the winter, closing down in November, but the little locomotives kept busy during the summer. Passengers rode where they were lucky enough to find space. Sightseers during 1901 and 1902 found Anvil City, the name tacked on the community at the mining site, consisted of several saloons, a restaurant or two, the mining company mess house and the Wild Goose Railroad station, plus hundreds of tents of prospectors and miners.

Despite an eight miles-per-hour speed limit, half of the train's crew time was spent jacking either the engine or train of flat cars back on the tracks. A ride was enough to give "a timid man a feeling of seasickness."

The roadbed continued to sink into the marshy tundra, giving a roller-coaster effect.

Whenever one of the girls from the stockade made a strike in the creeks through grub-staking a miner, she invariably chartered the Paystreak Express to convey her guests to the party that she would throw at one of the roadhouses out of Nome. The singing, whooping gang would start out merrily enough, but it was not long before the men would be bending their backs putting the train back on the tracks with encouragement, vocal of course, from the ladies.

If the train reached its destination without several such derailments it was a miracle, but no one cared. It was all part of the fun. The girls enjoyed it immensely as it was practically the only wholesome enjoyment for them since their girlhood days.

Business thrived sufficiently that it was necessary to obtain a third Climax by 1902. It too, was a 15-ton

One of the Climax locomotives used by the Wild Goose (Nome version) is seen here as the crew pumps water from the river to replenish the boiler. The Wild Goose used several Climax narrow gauge locomotives during its short life in the early 1900s. (Yukon Archives)

Class A with a box cab to enclose the crew from the weather. A fourth Climax was added later.

The line originally began on the sandspit at the mouth of the Snake River, near the beach and opposite the center of Nome. Later a line was built into Nome itself, and two branches were built out at right angles along the old beach line.

As the Wild Goose company sought new operations in the Ophir Creek district out of Council City, Lane planned construction of a second Wild Goose Railroad, formally known as the Golofnin Bay Railway Co., to run between Council City and No. 15 Ophir Creek, a distance of eight miles or thereabouts.

Construction on the railroad started in late June 1902 and was finished by July 21. Lane moved equipment, rails, and the like to his new operation. Motive power on the second road was the No. 4 15-ton Climax brought over from Nome on July 26, 1902.

The first excursion train over this narrow gauge route was enjoyed by 150 persons who turned out on Aug. 17 to enjoy the ride on the Wild Goose Railroad. Planks were laid on boxes on open flat cars to accom-modate the merry crowd on its Sunday outing to the mines at Ophir Creek.

For a time, this road proved prosperous, too, as long as gold was plentiful, but folded in 1906 or thereabouts as did the Council City and Soloman Railroad, when gold petered out.

In the meantime, the original Wild Goose continued — under a variety of names and operators.

In 1903 Lane started disposing of some of his interests in the mining company and the original Wild Goose Railroad with the Pioneer Mining Company, headed by Lane's early-day partner, Jefet Lindeborg, one time reindeer herder and one of the original discoverers of gold in the Anvil Creek area, taking one-fourth of his interests and the Miocene Ditch Company taking another quarter. The railroad was reorganized as the Nome-Arctic Railroad.

Lindeborg later teamed up with Lane to play an important role in the efforts to thwart the nefarious McKenzie-Noyes conspiracy, as Judge Arthur J. Noyes would appoint Alex McKenzie as court receiver while the rights to some of the early discoverors were

First Train on Original Wild Goose. It was a foggy day when the first train left Anvil for Nome on the original Wild Goose Railroad on July 19, 1900. Passengers, mostly construction workers or miners, sat where they could on the open flat cars. (University of Washington Historical Library)

being argued in court. As Judge Noyes set legal blocks whenever possible to stall and delay the trial, McKenzie would be working the disputed claims for all they were worth and the miners were robbed of whatever prize they sought. In time, the Judge and McKenzie were exposed and convicted, but they had stolen millions in the meantime. (Rex Beach's novel, The Spoilers, was based largely on this affair.)

At about this time, the plan to bring the railroad into town was revived with a terminal on Second Street, from which a spur was run to the beach. The line ran along Fourth Street, back of St. Joseph's Church, across Stedman Ave., and then south to Second. Another branch line was built from Anvil Road to about a quarter mile beyond the Wild Goose Company's plant on the Snake River.

Work was suspended on the Nome-Artic in the fall of 1905, according to the Nome Nugget, with Major W.N. Monroe, manager of the company, giving as the reason the government tax of $100 per mile and the Nome city assessment of $20,000. There were troubles with longshoremen, also, and the road operated only four months of 1905, the final year of operation.

One of the "engines" used on the Wild Goose-Nome Arctic-Curly Q railroad in later years was the Fordson powered tractor with flanged wheels. This type of equipment was also used on some Seward Peninsula and possibly on the "other" Wild Goose trackage. The tractor is located near a Nome playfield where it is gradually being destroyed by vandals and the weather. (H. Clifford)

Terminus of the Wild Goose (Nome version) was Anvil Creek, where a small community known as Banner Station developed. Passengers and cargo rode on open cars in those days, sometimes a rather tricky ride as the rails were very uneven from the melting permafrost and oftimes cars tipped at a precarious angle. (University of Washington Historical Library—Northwest Collection)

Wild Goose engine roster.

No. 1   Climax 212 Class A geared. 15 tons. 4/1900. Acquired 1900. To Seward Peninsula No. 1, Pioneer Mining & Ditch Co., Territory of Alaska 1921.

No. 2   Climax 212 Class A geared. 15 tons. 4/1900. Acquired 1900. To Seward Peninsula No. 2, Pioneer Mining & Ditch Co., Territory of Alaska 1921.

No. 3   Climax 315 Class A geared. 15 tons. 4/1900. Acquired 1902. To Seward Peninsula No. 3, Pioneer Mining & Ditch Co., Territory of Alaska 1921.

No. 4   Climax 315 Class A geared. 15 tons. 4/1902. Acquired 1902. To Golofin Bay Railroad (2nd Wild Goose), July 1902. Believed to be locomotive sold to Charles Reader. Left on tundra and recently sold to Keith Christensen, Anchorage.

A Climax locomotive pulls an excursion train loaded with passenger riding on flat cars, out of Nome on the original Wild Goose Railroad. Generally such excursion were run on holidays, such as the Fourth of July. (University of Washington Historical Library—Northwest Collection)

Chapter 16
Council City & Solomon River Railroad

Little remains today of a railroad which at one time showed promise of becoming one of the most prosperous in Alaska. It was the Council City & Solomon River Railroad, also known as the North Star Line. Despite its name, the railroad never actually reached Council City, and perhaps that tells the story.

The Council City and Solomon River was chartered on March 27, 1902 under the laws of New Jersey. Incorporators included president, Edward A. Olds, New York; vice president, J. Warren Dickson, who also served as general manager; treasurer, Ernest S. Emanuel; and secretary, A. Dwight Keep. Among the directors were J.H. Emanuel Jr. of the J.P. Morgan Co., New York, a firm also active in construction of the Copper River and Northwestern Railroad out of Cordova.

In Sept. 1902, Herman Heinze, a U.S. deputy surveyor, revealed that he had completed a survey from the coast along the Solomon River and thence to Council City, and although he did not announce his employer or whether the road would be a wagon trail or a railroad, he did say that the route was a good one with easy grades.

On May 3, 1903 the Nome Nugget reported that the Western Alaska Construction Co., of Chicago, with capital of $1 million had been granted a right-of-way by the government to build the Council City & Solomon River Railroad, "to connect all the principal producing areas and centers of population known at present throughout the Solomon River, Council City, Ophir Creek, Bluestone, York and Nome regions with tidewater and vessel transportation at Solomon River, Grantley Harbor, Port Clarence and Good Hope Bay, thus gridironing the peninsula."

This was one of the rich and most promising mining districts in Alaska and despite "impossible" transporta-tion costs across the muck and mire of the tundra between the area and the closest major port, Nome, it was a prosperous one. By 1906 the mines at Ophir Creek had produced about $4,500,000 in gold. The Discovery Mining District was inland and its claims not as accessible to the miner as those at and near Nome, but Council City grew and thrived despite the excessive expense and inconvenience of freighting supplies from Nome at a cost of up to more than $55 per ton.

Preliminary work started on June 19, 1903, and a couple of weeks later the steamer Aztec arrived with 4,000 tons of cargo, including a pile driver and hoisting engine, two locomotives and box and flat cars.

J. Warren Dickson of Seattle, the firm's vice president, shortly thereafter imprinted his name on the maps of Alaska by naming the southern terminal of the railroad, Dickson.

Major activity was centered around Dickson with docks, a bridge over the lagoon, offices, waiting rooms and machine shops being constructed. The headquarters complex, located across the Solomon River from the village of Solomon, consisted of a large two-and-one-half story building with 12 rooms which was the residence of company officials, a 45-foot by 90-foot machine shop, a 16-foot by 48-foot two story office building and a 10,000-gallon water tank to supply the area.

In no time at all Solomon had six restaurants and five saloons which were open day and night and word shifted back to Nome that there was much need for a marshall or commissioner to keep order as "dance hall girls and brawls" were much of the scene.

Workers were paid $3 a day with room and board, and an initial payroll of $30,000 a month supported 160 laborers who worked 10 to 15 hours a day.

This impressive building (for the time) was the general office building for the Council City & Solomon River Railroad at Dickson. The railroad shops and freight yard is in the background. The bulding also served as headquarters for Western Alaska Construction Co., in charge of building the railroad. (University of Alaska Archives—Charles Bunnell Collection)

As mid-summer rolled around, additional employees were hired and soon 450 men were working with a payroll of $76,000 a month. The Aztec arrived with an additional 5,000 tons of supplies. Cargo landed at Dickson that first summer totaled more than 4 million board feet of lumber, 165,000 ties, 50 miles of rails, the locomotives and freight cars previously mentioned, and 104 miles of copper wire plus a number of "Bell telephones" as the railroad had become the exclusive licensee of the Bell Telephone Company on the Seward Peninsula.

By Aug. 19, seven miles of track had been completed, and by Sept. 2, ten miles had been laid and service inaugurated over that portion of the railroad to a point about a mile and one half below Big Hurrah. A passenger fare of $1 was advertised and service began.

Despite statements that "50 miles of track would be completed before the snow flys," that was the extent of progress that first construction season.

The summer of 1904 saw several new businesses at-

The boom following the start of work on the Council City & Solomon River Railroad in 1903 saw the town of Solomon grow by leaps and bounds. In no time at all there were six restaurants and five saloons and the word was sent back to Nome that a marshall was needed to keep order, as "dance hall girls and brawls" were much of the scene. Solomon was located across the Solomon River from Dickson, the western terminus of the railroad. (University of Alaska Archives—Cliff N. Allyn Collection)

Members of a work crew, along with locomotive No. 1 of the Council City & Solomon River railroad at Hard Rock Creek as they prepare the roadbed over the tundra. The photo was taken Sept. 25, 1903. All of the CC&SR locomotives were formerly New York City Elevated Railroad engines. (University of Alaska Archives—Charles Bunnell Collection)

tracted to Dickson, including the Northwestern Commercial Co. and Tanner and Clark Lumber Yard and warehouse. A 10-bed hospital was opened under direction of Dr. William Hopper and plans were announced for the Hotel Dickson — second largest on the Seward Peninsula.

The railroad officials completed arrangements with the Alaska Pacific Express Co. so that miners could send money orders from Dickson and the various points along the line to anywhere in the world. Actual construction on the railroad, however, was slow. Only 1,000 feet of track had been added by July 1, 1904, and the company, instead, opened a stage service from Right Branch Station on the railroad to Council City. That was it for the season.

Dickson resigned from the company and some time later announced plans for the construction of a railroad from Nome to Kougarok region.

The year 1905 again saw many promises in the way of construction, but all that was added was a 927-foot bridge across the Solomon River and the laying of track to it and across the bridge, bringing the overall total to 13 miles.

The company was reorganized and a new contractor and general manager, Hugh F. Magee, arrived to take charge of the operation.

In the meantime, Major Wilds P. Richardson, president of the Alaska Road Commission, visited Council and stated that a road was needed and that it would be one of the first projects of the 1906 season. Transpor-

Locomotive No. 1 on the Council City & Solomon River Railroad was a former New York Elevated Railroad engine built in 1886. The CC&SR was the farthest north and farthest west standard guage railroad in the country. Remains of this 0-4-2 locomotive along with a couple of other CC&SR engines may still be seen on the flats near the ghost town of Dickson on the Solomon River south of Nome. (University of Alaska Archives—Charles Bunnel Collection)

tation, however, seemed to go from bad to worse, and freight rates to the Council area from Nome rose to $66 a ton, ten times the cost of shipping from Seattle to Nome.

By April 1906 the Nome Nugget was predicting that construction of the Council City & Solomon River Railroad would be abandoned, but this appeared to be premature by about a year. The railroad, however, did sell rails and quantities of fish plates, ties and other construction material to the Seward Peninsula Railroad of Nome.

Perhaps Magee needed cash, but shortly thereafter he was replaced by Theodore Knowlton who took over the job in June 1906 and pushed construction work through Cheyenne Creek, bridged Coal Creek, and by August had added 10 miles of finished track. By Sept. 19 the trackage had reached Penelope

Creek, bringing the total to 35 miles. Construction stopped here because they ran out of fish plates — no less.

Knowlton, however, admitted that prospects for further construction were somewhat gloomy and depended upon his report to the Board of Directors in New York. He added that business in 1906 had not equaled that of 1905 and he foresaw further declines. He pointed out that it would cost about a quarter of a million dollars to extend the trackage to Council City.

Total rolling stock at the time consisted of three locomotives, two passenger cars and 17 freight cars.

The railroad operated at least part of the 1907 season, with the advertised schedule effective July 15, 1907 calling for trips to East Fork on Mondays, Wednesdays, Thursdays, Saturdays and Sundays only, and to Penelope Creek on Tuesdays and Fridays. Running time to East Fork was one hour and to Penelope three hours.

In Oct. 1907 Jerome D. Gedney of East Orange, N.J., was appointed receiver by the Court of Chancery of New Jersey. Of the $1,000,000 in authorized stock at $10 a share, $895,460 was outstanding, along with a funded debt of $347,000 first mortgage at six percent. Three-year gold bonds, due May 1, 1908, with interest payable May 1, and Nov. 1, each year were also outstanding with no payment made and money not available for payment.

And thus came the end of the Council City & Solomon River Railroad. Some trackage, collapsed buildings and the rusty ruins of three locomotives and a few flat cars are all that remains of a promised dream.

The Nome Nugget of April 28, 1906, commenting on the CR&SR blamed the failure of the project on "well planned but miserably executed enterprise. The original promoters' ideas were alright but his judgment wanting. The road started on a too elaborate scale and much money spent uselessly and needlessly. Had sound judgment coupled with practical experience prevailed, Solomon and Council would have been connected by rail.

"And now this seems far distant. Mr. Dickson was a sanguine. He did not consider carefully. He announced his intention to move Nome to Solomon (or Dickson) within two years"—and now his road is to be abandoned. Had he been less optimistic and more practical, the result might have been much different.

"The failure of an enterprise like the building of the Council City road is a detriment to the development of the country. And yet it is not the country's fault, but it is rather due to the short-sightedness of the promoters."

Although the train was standing still, high winds make it appear as if this Council City & Solomon River train was heading out under a full head of steam. The "passenger" car was built up from one of the railroad's flat cars. The locomotive was from the New York Elevated. The photo was taken in the early 1900s. (Clifford Collection)

Council City & Solomon River locomotives.

No. 1   0-4-4T. New York #137 Fornay-Type. 6/1886. Built for New York Elevated No. 21.
            Rebuilt by Manhattan Railway 10/19/94. Sold 4/28/03 to Western Alaska Construc-
            tion Co. and delivered to Seattle, Wash. To CC&SR No. 1.

No. 2   0-4-4T. New York #149 Fornay-Type 8/1886. Built for New York Elevated No. 159.
            Rebuilt by Manhattan Ry. 6/30/94. Sold 4/28/03 to Western Alaska Construction Co.
            for delivery to Seattle. To CC&SR No. 2.

No. 3   0-4-4T. Baldwin #5622 Fornay Type. 5/1881. Built for NY Elevated Ry., No. 303.
            Rebuilt by Manhattan Ry., 5/10/94. Sold 8/13/04 to Western Construction Co. and
            delivered to Seattle, Wash. To CC&SR No. 3.

All that remains of the Council City & Solomon River railroad are the rusting hulks of these locomotives and a few flat cars, deserted on the tundra near the ghost town of Dickson. These locomotives saw service on the New York Elevated Railroad before being shipped to Alaska. The CC&SR was the farthest north and farthest west standard guage railroad at the time. (Bruce Campbell photo)

Chapter 17

Seward Peninsula

As activity on the Nome-Arctic and the Council City & Solomon River roads began to diminish, plans for construction of a railroad from Nome to the Kougarok mining area continued to be discussed.

In June 1905 J. Warren Dickson, who had resigned as vice president and general manager of the CC&SR, announced plans for the Seward Peninsula Railroad Co., financed by New York money, to run from Nome to Kougarok.

The Nome Nugget of April 26, 1906 carried comments on a previous article on the organization of a company in New York by John Rosene and Major L.H. French called Northwestern Development Company, with capital of $2 million. The company was organized to build a railroad into the Kougarok country and to develop extensive mineral holdings which the company had acquired in that region.

The road was to be built from Nome and construction was to start with the opening of navigation and pushed forward as rapidly as possible.

Rosene was the initial president of the new firm, and Major French had previously obtained an option to purchase the Nome-Arctic Railroad, and eventually exercised this option through the new firm. Construction of the railroad was part of Rosene's plan to connect the Seward Peninsula with Valdez. He had been active in the project to build the Copper River and Northwestern Railroad from Valdez to the rich copper fields at the head of the Tanana River.

Actual officers of the developing company turned out to be H.C. Davis, president, and Eugene Small, Cable Whitehead and George Henderson, vice presidents. Headquarters was in the Hanover Bank Building in Manhattan. Whitehead was also president of the Alaska Bank and Trust Co., and later had the distinction of being the only officer of an Alaskan railroad to lose his life on the line. An engine he was riding flipped over near Salmon Lake, 42 miles out of Nome, and he was killed.

Meanwhile on April 27, 1906, the Seward Peninsula Railroad (both Peninsula and Peninsular were used) was incorporated in Nevada, to operate the road, to be built by the Northwestern Development Company. President was E.A. Mathews and T.A. Davis was vice president. Offices were in the Mutual Life Building in Seattle.

In 1910 Davis became president, and a new slate of vice presidents was named. Such was organization and promotion of railroads in Alaska in those days.

During the 1906 construction season the railroad reached Lane's Landing, or Shelton, on the Kuzitrim River, a distance of some 85 miles, the furthermost point reached during its operation. Shelton was the supply point for the Kougarok country, and served as the road's terminus.

The first few miles of the line were very inexpensive to construct, costing about $5,000 per mile. Later trackage, through the Pilgrim River and Nome Valley, proved to have cost more as the road had 128 bridges and trestles. One trestle, over the Kuzitrim River, was some 1,000 feet in length, and the ice took it out during the winter of 1907. Thereafter it was removed each winter and reinstalled in the spring.

As was the case with the Wild Goose, the thawing tundra presented many operational problems with the soggy mud presenting a roadbed with the stability of a wet sponge, and derailments were a normal pattern of the operation.

The extension of the railroad to Shelton and the increased business required additional locomotives. The Seward Peninsula had taken over the three remaining Climax "A's" from the Wild Goose (Nome-Arctic) — the fourth having gone to the "other" Wild Goose and apparently having been abandoned there.

The first of the "new" equipment was the road's first rod engine, already a museum piece, a small Porter 0-6-0 which had been built in Jan. 1878 and obtained from the Walla Walla & Columbia River Railroad in

Washington State, where it had been named "Blue Mountain." The engine had seen service on the Oregon Railway & Navigation Railroad at the Dalles until 1894, when it went to work on the former Mill Creek Flume & Manufacturing Co. line at Walla Walla. It was eventually purchased by the Northern Pacific in July 1905. The next year it was obtained by the Seward Peninsula.

The little Porter was the most popular locomotive owned by the company. It was "low slung and powerful" and the crews could make good time with her. Most of the other engines had to be handled with great care on the curves and poor roadbed.

The line also purchased three new, larger Climaxes in 1908. These were 36-ton "B" engines, and were numbered No. 5, No. 6, and No. 7. They were only in service one season, proving to be too heavy and cumbersome for the roller coaster trackage of the Seward Peninsula and were shipped back to the states for use on lumber lines in Washington and Oregon.

In 1907 another 0-6-0 was received and numbered No. 5. It was larger and newer than the little Porter. It was a Baldwin (10882) turned out in 1890 for the Alberta Railway and Coal Co. and used in the Lethbridge area as their No. 1 for years before the trackage was changed to standard gauge.

"End of Track" was the ultimate in 1906 rail excursions in the Nome area. From day to day where that would be nobody knew. A timetable was published in the Nome Gold Digger, announcing that trains left daily at 8 a.m. and 2 p.m. for Little Creek, Discovery, Banner, Summit, Dexter, Ex and End of Track. On the return, however, departure time was not given for End of Track, but only a warning that trains would leave Ex at 10:15 a.m. and 4:15 p.m.

Freight trains with a light load made the run from Nome to Lane's Landing in about 10 or 12 hours, but if many cars were added, the time could be extended to 16, 18 or even 20 hours. For a return trip the cars would usually be empty and would bounce along into Nome in a matter of only 6 or 8 hours.

Soon after the tracks finally reached Lane's Landing business on the Seward Peninsula began to decline. By the close of the first decade of the century the train schedule had been cut to two or three trips a week and in the fall of 1910, as gold mining declined railroading on any real commercial scale came to an end on the Seward Peninsula.

Nomeites were incovenienced by the lack of service, and the still-operating mines were in need of supplies. In 1911 the Seward Peninsula started changing hands, with the the Maine Northwestern Development Company gaining possession for $1,074, although

This is Warehouse No. 5 and the "Cannon Ball Express" of the Seward Peninsula Railroad in Nome. The "express" is composed of a caboose, flat car and locomotive. The photo was taken Oct. 1, 1906. (University of Washington Historical Library—Northwest Collection)

there were probably other considerations. The Nome court records show a quit claim deed from the Seward Peninsula Railroad to the Maine company on May 28, 1913 for the consideration of $1.

On that date Jefet Lindeborg, operator of the Pioneer Mining and Ditch Company, apparently leased the railroad and on Aug. 10, 1920 purchased it at a U.S. Marshall's sale for $10,100, as a result of a judgment amounting to $52,947.50 obtained by the State Street Trust Co. of Boston against the Maine Northwestern Development Company.

During the period of Lindeborg's operation, the line was used intermittently for the transportation of light freight, a few passengers, and the mail. It was during this period that a wide assortment of picturesque conveyances were used for travel over the tracks, including carts pulled by dogs—known as pupmobiles.

Shortly after Lindeborg's purchase, the Territory of Alaska Legislature passed a bill which was approved by the Governor on May 5, 1921, providing for the purchase of the road and all equipment at a price not to exceed $30,000, and further provided that "it shall be put in good operating condition and operated as a public tram and highway."

Later that same year Lindeborg transferred the property to the Pioneer Mining and Ditch Company, which he was a principal. The bill of sale was dated

One of the several locomotives (No. 5) used by the Seward Peninsula Railroad, along with the tender. This locomotive is the 0-6-0 Baldwin built in 1890 for the Alberta Railway and Coal Co. as their No. 1. It was obtained by the Seward Peninsula in 1906. (University of Alaska Archives—Henderson Collection)

Nov. 18, 1921, but no amount was mentioned. Then a month later, on Dec. 19, 1921, the property was deeded to the Territory of Alaska by Pioneer Mining in consideration of $30,000. The sale included, besides the roadbed and certain real estate in Nome, five locomotives, Nos. 1, 2, 3, 4, and 5; a coach, No. 92; a box car, No. 1; a cook car, No. 97; a bunk car, No. 109; and twelve flat cars and two roll-top desks.

On Oct. 13, 1922, the Alaska Road Commission, a federal agency which handled road and trail construction, took over the road for the Territory at a purchase price listed as $24,000 and noted that repair of the "87-mile tram" was of "great public interest."

During the summer of 1924 the portion of the line between Little Creek and Nugget Roadhouse was rehabilitated at a cost of between $20,000 and $25,000. By the end of the year the Alaska Road Commission had spent $32,653.85 and 42 miles of line had been put in good operating conditions for light loads.

Again arrangements were made for draft animals, etc., to use the right-of-way and planks were placed between the rails on bridges and trestles. A light gasoline locomotive was purchased by the Commission for use over the road.

Regulations were put into effect. A powered vehicle was required to have a siren, suitable brakes, a sander and if pulling a loaded car, a "hired employee." Each locomotive was to be numbered, and if one planned to wander beyond the Nome River area, a "travel plan" was to be filed giving destination and time of departure.

Dog powered rigs, however, proved to be the most practical as such could be derailed and launched again upon meeting an oncomer. In such cases the vehicle with the heavier load had the right-of-way, with the vehicle being derailed going to the high side of the track, so that the owner operator could put it back on the rails.

Such operations continued until the war years, with everything imaginable that had wheels being used on the track at one time or another.

During World War II the military made some repairs and controlled traffic and brought a couple of LeRoy-powered Plymouth locomotives for use on the trackage as far north as Little Creek.

In the post-war years the line returned to the Territory and maintenance and repair again became top priority. The trackage, however, was used only occasionally. In 1953 Charles M. Reader dubbed the line the "Curly Q" and operated a small gasoline rail bus as far as Salmon Lake, carrying tourists each summer.

He sold out to Thomas Martin a few years later, but by 1955 people stopped using the tramway and the Highway Commission converted some of the roadway into highway use.

In 1963 August Krutzsch purchased some 70 miles of trackage for $6,501 along with the remains of the little No. 4 locomotive, which in the meantime had been used as part of the Nome seawall before finally being rescued by history-minded Nomeites. Hopes of restoring the little engine never came about and the Porter was shipped south to California where it is planned to restore it and use it in the operation of a tourist railroad in San Diego.

Other railroads were planned for the Nome-Seward Peninsula area. There was the Norton Bay and Yukon Railway and Navigation Co. of Washington, which planned to build from Norton Bay to the Yukon River, a distance of 76.5 miles, with extensions. Filings were in Oct. 1898.

The Bering Sea Council City Railroad was another that was planned but soon fell by the wayside. It was a New Jersey corporation.

Another was the Nebraska, Kansas and Gulf Railway Co. of Kansas, with plans to build from Nome to Port Clarence and from Nome to Golovin Sound, a total distance of 227.12 miles. Filings were made in July 1901.

The Yukon River and Bering Strait Railroad Co. planned to build from Teller City on Grantly Harbor to

A favorite way of getting around in the Nome area following the demise of the Seward Peninsula Railroad was by "pup-mobile." Residents used dog teams and a flanged wheel cart on the tracks of the old SPRR, rather than try to cross the mushy tundra in the summer months. This photo shows a team in action in 1914. (University of Alaska Archives)

Council City, with various branches. Filing was in Jan. 1901.

The DeSoto Mining Co. planned to build a standard gauge line from Nome to Council City, according to Dr. DeSoto, president of the firm. This road, proposed during the summer of 1903, would go by way of Osborne Creek and St. Michael Gulch, thence across country, taping the Eldorado, Bonanza and Solomon districts along with the Casadepogo and the Neukluk.

The Tin City and Arctic Railroad Co. of Washington, planned to build from Lost River on the Bering Sea to a point near Shishmaref Inlet, a distance of 20 miles. Filings were in Nov. 1904.

The Alaska Northern Railroad Co. of Maine (not to be confused with the Alaska Northern which eventually became the Alaska Railroad) planned to build northwesterly from Port Clarence, a distance of 68 miles. Filings were in April 1906. Another was the Alaska Coast Line Railroad Co. of Alaska, planned as a route from Nome along the coast of the Bering Sea to the U.S. Military Reservation at Port Clarence. Filings were in Nov. 1907.

Seward Peninsula engine roster.

No. 1	Climax 212 Class A geared. 15 tons. 4/1900. Ex-Wild Goose (Nome Arctic RR). To Pioneer Mining & Ditch Co.; Territory of Alaska 1921.
No. 2	Climax 212 Class A geared. 15 tons. 4/1900. Ex-Wild Goose (Nome Arctic RR). To Pioneer Mining & Ditch Co.; Territory of Alaska 1921.
No. 3	Climax 315 Class A geared. 15 tons. 4/1902. Ex-Wild Goose (Nome Arctic RR). To Pioneer Mining & Ditch Co.; Territory of Alaska 1921.
No. 4	0-6-0 Porter #283 1878. Ex-Walla Walla & Columbia River RR "Blue Mountain";Oregon Railway & Navigation Co., No. 4, Northern Pacific No. 291, OR&N No. 3. Seward Peninsula No. 4 1906. To Pioneer Mining & Ditch Co.; Territory of Alaska 1921, Scrapped and used for rip-rap in Nome breakwater. Later rescued and shipped to San Diego for restoration.
No. 5 (1st)	Climax 670 Class B geared. 23 tons. 1906. To lumber company in Oregon or Washington, 1906.
No. 5 (2nd)	0-6-0 Baldwin #10882. Built 1890 for Alberta Railway and Coal Co. No. 1. Seward Peninsula No. 5 1906. To Pioneer Mining and Ditch Co.; Territory of Alaska 1921.
No. 6	Climax 672 Class B geared. 23 tons. 1906. To Crown Timber Co. 1906.
No. 7	Climax 682 Class B geared. 28 tons. 1906. To lumber company in Oregon or Washington 1906.

Chapter 18

On the Drawing Board

Over the years, many railroads were planned for Alaska and the Yukon but never really got into operation. Some were merely stock promotion schemes. Other were seriously planned and fell by the wayside due to lack of funds or for other reasons. Others were well planned, seriously considered, and apparently had funds available, but were dropped due to changing times or conditions.

The most recent proposal for a new rail line in Alaska followed the difficulty of the summer of 1975, when severe ice conditions in the Arctic disrupted the shipment of vital oil pipeline construction materials to the North Slope. Former Alaska Governor Walter J. Hickel renewed efforts to extend the Alaska Railroad to the North Slope, as had the NORTH Commission (Northern Operations of Rail Transportation and Highways) a few years previous.

Gov. Hickel's 1975 proposal called for an extension of the Alaska Railroad northward from Nenana to Deadhorse on the North Slope. A line would also branch west from Alatna to Kobuk, and then to Teller and Nome. Another branch would extend eastward from the Fairbanks area to Whitehorse to connect with Canadian operations.

The NORTH Commission originally made a similar proposal in 1967-68 in conjunction with the proposed development of Alaska's North Slope.

The Commission was charged with pushing major development in the Arctic northland and favored the building of an extension of the Alaska Railroad to serve the petroleum and mineral rich areas of the north.

The proposed program involved extending the federally-owned Alaska Railroad northwest from the Dunbar areas, south of Fairbanks, to a point where two lines would branch off—one west to Bornite and eventually to Nome; the other north through the Brooks Range and Anaktuvuk Pass to the Prudhoe Bay area.

The program was favored strongly by then Gov. Hickel, and the late Senator Bob Bartlett.

Chairman of the NORTH Commission was Albert Swalling. During the winter of 1967-68 a crew hacked a survey trail into the Kobuk River country, using two electrotape units, a highly accurate instrument which enabled a survey line to be laid out in far less time and with more accuracy than older techniques.

In making the survey, it was recalled that the Army Corps of Engineers made a similar survey in 1942, for a railroad between Dunbar and the Nome area. It was also noted that this was the fourth time since 1900 that a railroad survey had been made from Fairbanks area to the vicinity of Nome.

A major military program for the north was one of the most ambitious ever proposed. It was in reality two separate railroads which would serve as one, with Fairbanks the division point. To the east it would run to Prince George, where it would connect with the trans-continental railroads of Canada, and would be known as the Trans-Canadian, Alaska Railroad. The actual distance of this section was to be 1,417 miles. West of Fairbanks, the road would run to the ocean terminal to be established at Teller, and would be known as the Western Railroad. It would be 735 miles in length.

The Trans-Canadian, Alaska and Western Railroads were the brainchild of Frederic A. Delano, a relative of President Franklin D. Roosevelt, and came at a time when the United States was desperate to get materials to its ally, Russia, battling the Germans on the Eastern Front. Delano was an experienced railroad man, a former president of the Burlington Route, and an official of other companies. The suggestion was reportedly made before the planning of the Alcan Highway, which started March 17, 1942.

One hitch in the building of the railroad — a major one, was the shortage of steel in 1942. The War Department, however, was interested in the project,

Stock certificate for The Trans-Alaskan Railroad Company, just one of many promotions by organizers of railroads in various parts of the Territory of Alaska. This one was organized in 1913 under the laws of the State of Arizona and was planned to operate from Iliamna Bay near the mouth of Cook Inlet to Railroad City near Holy Cross, a distance of about 350 miles. (Clifford Collection)

and a week before work on the Alcan started, the Department ordered the rail route surveyed.

The route was to go via the Rocky Mountain Trench from Prince George to Fairbanks. The survey was to be pushed to completion during the summer of 1942. The plan also called for reconnaissance of the area west of Fairbanks. About $2.8 million was earmarked for both projects. Canadian approval for the project was secured.

Among the projects of the western reconnaissance was the location of suitable sites for ocean terminals from Norton Sound to Point Barrow, the practicability of both rail and highway routes, and general features such as topography, climate, soil, forest growth, in-

habitants, and existing roads, trails and waterways. A preliminary report was to be completed by June 1, 1942.

One of the requirements for the ocean terminal was a sheltered, deep-water harbor large enough to accommodate the maximum traffic density anticipated over the military railroad, up to 20 trains of 1,000 tons each day, each way. This was the equivalent of about 15 boxcars per train, plus locomotive and service car.

Port Clarence near Teller, was deemed the best protected deep-water harbor on the west coast of Alaska, north of the Aleutians. Other places considered were Golovnin Bay on the south shore of the Seward Peninsula, Unalakleet, St. Michael, Nome, Kotzebue and Deering. Reconnaissance on routes to all suggested destinations was completed via air and ground. The report submitted in June stated that a railroad or highway was feasible between Fairbanks and Port Clarence, although such would be difficult as in all Alaska construction, due mainly to inaccessibility of sites, making uncertain the supply of materials and construction machinery.

The shortest and most logical route west of Fairbanks would be through the Yukon River valley. The existing Alaska Railroad would be used from Fairbanks to Dunbar, a distance of 39 miles. In event a highway seemed suitable, the highway would parallel the railroad at this point.

The route from Fairbanks to Council for 300 miles was the same as had been selected in a reconnaissance under Major Wilds P. Richardson of the 9th U.S. Infantry in 1906, when he was president of the Alaska Railroad Commission.

The favored Trans-Canadian, Alaska R.R. route went from Prince George, along the main line of the Canadian National Railroad to Fort Frances, then along the Pelly River valley to the Yukon River, along the White River from its mouth to Ladue River and down the Tanana River valley to Kobe (now Rex) on the Alaska Railroad, some 84 miles south of Fairbanks. Sifton Pass, an elevation of 3,273 feet was the highest point on this route.

The railroad would be built of 60-pound rails, standard gauge, with diesel-electric locomotives specified. The actual construction was to require 400 days, with 16,937 workers involved.

The project, was to cost a total of $86,576,000 for the Trans-Canada, Alaska Railroad; and $60,222,000 for the Western Railroad; plus $23,187,000 for the port; $11,500,000 for an oil pipeline; and $420,000 for two rail-river terminals. It was given the go ahead on Feb. 17, 1943 with construction to start on May 15, 1943.

Meanwhile, however, military action was underway towards regaining the Aleutian Islands and thousands of American aircraft were being moved to Russia via Canada and Alaska, the Germans had been repulsed by the Russians at Stalingrad, and the tide of war was beginning to change in Europe.

As a result, the need for the Trans-Canada, Alaska and Western Railroads and a military port on Alaska's Western shore diminished and the Delano program was filed away—possibly never again to be revived.

Some 37 years earlier, in 1906, the American Trans-Siberian Co. announced plans in Russia and the United States for a railroad with the Alaskan routes to run from Cape Prince of Wales via one of two routes.

One was from Kingegan eastward following the shores of Kotzebue Sound and thence over to the vicinity of Nulato on the north bank of the Yukon, and up the river to Dawson City. The other would run from Kingegan southward through the Kavizagemut to Nome, and thence along the shore of Norton Sound to a point opposite St. Michael and thence across the Yukon eastward from that point.

The company, incorporated for $250,000,000 had plans to tunnel under the Bering Straits from Cape Prince of Wales to East Cape in Siberia.

One condition in the building of the road through Alaska was that the company would receive alternate sections of eight miles on each side of the line, together with mining concessions.

Another of the early day imaginative railroad proposals was the development of a line of railroads thousands of miles in extent, over the vast territory of Siberia and through the uninhabited arctic tundra of the Chukotsk Peninsula; the construction of a submarine tunnel forty miles in length under the Bering Strait, and the continuation of the line through Alaska and British Columbia to connect with existing railroads on the American continent.

No one company would operate such a system, but it would be a series of companies. Such would include the Grand Trunk Pacific Railroad which was incorporated by an act of the Dominion of Canada Parliament in 1903. It would reach 3,600 miles across Canada from the Atlantic to the Pacific. One branch would extend from Edmonton to Dawson City in the Yukon, and thence across Alaska—involving some of the railroads already built, under construction, or planned in the areas between Dawson City and Nome.

Another was the Trans-Alaska Siberian Co., a French-Russian-American firm headed by Baron Loug de Lobel, a noted French engineer. The firm, incorporated in New Jersey with capitalization of $6 million, had obtained concessions from the Russian government which would tie the line in with the Siberian railroad. A 3,000 mile route across the United States, through Alaska, under the Bering Straits via the Diomede Islands, to East Cape was planned. One of the conditions of the project was that alternate sections of eight miles on either side of the line, together with mining concessions, would be granted the company.

Although various parts of the project were completed at one time or another, the promoters were unable to tie it all together and the plan went by the boards.

Another proposal was by the Alaska-Northwestern

Railroad Co., incorporated under the laws of the Territory of Arizona with capitalization of $60 million, "to build a single track, standard gauge steam passenger and freight railroad from the City of Vancouver B.C. to Cape Prince of Wales (Tin City) Alaska, a surveyed distance of 2,300 miles between terminals." The firm was headed by Cesilius Swenson of New York.

There was also an Alaska and Northwestern Railway Co., incorporated under the laws of West Virginia to build from Portage Cove on Lynn Canal to the international boundary, a distance of 36 miles. This firm filed in May 1898.

The Alaska Short Line Railway and Navigation Co. of Washington, planned to build from Iliamna Bay to Anvik on the Yukon, a distance of 369.2 miles, and then to the Bering Strait. Filing was in Jan. 1904, and the estimated cost was $44,300 per mile which included a tunnel through the Coast Range at 475 foot elevation and the greatest pass height would be 975 feet, thus giving easy gradients and favorable alignments. It was proposed that this railroad would connect with the Trans-Siberian railroad via the Bering Straits.

Capitalization was $15 million, with Colonel J.T. Cormforth as president.

The Trans-Alaska Railroad & Navigation Co. with capital of $50 million, was incorporated in 1902 under the laws of the State of Arizona by a group of Colorado capitalists. The Trans-Alaska was to run from Iliamna Bay on Cook Inlet to Port Clarence on the Bering Strait, where the road would connect with the Trans-Siberian Railroad by use of immense steel ferries, which would carry the trains across the Strait. Steamers would connect the Alaska portion of the route with Puget Sound, with headquarters in Tacoma or Seattle.

This railroad was said to have been started by a group of wealthy freelovers and that colonization was a large part of the overall planning.

A large amount of timbers, ties, rails, and camp equipment was loaded at Iliamna Bay and some offices and headquarters buildings erected along with line grading being completed. A tunnel was started through the mountains. Shops and office buildings were also constructed at the northern terminus, but the line died an inglorious death through lack of capital. Some of the materials are still visible at Iliamna and Railroad City.

A rival company, bearing much the same name, was the Trans Alaska Co., incorporated in California at $100,000. This caused considerable trouble in stock selling programs for the other firm, and is given as one

of the reasons for its failure. The second company failed within months.

About the same time a Chicago company proposed a railroad from Iliamna on Cook Inlet north to the Kuskokwim River, thence along its upper course and across the divide to Nulato, at a point where the Koyukuk flows into the Lower Yukon. From Nulato it was proposed to continue the line to Nome.

In 1891 a bill was introduced in the Senate authorizing construction of a railroad in Alaska and granted the Alaska Coal Mining and Development Co. the right to construct a railroad and telegraph line on the most eligible route from Portage Bay to Herendeen Bay on the Bering Sea and to develop coal deposits on the Alaskan Peninsula.

The Sitka Alaskan, the leading newspaper of the time in the Territory of Alaska, carried several stories in the late 1800s regarding railroads to be constructed to and within the Territory.

On Feb. 6, 1886 a story appeared stating that the Canadian Pacific Railroad proposed to extend its routes from British Columbia along the coast of Alaska to Mt. St. Elias, and then across Alaska to the Behring (Bering) Straits, which would be bridged to connect with a Siberian line and continue on to Europe.

In April of that year a story related to a proposal to connect the Western States with Alaska through New Westminster, B.C. and then on July 6, 1889 a similar line was proposed from Victoria, B.C.

A railroad from Vancouver, B.C. to Cape Prince of Wales, Alaska, was in the headllines several times between 1891 and 1893 when it was announced that the survey had been completed, with the route found easy as far as Juneau, and not exceedingly difficult beyond that point. This proposed line would also connect with Siberian and Russian railroads, and thence to Europe. It was pointed out that the present Trans-Siberian Railroad was to end at Vladivostock and that it would be necessary to extend that line approximately 1,000 miles to connect with the Alaska railroad.

There were other railroads proposed, too, of which little was heard after their filings with the Land Office of the Department of the Interior. There were such as the Alaska-Yukon Railroad and Navigation Co., of New Jersey, which proposed to build from the Unalaklik River on North Sound to the junction of the Kaltag and Yukon Rivers, a distance of 79.19 miles, which was filed in March 1899.

Another was the Pacific Alaska Transportation and Coal Company of New Jersey with a route from Portage Bay to Herendeen Bay and from Northwest Harbor to the mouth of the Chignik River, with branches to other areas. The filing was in January 1903.

Chapter 19

Hither and Yon In
Southeast Alaska.

Alaska's First Railroad.

Written records giving the name of Alaska's first railroad, have been lost, but a photograph taken on May 15, 1894 showing a little 0-4-0 narrow gauge locomotive pushing a flat car loaded with passengers exists.

The locomotive, the first in Alaska, operated over three and one-half miles of track between Seward City and Berners Bay Gold Manufacturing Co.'s mine. The trains carried workers to the mine and ore back to the waterfront on Lynn Canal.

Alaska-Juneau Gold Mine Railroad.

Several mining railroads operated in the Juneau-Douglas area during the height of the Southeast Alaska gold rush.

One of the largest was the Alaska-Juneau Gold Mine Railroad which operated over about seven miles of track, not including sidings going to the waste dump and various nearby shops and warehouses.

During its operation in 1911 the company drilled a tunnel through Mt. Juneau from a position on the hillside above Juneau and adjacent to the milling plant overlooking Gastineau Channel to Silverbow Basin.

Trackage through the tunnel was 50-pound rails at first but later upgraded to 72-pound, set on 30-inch gauge. The equipment was electrically operated, being 600-volt D.C. overhead trolley locomotives. All hauling motors were two units, operating as cow and calf units. Personnel and ore were hauled throughout the mine area.

The mine was closed in April 1944 and most of the trackage and equipment sold as junk and hauled out during 1964-65. Some, however, was retained and a tour train operated in the mine for about 10 years,

using four rebuilt personnel shift cars pulled by a battery-operated locomotive brought in from the Lower 48.

A partial roster of the original equipment included:

4 Four-ton battery locomotives, Baldwin-Westinghouse #41326, 42629, 42592, and 43942. Motor type V-50, V-43X, V-50-4. Mechanical brakes.

5 General Electric trolley six-ton locomotives. Mechanical brakes.

3 General Electric trolley nine-ton locomotives. Mechanical brakes.

1 Jeffrey trolley 10-ton. Mechanical brakes.

5 Baldwin-Westinghouse trolley 18-ton locomotives. Air brakes.

250 Ten-ton ore cars, and miscellaneous other equipment.

Alaska-Gastineau Mining Company Railroad.

Another mining railroad in the Juneau area was operated by the Alaska-Gastineau Mining Co., of New York, which in Jan. 1913 had taken over the properties at Sheep Creek (Thane) formerly operated by the Howell Company, the Perseverance Mine and other properties which had started in the area as early as 1896.

In April 1914 the firm built a two-mile tunnel through the mountains from Sheep Creek to the Perseverance propertries and built a three-foot narrow gauge mining railroad through the tunnel.

Two used 18-ton 0-4-0 mining-type electric locomotives built in April 1914 by Baldwin-Westinghouse, #41328 and #41329, powered by 90-horsepower motors were put into operation. The 600-volt D.C. power was supplied by overhead trolley lines. Twelve-ton capacity four-wheel ore cars were used over the approximate five miles of track.

Alaska's first railroad operated between Seward City on Lynn Canal and the Berners Bay Manufacturing Co.'s gold mill. Constructed in early 1894, the railroad used a little 0-4-0 narrow gauge saddle-tanker, the first steam locomotive in the territory. The railroad carried workers up to the mine and gold ore down to the waterfront, a distance of three and one-half miles over an average seven percent grade.

The mining properties became unprofitable and closed down in 1921 as a result of increased operating costs and other factors. In 1923 the locomotives and other equipment was sold to the Pacific Cement & Aggregate Co., located at Davenport, Calif., a part of the Lone Star Cement Co.

Salmon Creek Railroad.

In 1913 the Alaska-Gastineau Mining Company built a construction railroad starting at a point 2.5 miles north of Juneau on the Gastineau Channel, and followed upstream along Salmon Creek for a distance of 2.6 miles. Here the firm built a concrete dam, 170 feet high with a crest 648 feet long. Water from the dam was utilized by two hydro-electric power plants, one near the dam and the other on the beach, which supplied electricity for the city of Juneau and the Alaska-Juneau Gold Mining Co.

The Salmon Creek Railroad was three-foot narrow gauge and used a two-truck Shay during construction. This was the only known Shay to have operated in Alaska. At least two 0-4-0 locomotives were also used for switching, one at the beginning on the beach and another at the upper end near the dam. The first 500 feet of road ran up a grade of about 20 degrees and the cars were pulled up with a cable. At that point the motive power could handle a couple of cars to the upper powerhouse, a distance of about two miles.

Treadwell Mine Railroad.

A two-foot narrow gauge railroad was used to connect the various mines just south of the city of Douglas on Douglas Island, including the Treadwell, the 700, Mexican, and Ready Bullion.

These various mines started operation around the turn of the century, with the Treadwell working under Gastineau Channel until a cave-in closed the operation in April 1917. The others closed down shortly thereafter with the Ready Bullion the last to cease operation in Dec. 1922. Nearly $70 million in gold was taken out of this operation.

Two other railroads were proposed in the Juneau area. The Juneau, Douglas and Treadwell Railroad Co. of Washington, filed in October 1902 to build from Juneau to Douglas, a distance of six miles and the Alaska Southern Railway Co. of Washington, filed in Feb. 1907 to build from the city limits of Juneau to the city limits of Douglas via a 7.2 mile routing.

Rush and Brown Copper Mine Railroad.

One of several mining railroads in Southeast Alaska which operated just after the turn of the century was the Rush and Brown Copper Mine Railroad on the Kaasan Peninsula on Prince of Wales Island.

About three miles of narrow gauge track, plus tramways were operated by the Rush and Brown firm for the Jumbo, the Mamie and other mines to move their copper ore output to the Hadley Smelter.

Some of the equipment used in this operation still remains in the bush on Prince of Wales Island. Recently one of the narrow-gauge locomotives, a H.K. Porter 0-6-0 of unknown vintage was removed from the Island to Ketchikan and then shipped to Reno, Nev., where it is being restored by Jim Walsh of Sacramento, who plans to display the relic.

Copper was first discovered on the Kaasan Peninsula by the Russians in 1865. Production at the mines began in 1905 and by 1906 the Hadley Smelter had been put into operation. Mining began to taper off in 1908 due to the lack of ore in the area, and closed down shortly thereafter.

One of several battery operated Baldwin-Westinghouse locomotives used in the Alaska Juneau Gold Mine at Juneau. These units pulled ore trains and carried workers to the far reaches of the mine in personnel cars. The mine is located above the city of Juneau. (H. Clifford)

Alaska Marble Company Tramway.

A gravity tramway some 3,200 feet in length operated by the Alaska Marble Company at Calder, on Prince of Wales Island, was another mining operation in Southeast Alaska.

The tram was used to move marble from a quarry on the mountainside 75 feet above the beach. The tramway was built of heavy timber, 30 to 40 feet in the air and 20 feet wide with a standard gauge of three rails. The center rail serving two tracks, which switched into one track at the dock.

A loaded car served as a counter-balance to bring up the empty cars. The quarry operated in the early 1900s and supplied pure white, blue veined marble, and a light blue with mottled background marble. The stone was not equal to the top Italian marble, but was better than most American grades.

Ketchikan Pulp Co.

There are two diesels in operation at Ketchikan Pulp Co., north of Ketchikan. One is a Baldwin S12 120 horsepower, #2124 built in Nov. 1952 for the Southern Pacific Railroad and later acquired by Ket-

This narrow gauge 0-6-0 Porter was recovered from the Rush and Brown copper mine on Prince of Wales Island in Southeastern Alaska. It has been moved to Southern California where it is being restored. The locomotive operated over two and three-quarters miles of narrow gauge track hauling ore to the bunkers prior to shipment. Copper was discovered in the area in 1865 by the Russians and production started in 1905 but was closed down by 1908. (Clifford Collection)

chikan Pulp. The second is a Whitecombe 50-tonner also built in 1952.

The locomotives are used for switching purposed to load and unload rail barges brought in twice weekly.

Ketchikan and Northern Terminal Co.

There is about 2,000 feet of track at Ketchikan and Northern Terminal Co., used in the loading and unloading of rail barges at this facility. Motive power is a front loader with a coupler on the back and it can put a coupler on instead of a bucket in front if needed.

Unuk River Mining & Smelting Co.

An electric railroad, to be built from Ketchikan to the Unuk River was planned by the Unuk River Mining and Smelting Co. Such never was constructed,

although a wagon road operation was complete over the 42-mile route in 1906.

Gold and silver were produced in the area.

Alaska Lumber and Pulp Co.

There are two locomotives at the Sitka plant of the Alaska Lumber and Pulp Co. One is a former U.S. Navy #17881 GE 45-tonner, built in June 1943 and which was brought to Sitka in 1965-66. A second locomotive formerly in operation is out of service at present.

* * *

Maps and early reports show mining railroads of varying types and lengths in the following areas, although very little other information is available.

Goulding Railroad—Goulding Harbor on West Side of Chicago Island

Eagle Harbor to Eagle Glacier—Serving Eagle River Gold Mine, Alice Gold Mine and Amalga Gold Mine.

Chapter 20

Railroads Elsewhere in Alaska.

Cook Inlet Coal Field Co. Railroad.

A three-foot narrow gauge railroad was constructed in early 1900 on the Kenai Peninsula from the bluffs west of Homer to the end of the Homer Spit by a British company which had set up coal mining operations in the area.

Passengers were carried along with cargo over the eight and one-half miles from the dock on the Spit to the town of Homer.

A 0-4-0 coal burning steam locomotive was put into operation hauling the wooden coal cars which delivered coal to the dock for shipment to the boom towns of Hope and Sunrise on Turnagain Arm. Some coal was also shipped to Europe from the Homer mines.

Some two-foot narrow gauge cars were also used in the mine and one is on display in Homer. This operation was abandoned in 1907 by the conservation act which withdrew mineral rights in Alaska.

Apollo Consolidated Mining Co.

The farthest west railroad in America was the Apollo Consolidated Mining Co. railroad on Unga Island, located near Cold Bay on the Alaska Peninsula.

The mine started operating in 1886 and had numerous substantial buildings, tramways, tunnels and shafts which yielded low grade gold quartz. The properties continued to prosper and in 1897 a 0-6-0 Baldwin narrow gauge locomotive #15273, built in April.1897, was put into operation.

As the supply of gold ore diminished, the mine was gradually phased out and the remains of track, locomotive and many of the buildings may still be seen in the area.

Crooked Creek and Whiskey Island Railroad.

A unique little attraction, the Crooked Creek and Whiskey Island Railroad, operates as a tourist attraction during the summer months at Alaskaland, the former Alaska Centennial site at Fairbanks. The three-foot narrow gauge scenic train runs around the 40-acre site. There is an old-time depot, water tower, etc., to add authenticity to this gasoline powered operation.

The locomotive is a Fornay type 0-4-0 built by C.M. Lovsted, Inc., of Seattle. The 131-horsepower gasoline engine moves the train at a top speed of 15 miles an hour with a train of four cars.

Also on display at Alaskaland is the observation car "Denali" which was used by President Warren G. Harding to travel over the Alaska Railroad to Nenana for the Golden Spike ceremony in 1923.

The little Tanana Valley Railroad No. 1 locomotive (also formerly Alaska Railroad No. 1) a 0-4-0 H.K. Porter #1972, built in 1899 and fully restored is also on display on the grounds.

* * *

A couple of other railroads planned for Alaska in the early days, but which did not fit into the usual scheme of things were the Setuck Company of Washington which filed in Jan. 1903 to build a road from a point near Ocean Cape to a point near Setuck River, with two spur lines for a total of 12 miles; and the Alaska Coal and Coke Company of California, which proposed to build from Yukon River, along Washington Creek to California Creek, a distance of 10 miles. Filing was also in January 1903.

A group of women and children on an outing on the Apollo Consolidated Mining Co. Railroad on Unga Island is pictured in front of the little Baldwin locomotive used by the "farthest west railroad in America." The 0-6-0 locomotive was abandoned in the wilderness, but has been rescued and restored by an Anchorage rail buff.

Bibliography

Books

Andrews, C. L. *The Story of Alaska.* Caxton Printers Ltd. Caldwell, Idaho, 1944.

Beach, Rex. *The Iron Trail.* A. L. Burt Co., Publishers, New York, N.Y. 1913.

Bearss, Edwin C. *Proposed Klondike Gold Rush National Historical Park.* National Park Service, Department of Interior, Washington D.C., 1970.

Clifford, Howard. *Skagway Story.* Alaska Northwest Publishing Co., Anchorage, Ak., 1975.

Colby, Merle. *A Guide To Alaska.* MacMillan Co., New York, N.Y., 1939.

Downs, Art (edited by). *Pioneer Days in British Columbia.* Outdoors, Vancouver, B.C., 1973.

Fitch, Edwin M. *The Alaska Railroad.* Frederick A. Praeger, publishers. New York, 1967.

Graves, Samuel H. *On the White Pass Payroll.* Lakeside Press, Chicago, Ill, 1908.

Gruening, Ernest. *The State of Alaska.* Random House, New York, N.Y. 1954.

Hauck, Cornelius W. (edited by). *Collected Colorado Rail Annual.* Colorado Railroad Museum, Golden, Colo., 1974.

Heilprin, Angelo. *Alaska and the Klondike.* C. Arthur Pearson, Ltd., London, 1899.

Herron, Ed. *Alaska's Railroad Builder. Michael Heney.* Mesaner, N.Y. 1960.

Hulley, Clarence C. *Alaska 1741-1953.* Binfords & Mort, Portland Ore., 1953.

The former cannery tender S.B. Matthews was one of the river steamers used in the construction of the Copper River and Northwestern Railroad. All of these little vessels did yeoman work in hauling supplies and equipment. (Clifford Collection)

Books

Janson, Lone E. *The Copper Spike.* Alaska Northwest Publishing Co., Anchorage, Ak., 1975.

Kirk, R. C. *Twelve Months in the Klondike.* William Heinemann, London, 1899.

Kitchener, L. D. *Flag Over The North.* Superior Publishing Co., Seattle, 1954.

LaVelle, Omar. *Narrow Gauge Railways of Canada.* Railfare Enterprises Ltd., Montreal, Canada. 1972.

Martin, Cy. *Gold Rush Narrow Gauge.* Trans-angelo Books, Los Angeles, 1969.

Moore, J. Bernard. *Skagway In Days Primeval.* Vantage Press, New York, 1968.

Naske, Claus M. *Interpretive History of Alaskan Statehood.* Alaska-Northwest Publishing Co., Anchorage, Ak., 1973.

Nichols, Jeanette Paddock. *History of Alaska Under Rule of The United States.* Arthur H. Clark, Co., Cleveland, 1924.

Poor. *Poor's Manual of Railroads.* Dow-Jones, New York., 1900, 1908, 1910, 1915.

Prince, Bernadine. *The Alaska Railroad,* Vols. I & II. Ken Wray Printing, Anchorage, Ak., 1969.

Richards, T. A. *Through the Yukon and Alaska.* Mining & Scientific Press, San Francisco, 1909.

Twekesbury, William. *Alaska Almanac.* Twekesbury Publishers, Seattle, 1949.

Westing, Fred. *Locomotives That Baldwin Built.* Superior Publishing Co., Seattle 1966.

Wharton, David B. *The Alaska Gold Rush.* Indiana University Press, Bloomington & London, 1972.

Whiting, Dr. F. B. *Grit, Grief and Gold.* Peacock Publishing Co., Seattle, 1933.

Wickersham, James. *Old Yukon.* Washington Law Book Co., Washington D.C., 1938.

Wickersham, James. *A Bibliography of Alaskan Literature, 1724-1924.* Alaska Agricultural College and School of Mines, Fairbanks, 1927.

Magazines

Alaska Journal, Vol. 2, No. 3, Summer 1972. "Rails Across the Tundra," Alice Osborne.

Alaska Journal, Vol. 4, No. 4, Autumn 1974 "Trans-Canadian, Alaska and Western Railroad," Lyman L. Woodman.

...."White Pass Aviation and Its Rivals," Jeanne Harbottle.

Alaska Journal, Vol. 5, No. 1, Winter 1975. "The Council City & Solomon River Railroad," Alice Osborne.

Alaska Industry Magazine, Jan. 1969. "The Little Railroad That Could Make a Profit," Robert G. Knox.

Alaska Industry Magazine, Oct. 1969. "Eskimos Mined It, Russians Ignored It," A. Cameron Edmondson.

Alaska Life, Oct. 1942. "Uncompleted Railways in Alaska," C. L. Andrews.

Alaska Life, Feb. 1944. "Railroad Saga of the North," Capt. Richard L. Neuberger.

Alaska Magazine, Jan. 1965. "Katalla and Cordova, Alaska Sojourn," Emma A. Davis.

Alaska Magazine, Feb. 1970. "The Seattle Kid," Berne Jacobsen.

Alaskana n.d. "By Way of History, Cordova 1924," Katherine Wilson.

................"L. V. Ray and the Keystone Canyon Caper," Elsa Pedersen.

................"Guns of Keystone Canyon," Lone E. Janson.

Alaskan Magazine, (and Canadian Yukoner), June 1900. "A Botanists's Trip on the Upper Yukon, J. B. Tarleton.

Alaska Monthly, Nov. 1906. "Reynolds Alaska Development Co."

Alaska Review, Spring-Summer 1969. "The White Pass Railroad," W. G. Godbey.

Alaska Sportsman, Oct. 1943. "Gold Rush Railroad," Charles O. Cole.

Alaska Sportsman, Jan. 1945. "A Sturdy Little Line," Cecil E. Barger.

Alaska Sportsman, Nov. 1949. "Copper River Railroad," Lawrence I. Williams and Oscar L. Brauer.

Alaska Sportsman, April 1958. "Thunder In the Mountains," Cecelia Selmar Price.

Alaska Sportsman, March 1962. "Rapuzzi, Dean of Alaskan Railroaders," Barbara Kalen.

Alaska Sportsman, May 1963. "Yakutat & Southern Railroad," E. M. McCracken.

Alaska Sportsman, Oct. 1968. "This Month in the Northland," Bob DeArmond.

Alaska-Yukon Magazine, n.d. "Renascent Valdez."

Alaska-Yukon Magazine, Jan. 1909. "Railroad Building in Alaska," Falcon Joslin.

Alaska-Yukon Magazine, Aug. 1909. "An Alaska Railroad, The Copper River and Northwestern," Joe King.

...."Alaska Railroad and the Country It Will Develop," Joe King.

...."Building A Railroad In Alaska," May Grinnell.

Alaska-Yukon Magazine, June 1910. "The Winter's Crucial Battle on the Copper River," Charlye Ellis.

Alaska-Yukon Magazine, Dec. 1910. "Conquering the Copper," Sidney D. Charles.

Alaska-Yukon Magazine, March 1911. "Another Northern Triumph — The Copper River-Kuskulana Bridge."

...."History of Alaska's Longest Railroad," F. F. Swergal.

Alaska-Yukon Magazine, Aug. 1911. "Transportation on the Seward Peninsula."

Beaver, Sept. 1954 "White Pass Route," W. D. MacBride.

British Columbia Outdoors, June 1972—Aug. 1972, "Captain William Moore, Frontiersman," Norman Hackling.

Commonwealth, 1903. "Alaska Short Line Railroad and Navigation Co."

Cosmopolitan, May 1899. "Railroad to the Klondike," W. M. Sheffield.

Engineer & Mining Journal, April 21, 1906. "The Alaska Central Railroad," M. S. Duffield.

Frontier Times, June 1969. "Tanana Valley Narrow Gauge," Jack McPhee.

Leslie's Magazine, April 1909, "A Railroad to the Yukon," W. A. Croffut.

Literary Digest, Jan. 3, 1920. "Uncle Sam's Alaskan Railroads."

McClures's Magazine, March 1900. "Building a Railroad Into the Klondike," Cy Warman.

National Geographic, Dec 15, 1915. "Alaska's New Railroad."

National Geographic, Feb. 1943. "Alaska Highway, an Engineering Epic."

Okuruk, June 1973. "Transportation in the North, the Incredible WP & YR Story."

Outlook, April 28, 1915. "Seward Route for Alaskan Railroad."

Overland Magazine, May 1902. "A Day's Journey on the Wild Goose Railway," Josephine Vrelle Scroggs.

Pathfinder, Dec. 1921—Jan. 1922. "The Alaskan Government Railroad."

Pacific Monthly, Nov. 1906. "The Connecting Link of the World's Railroads," George Sherman.

Pacific Northwest Quarterly, Jan. 1954. "Ghost Railway in Alaska," Duane Koenig.

Review of Reviews, March 1904. "Alaska's Railroads."

Review of Reviews, Dec. 1908. "Alaska's Railroad Development," Frederick H. Chase.

Saturday Evening Post, Feb. 27, 1942. "Highballing at Sixty Below," Capt. Richard L. Neuberger.

Scientific American, Jan. 1922. "Government Railroad in Alaska Nears Completion."

Scientific American, Jan. 1923. "Building a Railroad in the Frozen North."

Scientific American, Dec. 1923. "Where Bridges Are Built in the Dead of Winter."

Technical World, March 1912. "It Had To Be Done," Charles Ellis.

Technical World, July 1921. "Moving a Railroad Six Thousand Miles," Rene Bache.

Technical World, Oct. 1913. "Farthest North in Railroading," Emil Hurja.

Technical World, Feb. 1914. "Rails to Revolutionize Alaska," Monroe Wooley.

The Flag, Nov. 1974.

The West, April 1965. "Tex Richard, the West's Incredible Promoter," Julian R. Green.

Having battled winter storms through the White Pass, this WP&YR locomotive makes its way up Broadway in Skagway, its front end covered with snow and ice. The photo was taken in 1901. (Yukon Archives)

Newspapers

Alaska Dispatch. Golden Spike Edition, 24th Year, 1923.

Alaska Empire, March 7, 1969.

Anchorage Times, July 12, 13, 14, 16, 1973; Feb. 3, 1975; Aug. 11, 1975, and various other issues.

Anchorage News, Aug. 18, 1974, and other issues.

Cordova Alaskan, various issues.

Cordova Daily Times. All Alaska Review, 1927, 1929, 1930, 1931, and various other issues.

Council City News, various issues.

Dawson City Daily News, July 21, 1909.

Fairbanks News Miner, Nov. 24, 1973; Oct. 31, 1974; Nov. 7, 14, 21, 29, 1974; and various other issues.

Fairbanks Times, Sept. 1, 1908; Oct. 21, 1908; April 10, 1910; Tanana Magazine Issue, Dec. 1912, Feb. 23, 1914.

Juneau Alaska Empire, July 31, 1975.

Katala Herald, Sept. 25, 1907; and other 1907-09 issues.

Klondike Nugget, Dawson City, various 1906 issues.

Nome Nugget, various 1906 issues.

Seattle Post Intelligencer, June 23, 1974.

Seattle Times, May 6, 1973.

Seward Gateway, Sept. 9, 1927.

Sitka Alaskan, Jan 24, 1891 and various other issues, 1899—1906.

Skagway Northwind, various issues.

Valdez Prospector (Valdez News) various issues Aug. 15—Oct. 3, 1907.

Whitehorse Star, May 1, 1901; Oct. 4, 1969; Jan. 9, 1974; and various other issues.

Miscellaneous Maps, Papers, Pamphlets and Reports

Alaska Central Railroad Prospectus. Seattle, 1906.

Alaskan Engineering Commission Report, Joshau Barnhadt. 1922.

Alaska Northwestern Railroad Co. Prospectus. New York. n.d.

Alaska Railroad Commission Report. Washington, D.C. Jan. 20, 1923.

Alaska Railroad files, 1923-1960. National Archives, Seattle.

Alaska Railroad Record, Vol. 4, 12/5/16—12/12/16.

Alaska Short Line Railway & Navigation Co. Prospectus. Seattle, 1903.

Alaska-Yukon Area Railfan's Guide. Alaska-Yukon Railroad Historical Society, Anchorage, n.d.

Atlin, 1892—1910. Atlin Centennial Committee, Atlin B.C., 1971.

Canadian Government files, 1899—1931, Yukon Archives, Whitehorse, Y.T.

Canadian Pacific Railroad Archives, Montreal.

Catalogue No. 1, Dawson City Hardware Co., Ltd., Dawson City, March 1903.

"Comprehensive Inventory of Sites and Areas of Historical Significance in the Yukon Territory," Alan Innes-Taylor.

Clifton Museum, Valdez. Misc. reports, maps and papers.

Horback, Helen, "Notes on Norman Macaulay." Yukon Archives, Whitehorse Y.T.

Innes-Taylor, Alan, "Papers in Yukon Archives." Whitehorse Y.T.

Map of Canyon Townsite (Canyon City), Nov. 10, 1900.

Map of Whitehorse Townsite (original Townsite east of river) Sept. 1899.

Map of White Pass & Yukon Railroad Right-of-way, Whitehorse (BYMT&T Co.), March 22, 1900.

Moose Gooser, 1967—1975. Alaska-Yukon Railroad Historical Society, Anchorage.

Northwest Mounted Police, Annual Reports 1894, 1897, 1898, Yukon Archives.

Quitsch, William, "My First 80 Years." Unpublished paper. Valdez Public Library.

"Strangling the Alaska Railroad," John Ballaine. Seattle, 1923.

"The Steel Went North," Ray Minter. Vancouver, B.C.

"Treasures of Alaska Maps," Van Winkle Publishing Co., Holland, Mich.

White Pass Container Route News, various issues.

White Pass & Yukon Railroad Folders, 1906, 1909 and various other dates.

First to flash word to the outside world of the landing in Seattle of the S.S. Portland with its "ton of gold" from the Klondike, the Seattle Post Intelligencer was the first outside sponsor of an excursion over the White Pass & Yukon Route, built as a result of the Klondike rush. Here is the Seattle PI excursion party on the shores of Lake Bennett on August 22, 1899.

Loaded flat cars built up with side rails, benches and roof carry tourist over the White Pass & Yukon during the early 1900s. The scenic trip is still one of the most exciting and most interesting in North America. The narrow gauge line runs on a regular schedule on the 110 miles between Skagway and Whitehorse, following closely the route of the Klondike stampeders. (Clifford Collection)

Summer Excursion—One of the most enjoyable outings for early day Skagway residents was an excursion on the White Pass & Yukon Railroad. Here a group is pictured at Glacier during the summer of 1899. Note wooden benches placed on flat cars to serve as "observation cars." The coach in the foreground carries the P&AR&N Co., (Pacific and Arctic Railway and Navigation Co.,) one of the three companies which made up the White Pass & Yukon. (Yukon Archives)

Alaska Railroad "rubberneck" car. This odd, experimental car was built and used by the Alaska railroad whenever there were spectator events along its route. Passengers could remain in their "grandstand" seats and view the goings on, such as the Matanuska Valley Fair at Palmer, sled dog races at various points, and other attractions. (Clifford Collection)

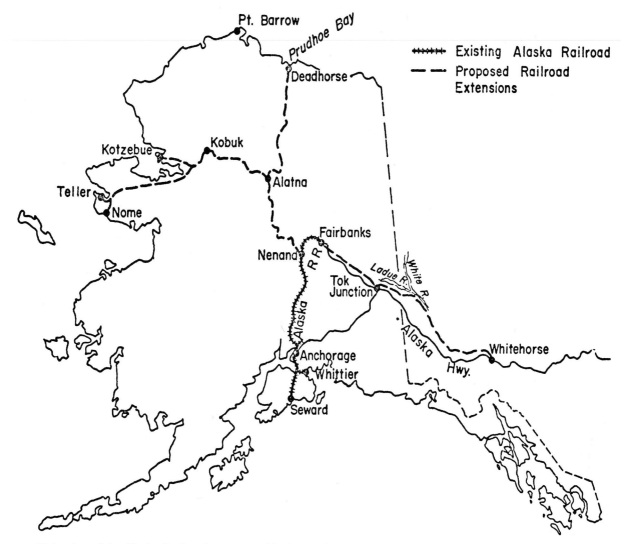

Extension of the Alaska Railroad as proposed by former Governor Walter J. Hickel would go east to Whitehorse in the Yukon Territory, north to Alatna and Deadhorse, and west to Kobuk, Kotze-bue, Teller and Nome.

Index